World Wisdom
The Library of Perennial Philosophy

The Library of Perennial Philosophy is dedicated to the exposition of the timeless Truth underlying the diverse religions. This Truth, often referred to as the *Sophia Perennis*—or Perennial Wisdom—finds its expression in the revealed Scriptures as well as the writings of the great sages and the artistic creations of the traditional worlds.

The Eye of the Heart appears as one of our selections in the Writings of Frithjof Schuon series.

The Writings of Frithjof Schuon

The Writings of Frithjof Schuon form the foundation of our library because he is the pre-eminent exponent of the Perennial Philosophy. His work illuminates this perspective in both an essential and comprehensive manner like none other.

T0170045

English Language Writings of Frithjof Schuon

Original Books

The Transcendent Unity of Religions
Spiritual Perspectives and Human Facts
Gnosis: Divine Wisdom
Language of the Self
Stations of Wisdom
Understanding Islam
Light on the Ancient Worlds
Treasures of Buddhism (In the Tracks of Buddhism)
Logic and Transcendence
Esoterism as Principle and as Way
Castes and Races
Sufism: Veil and Quintessence
From the Divine to the Human
Christianity/Islam: Essays on Esoteric Ecumenicism
Survey of Metaphysics and Esoterism
In the Face of the Absolute
The Feathered Sun: Plains Indians in Art and Philosophy
To Have a Center
Roots of the Human Condition
Images of Primordial and Mystic Beauty: Paintings by Frithjof Schuon
Echoes of Perennial Wisdom
The Play of Masks
Road to the Heart: Poems
The Transfiguration of Man
The Eye of the Heart
Form and Substance in the Religions
Adastra & Stella Maris: Poems by Frithjof Schuon (bilingual edition)
Autumn Leaves & The Ring: Poems by Frithjof Schuon (bilingual edition)
Songs without Names, Volumes I-VI: Poems by Frithjof Schuon
Songs without Names, Volumes VII-XII: Poems by Frithjof Schuon
World Wheel, Volumes I-III: Poems by Frithjof Schuon
World Wheel, Volumes IV-VII: Poems by Frithjof Schuon
Primordial Meditation: Contemplating the Real

Edited Writings

The Essential Frithjof Schuon, ed. Seyyed Hossein Nasr
Songs for a Spiritual Traveler: Selected Poems (bilingual edition)
René Guénon: Some Observations, ed. William Stoddart
The Fullness of God: Frithjof Schuon on Christianity, ed. James S. Cutsinger
Prayer Fashions Man: Frithjof Schuon on the Spiritual Life, ed. James S. Cutsinger
Art from the Sacred to the Profane: East and West, ed. Catherine Schuon
Splendor of the True: A Frithjof Schuon Reader, ed. James S. Cutsinger
Letters of Frithjof Schuon: Reflections on the Perennial Philosophy,
ed. Michael Oren Fitzgerald (forthcoming)

The Eye of the Heart

Metaphysics, Cosmology, Spiritual Life

A New Translation with Selected Letters

by

Frithjof Schuon

Includes Other Previously
Unpublished Writings

Edited by
Harry Oldmeadow

Foreword by
Huston Smith

World Wisdom

The Eye of the Heart: Metaphysics, Cosmology, Spiritual Life
A New Translation with Selected Letters
© 2021 World Wisdom, Inc.

Translated by Mark Perry and Jean-Pierre Lafouge

Published in French as L'Oeil du Coeur,
Gallimard, 1950, Dervy-Livres, 1974,
L'Age d'Homme, 1995, L'Harmattan, 2017

Library of Congress Cataloging-in-Publication Data

Names: Schuon, Frithjof, 1907-1998, author. | Oldmeadow, Harry, 1947-
editor. | Smith, Huston, writer of foreword.. | Perry, Mark, 1951-
translator. | Lafouge, Jean-Pierre, 1944- translator.
Title: The eye of the heart : a new translation with selected letters / by
Frithjof Schuon ; edited by Harry Oldmeadow ; foreword by Huston Smith ;
translated by Mark Perry and Jean-Pierre Lafouge.
Other titles: Oeil du coeur. English
Description: Bloomington, Indiana : World Wisdom, [2021] | Series: The
library of perennial philosophy | "Translation of: L'oeil du coeur. |
Includes bibliographical references and index.
Identifiers: LCCN 2021001861 (print) | LCCN 2021001862 (ebook) | ISBN
9781936597703 (paperback ; acid-free paper) | ISBN 9781936597710 (epub)
Subjects: LCSH: Religion.
Classification: LCC BL48 .S3813 2021 (print) | LCC BL48 (ebook) | DDC
200--dc23
LC record available at https://lccn.loc.gov/2021001861
LC ebook record available at https://lccn.loc.gov/2021001862

Cover:
Our Lady of the Great Panagia (Orante),
Yaroslavl, early 13th century, Tretyakov Gallery, Moscow

Printed on acid-free paper in the United States of America

For information address World Wisdom, Inc.
P.O. Box 2682, Bloomington, Indiana 47402
www.worldwisdom.com

CONTENTS

LIST OF ILLUSTRATIONS

FOREWORD

Frithjof Schuon's writings are studded with passages of indescribable beauty, but no one has ever charged them with being easy reading; out of incomprehension, I myself almost gave up on the first of his books that I came upon. And so, as one who providentially got over the hump and has continued to read him for thirty years, I propose to use this foreword to say in the simplest possible way why I consider him to be the most important religious thinker of the twentieth century.

Human beings need two things. We need to be anchored vertically in the Absolute; to be redeemed from loneliness, confusion, and lassitude, the human heart must be pierced, centrally and solidly, by the *axis mundi*. Concomitantly and horizontally, we need to reach out with open arms towards our fellow men and bear one another's burdens. The mission of the world's religions is to meet these twin needs, but on the surface they seem to conflict. The revelations that launched them differ, and this seems to present their adherents with an impossible choice. They can either adhere to their religions' absolutes and find themselves separated from people who live by different absolutes; or they can ignore the distinctive teachings of their revelations that give them their cutting edge, and thus reduce them to vague generalities that cover all religions. The latter choice eases religious friction, but at the cost of denaturing revelation, whose power requires concreteness. Facing this disjunction, religious conservatives take the right fork in the road, holding to their absolutes and risking dissension. Religious liberals choose the other fork and turn left. They cash in absolutes in the interests of presumptive social harmony.

Modern philosophy and theology have not been able to solve this problem. Frithjof Schuon, riding the wave of the timeless perennialist position which he has detailed with unprecedented completeness, solves it by stepping out of it. His step is an upward one which introduces a third dimension into the picture and solves the dilemma in the way a three-dimensional globe resolves the spatial distortions that two-dimensional map makers cannot escape. There is a type of person for whom formlessness—being free of boundaries that "cabin, crib, and confine"—tokens greater concreteness and reality, not less. Saint Dionysius, Meister Eckhart, and Shankara are classic instances of such persons, but their type surfaces everywhere. For such people, the Absolute in its fullness exceeds all of its formal, historical instantiations, including the great, enduring revelations that are its expressions in history. These revelations are the clearest depictions of itself that the Absolute can effect in the world of forms.

Only two points need be added. First, perennialists do not, as is often charged, make end runs around the revealed religions to create a religion of their own. They are fully aware that, being as human as everyone else, their lives too must traffic mostly in forms, and that the configurations of forms that mortals slap together cannot match those that God has ordained. The second required addendum is that perennialists are not utopian. Their stance towards their co-religionists is that of the author of *The Cloud of Unknowing* who wrote, "The point I am making is correct, but if you cannot grasp it, then let it be, until God himself helps you to understand" (chap. 34).

Having decided that most readers of this book would find it useful to have it placed against its orienting backdrop, I have turned this foreword to that end and will be brief about the book itself. Originally published in Paris at exactly mid-century, *L'Oeil du Coeur* was one of Schuon's earliest books. As if in tribute to God's infinity, the topics the book covers are wide-ranging; they include the issues of free will's relation to predestination, God's omnipotence in the face of evil, and faith's interface with intelligence. Threading these diverse issues is the clear enunciation of God's "simplicity" in the technical sense of that word. In its Vedantic formulation, "*Brahma* is Reality, the world is appearance; the soul is not other than *Brahma*."

Again in this book, as everywhere in Schuon's writing, one is struck by the hierarchical, vertical character of his thinking—his depiction of an absolute and transcendent Reality that deploys itself through All-Possibility and ultimately returns to Itself through human beings "made in the image of God". Beauty is the vehicle for this return: outward beauty which comes from God and leads back to Him; and inward beauty—virtue—which is essential for human participation in the Divine Nature.

Huston Smith

EDITOR'S PREFACE

St. Augustine writes of "Wisdom uncreate, the same now as it ever was, and the same to be for evermore";[1] the self-same wisdom was affirmed early in the twentieth century in the metaphysical writings of René Guénon. Guénon's work inaugurated a movement which has come to be known as traditionalism, or perennialism, a perspective recalling humankind to the *sophia perennis* which informs the world's manifold religious and sapiential traditions and which has been obscured "in a world depleted of the sacred, and therefore of meaning".[2] Along with the French metaphysician, the most authoritative exponents of this outlook have been Ananda Coomaraswamy, Titus Burckhardt, and Frithjof Schuon.[3] These figures not only avow the perennial philosophy but are also committed to the defence of the particular forms which safeguard the integrity of each religious heritage and ensure its spiritual efficacy. From our present vantage-point we can now see that the culmination of this movement, or "school", is to be found in the works of Frithjof Schuon (1907-1998) who is not only the master metaphysician of our times—properly compared with the likes of Plato, Shankara, and Meister Eckhart—but also a peerless expositor of religious forms and an unerring guide to the spiritual life itself. Schuon's general position—or better, the position to which he adhered, for "clearly truth is not a personal affair"[4]— was defined in his first work to appear in English, *The Transcendent Unity of Religions* (1953, first published in French in 1948). Here he elaborated the distinction between the outer and inner, the exoteric and esoteric dimensions of religious traditions and, by uncovering the metaphysical convergence of all integral religions, provided a coherent and irrefutable basis for a properly constituted inter-religious ecumenicism—one may well say the *only* possible basis.

[1] *Confessions*, IX.10.

[2] Seyyed Hossein Nasr, *Knowledge and the Sacred* (New York: Crossroad, 1981), p. 65.

[3] Other leading figures include Marco Pallis, Martin Lings, and Seyyed Hossein Nasr.

[4] Frithjof Schuon, *Light on the Ancient Worlds: A New Translation with Selected Letters*, ed. Deborah Casey (Bloomington, Indiana: World Wisdom, 2006), p. 24.

Schuon's writings encompass an astonishing range of religious phenomena from all parts of the globe. In more than two dozen books he has explicated the metaphysical and cosmological doctrines, the religious forms and the spiritual paths of all of the world's major traditions. His writings are always attentive to the claims of religious orthodoxy—there is nothing iconoclastic in his outlook—but, at the same time, they surpass the limits of any exoteric or purely theological understanding. The explanation of the exoteric-esoteric distinction is fundamental in Schuon's work but, unlike Guénon, he does not restrict himself to the latter domain alone. Certainly the bedrock of Schuon's work is "the totality of primordial and universal truths—and therefore of the metaphysical axioms—whose formulation does not belong to any particular system".[5] But this is combined with a unique sensitivity to the distinctive forms and the varying symbolic languages of the diverse religious traditions. One might say that Schuon gives to both Revelation, the divine source of all religious dispensations, and Intellection, the immediate and supra-rational apprehension of metacosmic realities, their full due. Gnosis—that is, the divine wisdom espoused by the great sages and mystics—must ever be the primary focus of any properly constituted esoterism. However, in the writings of many of those in pursuit of the *sophia perennis*, a recognition of this patrimony has all too often been accompanied by a dismissive, even disdainful, attitude to the claims of religious orthodoxy.[6]

For Schuon the study of tradition has meant, primarily, the study of religion within a metaphysical framework. He has written of religion in all its aspects and in the full plenitude of both its formal and mystical dimensions. He is equally at home with, say, the most abstruse subtleties of Eckhart's exposition of metaphysical knowledge, the dense symbolism of the medieval cathedral, and the simple pieties of a European peasant. We might also note that Schuon writes with equal authority on the traditions of the East and those of primordial non-literate peoples. He exhibits what Marco Pallis has called "'the gift of tongues'. . . the ability, that is to say, both to speak and to

---

[5] Frithjof Schuon, "The Perennial Philosophy", in *The Unanimous Tradition*, ed. Ranjit Fernando (Colombo: Sri Lanka Institute of Traditional Studies, 1991), p. 21.

[6] One thinks primarily of various twentieth century sub-continental "neo-Hindus" as well as the self-styled "California Vedantins". The charge certainly cannot be leveled at any of the traditionalists associated with Guénon and Schuon.

understand the various dialects through which the Spirit has chosen to communicate itself . . . the power to penetrate all traditional forms".[7] One aspect of this gift is Schuon's preternatural sensitivity to Beauty as a vehicle of the Spirit, for "Verily God is beautiful and He loves beauty" (*hadīth*) (p. 172); furthermore, as the author states, "Truth . . . wishes to be 'seen' and not merely 'thought'" (p. xviii).

Schuon's books are compilations of free-standing essays written in different places at sundry times, only brought together under a single canopy at a later date.[8] Each book covers a diversity of subjects such as might initially bewilder an uninitiated reader. The present volume is no exception. As the author states in his prefatory remarks, "This book . . . has no homogeneity other than that of doctrine" (p. xv). However, readers who have spent some time with Schuon's *oeuvre* will discern an underlying unity in all his writings and a pattern of recurring and interfused themes and motifs. These concerns can be readily identified in the structure of the present volume and in the headings which flag its three segments: "Metaphysics and Cosmology", "Forms of the Spirit", and "Spiritual Life", which might be thought of as three dimensions of Tradition—in a manner of speaking, height, breadth, and depth respectively. We might also identify these parts as being fundamentally concerned with *principles*, *forms*, and *practices*.

Part I focuses on *metaphysics*, the science of the Real, of the Absolute, and in its light, the world of relativities. In Hindu terms, metaphysics is concerned with *Ātmā* or *Brahman* (the Supreme Reality) and, *sub specie aeternitatis*, with *māyā* (the time-space tissue of relativities which the modern mind so often mistakes for "reality" unqualified). Metaphysical principles are true and valid once and for all and not only for this particular age or mentality, and could not, in any sense, "evolve"; neither an empirical and materialistic science, nor a profane and rationalistic "philosophy", can add anything or affect these axioms in any way whatever. *Cosmology*, concerned with the visible universe and couched in the inexhaustible language of symbols, is the extension and application of metaphysical principles to macrocosmic time-space phenomena.

---

[7] Marco Pallis, *The Way and the Mountain* (Peter Owen, London, 1960), p. 78.

[8] The one exception is *Understanding Islam* (first published in 1961), which the author conceived and wrote as a single volume.

Part II addresses a range of diverse religious *forms of the spirit*, embracing doctrines, myths, scriptures, symbols, rituals, ethical codes, sacred art, and all manner of institutions—in short, all that goes to make up this or that "religion" and which bears the imprint of the Revelation from which the tradition in question issued. The author's inquiry is always shaped by the esoteric viewpoint, one which penetrates, universalizes, and interiorizes the truths vouchsafed by the providentially appointed but necessarily limited dogmas and practices of each tradition.

Part III is concerned with the *spiritual life* itself and testifies to the proper relationship between metaphysical vision, religious forms, and the transformation of the human wayfarer by disciplined practice within the cadre of a religious tradition. As the author states elsewhere, "Knowledge saves only on condition that it engages all that we are: only when it constitutes a path that works and transforms and wounds our nature as the plough wounds the soil."[9] *The Eye of the Heart* is one of the author's earliest books; the metaphysical wisdom which he so clearly articulates in this work remained the touchstone of his whole corpus.

L'Oeil du Coeur (Paris: Gallimard) first appeared in 1950. This was followed by a revised and expanded edition in 1974, and another, more or less unchanged, in 1995. In 1997 the first English translation was published by World Wisdom; it included a Foreword by Huston Smith, three articles written since the book's first appearance, and some textual revisions by the author, these subsequently appearing in the fourth French edition of 2017. However, the 1997 edition omitted several articles, on Buddhist and Islamic subjects, which had appeared in the earlier versions. The present volume follows the second and third French editions while also incorporating some of the revisions and additions made to the 1997 version. It also includes the four illustrations especially chosen by the author for the first edition. Like its companions in the on-going World Wisdom series of new English-

---

[9] *Spiritual Perspectives and Human Facts: A New Translation with Selected Letters*, ed. James S. Cutsinger (Bloomington, Indiana: World Wisdom, 2007), p. 146.

language translations of Frithjof Schuon's books, it includes detailed editorial annotations, a comprehensive glossary of foreign words and phrases, and a selection of excerpts from the author's correspondence and previously unpublished writings.

Harry Oldmeadow

AUTHOR'S PREFACE

This book as a whole has no homogeneity other than that of doctrine. Some will doubtless find in the following pages nothing but dogmatic speculations and question-begging statements, and it will not be possible to make them understand that intrinsic truth is independent of any dialectic; indeed, from the standpoint of the truth, it is all the same whether the real be expressed this way or that, whether it finds expression through a dialectic finely-shaded with oratorical precautions or through apparently naive affirmations. Rationalism, for its part, admits as true only what can be proven, without taking into account, on the one hand, that truth is independent of our willingness to admit it or not, and on the other hand, that a proof is always proportioned to a particular understanding, so that there are truths that cannot be proven to everybody; strictly speaking, rationalist thought admits something not because it is true, but because it can be proven—or feigned to be proven—which amounts to saying that for rationalism dialectic outweighs truth, in fact, if not in theory. Specifically rationalist thought, moreover, readily overlooks the fact that there are mental needs due only to a deviation or a hypertrophy and which are consequently unable to provide legitimate points of departure for axiomatic formulations; if blind men could see light they would not dream of asking for proofs of its existence.

It is worth dwelling on this question of doctrinal proofs a little longer: firstly, a distinction must be made between rational or logical proof and intellectual or symbolic proof; the first is fallible to the extent that the propositions of the syllogism may be false, the likelihood of this increasing with the loftiness of the order of reality; the second, on the contrary, depends on premises that cannot but be exact, since they are identified with the very nature of things, that is to say, since the premises of the syllogism are inseparable from the realities being proven, the "proof" will be like a reflection enabling the syllogism to highlight them. The spiritual or symbolic proof—which could be termed "ontological" so as to distinguish it from the merely "logical" proof—thus depends on a direct knowledge that, as such, is exact by definition, and serves not to conclude from the known to the unknown, but to become aware of the unknown with the help of the known: consequently the link between the two will not be a rational operation, but intellectual intuition, even though reasoning, being natural to man, may obviously play a temporary supporting role or be an occasional cause. As a result, the symbolic proof—termed thus because its cogency lies in the analogy between the communicating symbol and the truth to be communicated, and not in the logical combination of two propositions—the symbolic proof, then, serves to actualize a knowledge that is not added somehow from without but is virtually contained in intelligence itself. One may even go further and say that the symbolic proof is identified with that which is to be proven, in the sense that it "is" that thing at a lesser level of reality, as for example water proves universal Substance by the fact that it "is" it on the plane of corporeal existence. What matters is not to confuse the materiality of the symbol with its ontological essence; this is why Hindu doctrine, when it advocates the worship of the Deity through a sacramental image, forbids the worshiper to think of the material substance of this image; and it is for the same reason that the North American Indians—those who take the sun as a support for worship—specify that it is not the sun they worship, but the "Father" or "Ancestor" who resides there invisibly. All the phenomena of nature are proofs of God, as the sacred Scriptures attest, and this is so for the common man as well as for the sage—albeit for very different reasons—but not necessarily so for the philosopher, who may have neither the eyes of Faith nor those of Knowledge, and who in this case struggles vainly with the contradictions of a sterile conceptualism.

The means of expression of metaphysical knowledge is a dialectic based either on logic or on symbols, with various degrees of accentuation and combination; this is what distinguishes Vedantism, for example, from Taoism, though the question of dialectic or expression does not separate or oppose them from the point of view of their common content, that of the pure truth. Most rationalists disregard doctrines having a symbolist form, but include *Vedānta* or Neoplatonism in their category of "philosophy", that is to say in their profane logic, while simultaneously affirming that their speculations were unable to resolve the "great problems" of the "human mind"; other rationalists, on the contrary, deny these same doctrines along with those of symbolist form on the pretext that they are "dogmatisms" unworthy of "philosophy". Indeed, nothing could be more convenient or consoling, when one is caught in a vicious circle, than to pretend either that others are likewise caught in it or else that they are unable to be caught in it; and some will even go so far as to blame intelligence itself for their impotence, the outcome of such an attitude being the grossly imaginative philosophy, supposedly "concrete" or "existential" and readily psychologist, that rules the mentality of our epoch.

In this vein of thought, we must note that the starting point of a doctrine is either definitive, static, or dogmatic if one will, or else a contradiction pure and simple: consequently, the starting point of a doctrine that posits a state of permanent flux and admits no stable truth is either definitively valid, in which case its reason for being, namely the theory of the indefinite evolution of truth, is false; or else the starting point attributes to itself the right to "evolve" and hence to change, in which case it is false by definition and could not be the premise of anything whatsoever. Analogously, absolute subjectivism collapses before its initial contradiction: its starting point is either objective, in which case the evident necessity of its own objectivity only proves the falsity of subjectivism, or else it is subjective, in which case it obviously has no objective value, and it is reduced to a meaningless monologue. It is assuredly absurd to affirm that no affirmation is true; similarly, it is senseless to speak to others to tell them that one does not believe in their existence; all that is being done in such cases is to deny the essential aspects of intelligence and truth, namely objective reality on the one hand and intellectual evidence on the other, both being inseparable in intellection.

The error of rationalism is not to prove that which reason can perfectly well grasp, namely the facts or laws of nature, but to wish to prove that of which reason can by its own means gain no certitude; everything that can be said about rationalism applies *a fortiori* to the more or less recent systems such as "intuitionism", the "philosophy of values", and "existentialism" which, far from going beyond the plane of reason, represent, and cannot do other than represent, merely the decomposition of rationalism at the end of its resources. Thus, the only thing we shall retain in this order of ideas is that the prejudice of enclosing intelligence within reason leads in practice to the denial of reason itself. It goes without saying that the so-called "realism" resulting therefrom—and which is merely nihilist "mysticism" fond of assuming a psychologistical style—can only envisage the "real" from a properly infra-human perspective. The current use of the term "abstractions" to designate principial realities is quite characteristic of this mentality: far from revealing a concrete vision of things, this term too often constitutes but one criterion among others of the incapacity to think posing as arbitrator of every possible thought.

Truth, in proportion to the loftiness of its aspects, wishes to be "seen" and not merely "thought"; when it is a question of transcendent truths, the mental operation can have only two functions, which are really the positive and negative modes of one function: to contribute to the individual's assimilation of the intellectual vision, and to eliminate the mental obstacles that are opposed to this vision, or in other words, that veil "the Eye of the Heart".

Part I

Metaphysics & Cosmology

The Eye of the Heart

The eye, owing to its particularly adequate correspondence with the Intellect, lends itself as it were spontaneously to traditional symbolism, and it is to be found, although varying widely in degree of importance, in the symbolic language of all Revelations. The other organs of sensation—or more generally, the faculties of which they are the vehicles—give rise, it is true, to analogous applications, but with a less central bearing, so to speak: they correspond rather to distinct and therefore secondary functions of the intelligence, or else to fundamental modes of receptivity and cognitive assimilation, which means that they demonstrate less directly than the eye—or sight—the analogy between sensible and spiritual knowledge; among the faculties of sensation, only sight represents the Intellect conceived of as such and in its principle. This evident correspondence between sight and the Intellect is due to the static and total character of the former: sight realizes in simultaneous mode—as does space, which among the conditions of corporeal existence corresponds to it—by far the widest possibilities in the domain of sensible knowledge, whereas the other senses react only to influences linked to vital sensibility; hearing should be excepted, however, for it reflects intellection not in its static and simultaneous, but in its dynamic and successive mode, and which plays what could be termed a "lunar" role in relation to sight; that is why it is linked, not to space, but to time, the audible being situated, finally, in duration.[1] Be that as it may, the most important sensation—or let us say the one which is intellectually the most explicit—is undeniably light, whatever might be the importance of primordial sound, and of spiritual perfumes, tastes, and touches. Sight alone communicates to our perception the existence of immeasurably remote heavenly bodies that are perfectly foreign to our vital interests, and it could therefore be said that it alone is essentially objective.[2] Consequently, it is only

---

[1] In a certain sense, the sun makes space known, and the moon time.

[2] Hearing is subjective—but not vital as are scent, taste, and touch—in the sense that it communicates things to us insofar as they concern us; sight communicates things to us only—and thereby all the more fully—insofar as they "are", not insofar as they "speak" to us. The comparison between music—an exclusively auditory art—and painting—an exclusively visual art—is altogether significant in this respect. As for speech, it is addressed by definition to an auditor; for instance, if a written divine

natural to compare light to knowledge and darkness to ignorance, and this is what explains the wide use made by the most diverse languages, and especially the sacred Scriptures, of the symbolism of light and sight on the one hand, and of darkness and blindness on the other.

The symbolic transposition of the visual act onto the intellectual plane provides a quite expressive image of identification through knowledge: in this process one must indeed see what one is and be what one sees or knows; the object in both cases is God, with the difference however that He appears as "concrete" in the first case and as "abstract" in the second. But the symbolism of sight is universal and is therefore applicable also to the macrocosm and to all its degrees: the world is an indefinitely differentiated vision whose object in the final analysis is the divine Prototype of all that exists and, conversely, God is the Eye that sees the world and which, being active where the creature is passive, creates the world by His vision, this vision being act and not passivity;[3] thus the eye becomes the metaphysical center of the world of which it is at once the sun and the heart.[4] God sees[5] not only the outward, but also—or rather with greater reason—the inward, and it is this latter vision that is the more real one, or strictly speaking, the only real one, since it is the absolute or infinite vision of which God is at once the Subject and the Object, the Knower and the Known. The universe is merely vision or knowledge, in whatever mode it may be realized, and its entire reality is God: the worlds are fabrics of visions,[6] and the content

Name appears to us with the impersonality of a doctrine, the same Name, as soon as it is uttered and heard, has the function of a call; the distinction between the metaphysical and the initiatic perspectives—insofar as such a distinction is possible and relatively legitimate—clearly appears here and also explains the fundamental part played by incantation in methods of spirituality.

[3] Here, traditional symbolism will preferably involve Speech—the Word—owing to its immediate intelligibility.

[4] There are numerous and profound correspondences between the eye, the heart, and the sun, which often makes it possible to consider them as synonymous. The eye is the sun of the body, as the heart is the sun of the soul, and the sun is at once the eye and the heart of the sky.

[5] God as "Seer", sees Himself as well as the world, including the minutest contingency—an "ant in the desert", to quote an expression of the Prophet. This, by the way, excludes all pantheism as well as all deism.

[6] A world is thus a collective and yet homogeneous dream whose constitutive elements are obviously compossibilities. Subjectivists falsely inspired by Hindu doctrine readily forget that the world is in nowise the illusion of a single individual; in reality it is a collective illusion within another collective illusion, that of the whole cosmos.

of these indefinitely repeated visions is always the Divine, which is thus the first Knowledge and the ultimate Reality[7]—Knowledge and Reality being two complementary aspects of the same divine Cause.

But let us now consider the function of the Eye of the Heart in the usual meaning of the expression, starting from the corporeal eye as the term of comparison: we would then say that the corporeal eye sees the relative, the so to speak broken aspect of God, whereas the Eye of the Heart[8] is identified with Him by the purity of its vision; the bodily eye is itself broken by its bipolarization that adapts it to perception, that is to say to the knowledge of the manifested as such; manifestation for its part proceeds from the principial bipolarization of Being into Word—or determining Essence, the domain of the Ideas in the Platonic sense—and into *Materia Prima*.[9] The Eye of the Heart, on the contrary, is unique and central, like the divine Face[10] which is its eternal vision, and which, being beyond all determination, is also beyond all duality. Thus the heart lies as if between two visions of God,

---

[7] In Hindu doctrine, the pole "Knowledge" is designated by the term *Chit* and the pole "Reality" by the term *Sat;* in the human microcosm, one can distinguish the poles intelligence and will or at a more outward degree, thought and action.

[8] Before the Sufis, this same expression (*Oculus Cordis*) was used by Saint Augustine and others; it is connected with the well-known theory of this Father and the Doctors who followed him, according to which the human intellect is enlightened by divine Wisdom. The question of knowing whether or not there is a historical connection between the "Eye of the Heart" of Plotinian doctrine (ὁ μόνος ὀφθαλμός), Augustinian doctrine, and Sufi doctrine (*'Ayn al-Qalb*) is doubtless unsolvable and in any case unimportant from the standpoint at which we place ourselves; it suffices to know that this idea is fundamental and is encountered almost everywhere. Let us not forget to mention that Saint Paul, in the Epistle to the Ephesians, speaks of the "eyes of your heart" (*illuminatos oculos cordis vestri, ut sciatis . . .*) (1:18). On the other hand, it is hardly necessary to recall that according to the eighth beatitude of the Sermon on the Mount, it is they whose hearts are pure who shall see God.

[9] In Hindu doctrine: *Purusha* and *Prakriti*, the male and female Principles. Sometimes the latter is considered as active and the former as passive, because woman is active as mother; she produces children, whereas man, in the sole respect of enjoyment, is passive.

[10] The "Face of God" (*Wajhu 'Llāh*) in Sufi symbolism, represents the divine essence (*Dhātu 'Llāh*, the Quiddity or Aseity, ὕπαρξις in Greek theology), that is to say, Reality veiled firstly by the innumerable degrees of universal Manifestation, then by the "Spirit" (*Ar-Rūh*) which is its center as well as its "luminous Essence" (*An-Nūr*), and finally by Being itself; that is why the "Face of God" is also called the "absolutely Invisible" (*Al-Ghayb al-mutlaq*), or the "Invisible of invisibles" (*Ghayb al-ghuyūb*).

one outward and indirect and the other inward and relatively direct,[11] and from this point of view the heart may be assigned a double role and a twofold meaning: firstly, it is the center of the individual as such and represents his fundamental limitation—his "hardening", as the Scriptures say—and thereby all his secondary limitations; secondly, it is the center of the individual insofar as he is mysteriously connected to his transcendent Principle: the heart is then identified with the Intellect,[12] with the Eye that sees God—and that consequently "is" God—and by which God sees man. In man, finally, it is only the heart that sees: outwardly, it sees the world through the mind and the senses, and inwardly, it sees the divine Reality in the Intellect; but strictly speaking, both visions—the outward as well as the inward— are but one, that of God. Between these two main visions there is an incompatibility in the sense that they cannot take place side by side in the same way and on the same level—notwithstanding the fact that the world can be seen in God and God in the world—firstly because the vision of the world is absorbed and annihilated by that of God, so that from this angle there cannot be a question of any reciprocity, and then because the created exists only due to its illusory particularization in relation to the Principle, so that its incompatibility with absolute Reality is implied by definition.

Returning to the duality of the bodily eye, it could be said that in the process of the bipolarization required by the projection of Being

---

[11] There is a contradiction in terms here that cannot be avoided in such a case.

[12] In this respect, it should be recalled that according to Meister Eckhart's expression, the Intellect is "uncreated": *Aliquid est in anima quod est increatum et increabile; si tota anima esset talis, esset increata et increabilis, et hoc est Intellectus.* One should never lose sight of the distinction between the uncreated and the created Intellect, the latter being the vehicle of the former. In Hindu doctrine, the first is *Chit* and the second *Buddhi*, both being, in Christian theology, the Holy Spirit, which is always envisaged in its aspect of essential unity and not that of the degrees of universal affirmation; furthermore, the Holy Spirit, in accordance with the specifically religious point of view, which is sacramental, hence excluding the natural aspects of the supernatural, is hardly considered as "naturally" inhering in man. The texts that speak only of the uncreated Intellect always imply the other, which amounts to saying that they mention it implicitly; on the other hand, when it is said that the seat or place of actualization of the Intellect is the subtle or animic heart, it is always the created Intellect that is in question *a priori* and in an immediate fashion, even when, through essential synthesis and by omitting a link in the train of thought, one attributes to this Intellect the uncreated character of the divine Intelligence. Be that as it may, it goes without saying that the created Intellect is supra-rational like its unmanifested prototype.

into manifested mode, the pair of eyes, along with hearing and the other senses, marks the outermost limit and outcome of this process;[13] this is what explains the organic equivalence and symmetrical position of the eyes, whereas between the heart and the brain there is at most a certain physiological equivalence. The two eyes represent a bipolar projection of the brain into a domain of lesser possibility; the brain thus is the intermediary between the analytical vision of the eyes and the synthetic vision of the heart, and this intermediary role is even, in a certain sense, its entire reason for being, since man, owing to his individuation, has illusorily separated himself from Reality and has to find it outside himself. If one represents the heart and the brain by the two extremities of a vertical element, and the eyes as the extremities of a horizontal axis placed upon the upper end of the vertical, we obtain the form of a T, which can be regarded as the geometrical formula of the process of bipolarization and which can therefore symbolize in this fashion the relationship between two dualities—in whatever manner these are conceived, on condition that the first couple be principial in relation to the second.

If the Eye of the Heart is generally thought of as being hidden in man and looking at God, although strictly speaking such a manner of expression is contradictory, this same Eye, as we have said, is also—and even above all—the Eye of God that looks at man; or, in other words, it is that of the divine Principle which encompasses manifestation in its Omniscience. Now, if on the one hand we say that the Eye of the Heart is the Eye of manifestation seeing the Principle, and on the other hand, that it is the Eye of the Principle seeing manifestation,[14] we are

---

[13] If it were not thus, the left eye, which corresponds to the brain and to the past as the right eye corresponds to the heart and to the future—the frontal Eye of Hindu symbolism corresponding to the present, hence to the timeless or to eternity—the left eye, we say, ought to give rise to a new bipolarization: which is not the case, since the ontological process of bipolarization comes to an end precisely with the organs of sensation.

[14] An entirely analogous teaching was given to us—long after we had written these lines—by a wise man of the Oglala Sioux: "I am blind and I do not see the things of this world; but when the Light comes from On High, it illuminates my heart and I can see, because the Eye of my heart (*Chante Ishta*) sees all things. The heart is the sanctuary at the center of which is a small space where the Great Spirit (*Wakan-Tanka*) lives, and this is the Eye. This is the Eye of the Great Spirit by which He sees everything, and by which we see Him. When the heart is not pure, the Great Spirit cannot be seen, and if you should die in this ignorance, your soul will not be able to return at once to the Great Spirit, but will have to be purified by wanderings across the Cosmos. To know

faced with a relationship of inverse analogy, since vision starting from manifestation has to function as a projection or inverse reflection of the vision deriving from the Principle; and if we determine the first of these two visions as being passive in relation to its divine Object, we must, as mentioned earlier, consider the divine vision as being active, which amounts to identifying it with the creative act. Thus God may be conceived in accordance with four great visions, that is to say as self-realizing Himself in His All-Knowledge in four ways: first of all, God sees Himself in Himself, in his Essence;[15] secondly, He sees Himself through Creation, which is none other than His vision of Himself by virtue of the realization of the negative, hence limiting, possibility included in His All-Possibility;[16] thirdly, He sees Himself through His creatures, which see Him in Creation;[17] fourthly, He sees Himself

the center of the heart where the Great Spirit dwells, you must be pure and good and live according to the way that the Great Spirit has taught us. The man who is pure in this way, contains the Universe in the Pocket of his Heart (*Chante Ognaka*)."

It is impossible not to recall here the Hindu theory of the "Abode of *Brahman*": this Abode (*Brahma-pura*) is in the minutest ventricle (*guhā*) of the heart (*hridaya*), which contains in its turn a small lotus with a small cavity (*dahara*) occupied by the ether (*ākāsha*), the symbolic support of *Brahman*. According to Saint John Climacus, the Eye of the Heart can see the divine "Sun of the Intelligence" and, in this case, the contemplative sees himself all luminous.

[15] Strictly speaking, this form of expression applies only to Being and not to That which transcends and as it were envelops it; however, since nothing is in Being that is not in this supreme Essence—for the "Son" has nothing that the "Father" does not possess—the symbolism of seeing must necessarily apply to God in His supreme Reality, even though, in this case, the visual act dissolves into an undifferentiated Knowledge in which there is no longer any trace of bipolarization. Be that as it may, when we say that "God sees Himself in Himself", we are thinking in the first place of the creator Being, since all other visions derive from it, and since it is the creator Being that primarily justifies the universal application of the symbolism of sight.

[16] Sufi symbolism frequently compares Creation to a mirror in which God is reflected.

[17] An *Upanishad* says that "it is not for love of the spouse that the spouse is dear, but for love of the *Ātman* that is in her". Without being aware of it and without willing it, and no matter what they do, beings therefore know and love God, and that is why Meister Eckhart could say: "The more he blasphemes, the more he praises God." This knowledge and this love, being universal, could not be limited to men alone, quite the contrary: for man by definition has the faculty of seeing God beyond appearances and, correlatively, he also has the possibility of denying God, which is not the case for peripheral creatures: a bird greeting the dawn or the sunrise is really and necessarily greeting God; a plant turning towards the light really turns towards Him.

through His creatures, which see Him through the Eye of the Heart.[18] The first of these visions is beyond all duality; the second is realized through the Eye of the Heart; the third function operates via the bodily eye, which represents the individual as such; the fourth again emanates from the Eye of the Heart, this time according to the usual meaning of the symbolism, namely that of the "inward" vision that the Intellect has of God. God's vision proceeds from Him and ends in Him, like a circle that originates and closes upon itself.

When an analogy is established between this inner Eye and the frontal Eye of Shiva, the latter corresponding in man to the consciousness of eternity—lost as a natural faculty to the fallen humanity of the "iron age"—it could be said that this third eye has withdrawn from the surface of being, just as the earthly Paradise, according to certain Asiatic traditions, has withdrawn under the earth;[19] and just as this kingdom is to reappear at the end of the "dark age", the Eye of the Heart may be conceived, in spiritual realization, as having to re-ascend, like the rising sun, to the forehead, which represents the surface, in order to illuminate and absorb the plane of individual obscuration, so that the outer world will be spontaneously conceived of in its essence and will be merged with inward Reality.[20] However, this way of looking at things is somewhat human, since fundamentally it is man who has withdrawn from the eternal Eye, and it is humanity that has withdrawn from Paradise and not the reverse, just as it is the earth that turns away from the sun, despite appearances to the contrary; thus it could be said that man in search of God must descend

---

[18] In the terrestrial world, these are the men who, in conformity with the sufficient reason of the human state, open themselves to the divine Light, and whose hearts are not hardened; although the perspective that we give here concerns only spirituality in the strict sense of the word, this category of men can include those individuals who, while not having a true intellectual intuition of God, nonetheless turn towards Him according to their capacities and thus conform to that which consists in their sufficient reason.

[19] It is in accordance with this same symbolism that certain sanctuaries, for instance those of the Pueblo Indians, are underground.

[20] The Hindu theory of the *Avatāra*s can be connected to the analogy just set forth: having been hidden—from the earthly point of view—beneath the veils of the created, God appears suddenly like a sun on the surface of the human world in order to illuminate and reintegrate it into His own invisible Reality.

into his own heart to rediscover the lost Paradise and to realize the "Unicity of Existence" (*Wahdat al-Wujūd*).[21]

This unicity or identity has been expressed by the Sufi Mansur Al-Hallaj in terms that are like a synthesis of the entire doctrine: "I saw my Lord with the Eye of my Heart; and I said: Who art Thou? He told me: Thyself!"

---

[21] The word *Wujūd* here has the meaning of Reality, without restriction. The term *Wahdat al-Wujūd* has also been translated as "Supreme Identity" and as "existential Monism".

On Knowledge

All knowledge is by definition knowledge of absolute Reality; which is to say that Reality is the necessary, unique, and essential object of all possible knowledge. While it is true that there are kinds of knowledge that seem to have other objects, it is not insofar as they are Knowledge but insofar as they are modalities or limitations of it that they have them; and if these objects seem not to be Reality, this is so not insofar as they are the Object of Knowledge, but insofar as they are modalities or limitations of that Object, which is God seen by God.

The very existence of the world seems to contradict these assertions; is the world not different from absolute Reality, from the one and divine Object? The answer is that the world, while not being this Reality, is nonetheless its expression and thereby its limitation; hence it is Reality not as such, but insofar as it affirms itself within given limits; and these limits result from its infinity, as we shall see later. Thus, to speak of the "world" is implicitly to speak of "God". In strict terms, the world, insofar as it is not God, is reduced to nothing; but insofar as it is not nothing, it is essentially God.[1] Knowledge of the world is less true than Knowledge of divine Reality, but in the final analysis it is always a knowledge of this Reality, for we know the world because it is real and for no other reason. In the order of principles, distinction is premised on ignorance, for the One alone is real, and not that which is distinguished; that is why distinction is premised on knowledge in

---

[1] Each thing is God and the sage sees the divine Face in each thing—howbeit according to very different relationships—or, more exactly, he sees the divine Face "through" each thing. This precision is imperative in order that no one be tempted to see pantheism in a conception that is as far from it as possible. The pantheistic error arises from the incapacity to see God in the appearances, whence the confusion—atheistic at the same time as being idolatrous—between the world and God; which is to say that pantheism consists in nothing other than the error of admitting an identity that is material and not essential between the Principle and manifestation. The idea of "God's existence", although it has a certain legitimacy from the purely human point of view—for which "existence" is synonymous with "reality"—is not foreign, however, to the genesis of the pantheistic conception, in the sense that "God's existence" is a first stage towards the "divinity of that which exists". If we too appear to attribute to the created a divine aspect, it is however in a totally different manner and in a purely metaphysical sense that has nothing either material or quantitative about it.

11

the manifested order, where the relationship is inverted with respect to the principial order.

But the objective world is not the only limitation in universal Knowledge; the world also presents a subjective aspect: it is the macrocosm, yet by very definition it implies the microcosm whose unity brings the cosmic diversity back to the Principle, symbolically at least. The distinction between the "I" and the "not-I" is spontaneous, hence real, even though the "I" is inseparable from the "outward" world, both aspects being complementary. It is necessarily so: once the Supreme Reality affirms itself distinctively and thus outside its own Aseity, the distinctive character of its affirmation must be expressed by the duality or complementarity of the knower and the known. Man is thus able to know, on the one hand, pure Reality, and on the other hand, the world and, within it, the I—Metacosm, macrocosm, and microcosm—without his being, insofar as he knows, anything but Knowledge, and without the external world and the ego, insofar as they are susceptible of being known, that is, insofar as they are real, being anything but Reality. To say that we know ourselves amounts to saying that we know Reality insofar as it is ourselves; for there is no object of knowledge, whether around or within us, that is not essentially—not existentially—the one Reality, and there is no one who knows, if it be not immanent Knowledge, which is infinite.

However, no one would deny that man does more than just know, he also acts and therefore necessarily distinguishes action from knowledge. Now, if knowledge reflects divine Reality, action must also reflect it; if God did not act—or rather, if He were in no way pure Act—the creature could not act. Yet the divine Act is nothing other than the expression or the secondary mode of the divine Knowledge. Just as the divine Object of divine Knowledge is subject to the limitation constituting the world, so too this Knowledge itself is subject to a universal limitation: this is the affirmation, the act, which seems to oppose Knowledge as the world seems to be opposed to God; but in reality, the divine Knowledge acts, and the divine Act knows. Created—or "acted"—by God, we know; that is why, knowing, we act. It is because the divine Omniscience knows us that we exist; our existence is the knowledge that the Infinite has of our possibility.

The meaning and sufficient reason of man is to know, and to know is ineluctably to know the Divinity. Knowing the Divinity, man has no choice but to affirm it, proclaim it, teach it, since action by definition manifests God, and since the creature can therefore do nothing that does not is some way affirm God; likewise, a being acts as soon as it begins to live, and its actions are the manifestation of its life. Man's existence, like the existence of every being, has no meaning if it is not the affirmation of the Divinity. The Divinity affirms man in giving him existence, and man affirms—and must affirm—the Divinity because he exists. Not to affirm the Divinity would only make sense if we did not exist; now this supposition is absurd, for we do exist.

Given that he exists, man cannot therefore keep himself from affirming the Divinity in one way or another. If he denies, or rather thinks that he denies the Divinity, the very existence of the denier affirms the One whom he denies. Man can say no, but his existence says yes. Whoso denies the Divinity denies his own existence and it will be taken from him—because he takes it from himself—even though it cannot be taken from him effectively, that is to say other than in symbolic fashion. If it happens that beings can unconsciously deny their existence by consciously denying the Divinity, but without being able to remove this existence since they have not given it to themselves, it is again because the Divinity is infinite, and thus affirmation of it must, in its own way, retrace this Infinity: indeed, the Divinity, being infinite, comprises all the possibilities inherent in Infinity; now nothingness is a possibility, at the degree assigned to it by All-Possibility, and the latter by definition cannot exclude any possibility. If Infinity did not comprise nothingness to the extent that nothingness is possible, it would be limited by the absence of this nothingness, and therefore it would not be Infinity. Now nothingness, while being impossibility, can be said to be possible in a certain sense, otherwise it would be altogether inconceivable and, with all the more reason, inexpressible. Certainly, it is not in itself possible, for in itself it has no reality or existence, but it is possible in Infinity and owing to it. In other words, if Infinity were to leave outside itself its own negation, or rather the appearance of its own negation, it would not be Infinity. Imperfection is nothing other than a necessary aspect of mani-fested Infinity; imperfection exists because the Infinite is infinite and consequently because the non-existence of imperfection would limit Infinity, which is Perfection in relation to this imperfection. Imperfection does not exist in any way outside Infinity, since, as we have said, it has neither reality nor existence in itself. The Word, which is the affirmation of the Infinite, must affirm all of its aspects or all of its possibilities. The Word must therefore affirm evil, not as such, but as the necessary shadow of the cosmic affirmation of the Infinite.[2]

If man were not essentially Knowledge, according to the fundamental modes just described, his end could not be Knowledge, for one can become only what one is. If the universe were not Knowledge, the way towards Reality could not be Knowledge. As everything is Knowledge, and as there is nothing except Knowledge—Love also being Knowledge—there is nothing that could lead to Knowledge except Knowledge.

If we say: we know a given thing, we mean: the Divinity, inasmuch as it is us, knows the Divinity inasmuch as it is a given thing; so that all knowledge is that which Divinity has of itself; and this Knowledge is absolute and infinite Plenitude.

---

[2] "Just as the sun, eye of the world, is not sullied by the outward impurities that our mortal eyes perceive, likewise the unique Being that is in all things is not sullied by the evil that reigns in the world, for It is distinct from it" (*Katha Upanishad*, V:11).

An-Nūr

According to a teaching (*hadīth*) of the Prophet, "the first of the things *Allāh* created (that is to say: the first unmanifested Reality in the divine tendency to manifestation, or the first divine self-determination with a view to creation) is the Pen (*Qalam*), which He created of Light (*Nūr*), and which is made of white pearl; its length is equal to the distance which is between the sky and the earth (the distance which separates them, that is to say: the incommensurability between form-less—or supra-formal—and formal Manifestation). Then He created the Tablet (*Lawh*, or *Lawh al-Mahfūz*, the 'Guarded Tablet'), and it is made of white pearl, and its surfaces are of red rubies; its length is equal to the distance which is between the sky and the earth, and its width stretches from the East to the West" (it embraces all the pos-sibilities of Manifestation).

According to another teaching "there is near to *Allāh* a Tablet one side of which is of red rubies and the other of green emerald (colors which, like red in relation to white, indicate the differentia-tion of cosmic tendencies, the *guna*s of Hindu doctrine), and its Pens (*Aqlām*) are of Light" (the Principle of universal Manifestation—the Hindu *Purusha*—is conceived here as a plurality of vertical rays, which correspond respectively to the essential possibilities derived from the divine Names or aspects of Being).[1]

---

[1] According to another possible interpretation of the colors of the Guarded Tablet, one of the colors represents universal Substance insofar as it retains its undifferenti-ated purity, and the other this same Substance insofar as it manifests the possibilities transmitted by the Pen; in the first case, Substance—like Mary who is an incarnation of it—is Virgin, and in the second it is Mother (of the manifested Universe); as Virgin, it is the undifferentiated Substance of universal manifestation (*Jawhar al-habā'*, literally "Substance comparable to a cloud of dust", that is to say, undifferentiated); as Mother, it is the differentiating Substance (*Tabī'at al-kull*, literally "total" or "universal Na-ture")—one might say the efficient Cause—of manifested things. In the first case, the Tablet is "white", and in the second it is "colored". This distinction between *Jawhar al-habā'* and *Tabī'at al-kull* is not without analogy with the distinction that Hindu doctrine establishes between *Prakriti* (which is none other than *Natura naturans*) and *Vikriti* (*Natura naturata*), this latter term signifying Substance insofar as it is differenti-ated or actualized in its productions. The expression *Jawhar al-habā'* is frequently em-ployed in the sense of *Materia secunda*; the term *Al-Jawhar al-hayūlāni* ("the material Substance"), very frequently too has the same sense; often, one simply says *Al-Habā*

Another tradition, reported by Ibn Abbas, says that "*Allāh* created the Pen before He created the Creation (*Khalq*), and He was on the Throne (*Allāh* is on the Throne when a relativity is envisaged, the Throne signifying here, not formless Manifestation, but the immutable Transcendence or the incommensurable 'discontinuity' of the Principle in relation to its more or less relative aspects, so that this second proposition means that the ontological Principle remains unaffected by its bi-polarization from which cosmic manifestation will proceed);[2] and the Pen looked towards Him with a look of reverential fear (*haybah*) and burst open; and the Ink (*Midād*, which represents the initial and undifferentiated possibility of manifestation, while the Letters—*Hurūf*—mark its indefinite differentiation) issued drop by drop from it". The divine Incommensurability having mirrored itself in the Pen—its existential self-determination—the latter could not contain within the limits of its determination the incommensurability of the divine Indetermination, and translated it into differentiated mode; the Ink is thus the reflection of All-Possibility—a reflection which, as

("the cloud of dust") or *Al-Hayūlā* (from ὕλη, "first Matter"). As for the expression *Al-'Unsur al-a'zam* ("the supreme Element"), it signifies exclusively *Prakriti* as such. Islamic symbolism views the universal Substance also as "the Book" (*Al-Kitāb*) or the "Mother of the Book" (*Umm al-Kitāb*, the Book being in this case the Revelation, or by extension the entire cosmos); the Pen, itself, often has the name of "supreme Pen" (*Al-Qalam al-a'lā*), which indicates its identification with the *Logos*. According to Ibn Arabi, the terms *Al-Qalam*, *Al-'Aql al-awwal* ("The first Intellect"), *Ar-Rūh al-kullī* ("The universal Spirit"), *Al-Haqq al-makhlūq bihi* ("The Truth by which the created exists"), and *Al-'Adl* ("Justice", "Equilibrium") are synonymous; *Al-Qalam* is then here not the Word, but its cosmic refraction, *Ar-Rūh*, "The Spirit", of which the passive or feminine aspect is *An-Nūr*, "The Light".

[2] Since the Throne indicates a relationship—that of the Principle in relation to its manifestation—this symbol can be applied at different levels. In his treatise *'Uqlat al-mustawfiz*, Ibn Arabi says that "the infinitely glorious Throne (*Al-'Arsh al-majīd*) is the uncreated Intellect (*Al-'Aql*, which is identical to the supreme Pen), and the immense Throne (*Al-'Arsh al-azīm*) is the uncreated Soul (*An-Nafs*), which is the Guarded Tablet; then comes (in descending order) the Throne of Clemency (*Al-'Arsh ar-rahmānī*), which is the sphere of spheres, and the generous Throne (*Al-'Arsh al-karīm*) which is none other than the Footstool (*Al-Kursī*)". Generally speaking the fundamental cosmological symbols of Islam can be applied at different levels, including the metacosmic sphere, and this is because of their concrete nature, which is the mark of their universality. To the objection that this imprecision of technical terms makes Sufi texts very difficult to read, it may be replied that the latter were always accompanied by the oral teaching of a school for which the terms in question had a perfectly precise meaning.

such, could correspond only to the possibility of manifestation—and it will be transmuted by the Pen into indefinitely diverse existential possibilities. All-Possibility is the totality of the divine Names (*Asmā'*) or Mysteries (*Asrār*), and that is also the higher meaning of the Letters, which will then be conceived as inherent either in the supreme Essence (*Dhāt*), and so in Non-Being or more precisely in Beyond-Being, or in the Qualities (*Sifāt*), and so in Being,[3] without prejudice to the fact that Being is "one" *ad intra* (*ittisālan*) as well as *ad extra* (*infisālan*);[4] it is in this sense that the higher Letters (purely principial, each being *Allāh*, but none being the others), are "mirrored" in the Pen which, "being made of Light", receives their reflection and "bursts open" under the pressure (symbolized by *al-haybah*, the reverential dread) of their incommensurability, to transcribe them in manifested, created, "broken" mode.

Ibn Abbas says that "the Pen burst open and the Ink flows from it until the Day of the Resurrection (*Yawm al-Qiyāmah*, that is to say so long as the cycle of universal manifestation lasts); and *Allāh* commanded the Pen: Write! And the Pen replied: Lord, what shall I write? He said: Transcribe my Science of my Creation; all that will exist until the Day of the Resurrection (the totality of the possibilities of manifestation included in the divine Omniscience)".[5] According to Said ibn

---

[3] The divine Names are divided into Names of the Essence or of the Quiddity (*Asmā' dhātiyyah*) and Names of the Qualities (*Asmā' sīfātiyyah*); these latter refer to the aspects of Being. For example, "the Holy" (*Al-Quddus*) is a Name of the Essence, for there is nothing in *Allāh* that is not holy; on the other hand, "He who is full of pardon" (*Al-Ghaffār*) is the Name of a Quality, not of the Essence, for all in God is not pardon, since he has also the Quality of "Avenger" (*Al-Muntaqim*). The Names of Quality are either "glorious" or "terrible" (*jalāliyyah*), or Names of "Beauty" (*jamāliyyah*), that is to say beneficent or merciful.

[4] Which means that Being is without associates and also without parts; in the first sense it is "unique" and in the second sense it is "one".

[5] This passage indicates the phallic symbolism of the Pen, which recalls the creator *lingam* of Shiva, and which moreover brings clearly to light the sacred character of sexual union. On the other hand, it is worth noting the relationship between the Pen and the prophetic function or—from another point of view—supreme sanctity: thus the Prophet Muhammad says of himself: "I am the Pen" (*Anā'l-Qalam*); similarly *Sayyidnā* Ali, the "Saint John of Islam", said: "I am the (diacritical) point beneath the letter *bā*; I am the side of *Allāh* (the Word 'seated on the right hand of God') ; I am the Pen; I am the Guarded Tablet; I am the Throne of *Allāh*; I am the seven Heavens". One will also notice the similarity between the command given by *Allāh* to the Pen: "Write!" and the command of the Archangel Jibrail to Muhammad: "Read!", as also

Mansur, "the first thing that the Pen wrote was: in truth my Mercy precedeth My Wrath" (*Inna Rahmatī sabaqat Ghadabī*).[6]

Ibn Abbas also relates that "the Pen set down in that hour that which will exist until the Day of the Resurrection (the *pralaya* of Hindu doctrine), and that which has been determined of good and of evil, of happiness and of unhappiness, in conformity with the divine Utterance: We have counted (predestined) every thing in a precise model (a prototype) (Koran, *Sūrah "Yā Sīn"* [36]:11); which is to say: on the Guarded Tablet". "In truth, there is next to *Allāh* a tablet of white pearl at which He looks each day and each night three hundred and sixty times;[7] and with every look, He creates and makes to subsist and kills and revives and dethrones and enthrones and does that which He wills" (that is to say: that which no individual will can ever modify, and that of which individuals as such do not know the causes).

Finally, one other *hadīth* of the Prophet may be mentioned: "*Allāh* has written the destinies of creatures fifty thousand years (a symbolical number expressing the incommensurability between the principial order and the manifested order) before He created the heavens (formless manifestation) and the earth (formal manifestation)." And a commentator adds: "This *hadīth* shows that the Pen preceded (principially and ontologically) the Throne, and that it is the first of created things (the word 'created' having here the meaning not of 'manifested', but of 'determined'); and He created the Tablet after it (the Pen)."[8]

---

between the reply of the Pen, "What shall I write?" and that of Muhammad: "I cannot read"—replies directly connected with the "illiterate" (*ummī*) quality appertaining to the Prophet; likewise, the annunciation made to the Virgin Mary presents, in all essential details, a remarkable analogy with the examples that we have just cited.

[6] *Allāh* is *Ar-Rahmān* ("the Clement") in Himself and in relation to the total Creation, and *Ar-Rahīm* ("the Merciful") in relation to creatures; it is said also that *Allāh* was *Ar-Rahmān* "before" the Creation (that is to say, beyond the latter, in Himself, in the sense of the Sanskrit term *Ānanda*), and that he is *Ar-Rahīm* "since" the Creation (that is to say, within the latter and "outside of Himself"); the first of these Qualities is intrinsic and the second extrinsic.

[7] The number three hundred and sixty glances of *Allāh* corresponds to the three hundred and sixty degrees of the Zodiac, the revolution of which takes place in one day and one night.

[8] A *hadīth* says: "I was Prophet when Adam was yet between water and mud"—a formulation that comprises the same meaning as this other: "I am the Pen". This calls to mind a saying of Christ: "In truth, before Abraham (as an individual) was, I am" (as God). The Holy Virgin too was created before the Creation, as the *Shakti* of Christ, to

If the Creation took place fifty thousand years after the inscription of the "destinies of creatures"—it is worth underscoring—this symbolically temporal gap indicates the transcendence of the Pen and of the Tablet in relation to the result of their common act; when this act is considered as a predestination, following Western terminology—it would be better to say "apportionment" (*qismah*, whence the Turkish word *kismet*) or "choice" (*ikhtiyār*)—care must be taken to understand this in the sense of a purely principial and so extra-temporal relationship. The two instruments of universal manifestation are themselves the two first Letters of the divine Alphabet respectively, that is to say the *alif* and the *bā*; all the other Letters are contained virtually in the diacritical point under the *bā*, this point being the reflected image of the divine Unity; it is the first drop of Ink that escaped from the Pen and its meaning is "Mercy" (*Rahmah*).

The common act of the two divine instruments has two aspects, the one principial and the other effective, in conformity with the teachings quoted above; thus "the Pen set down at that moment that which will exist until the Day of the Resurrection", and "*Allāh* inscribed the destinies of fifty thousand years before He created the heavens and the earth"; on the other hand, "the Ink runs until the Day of the Resurrection"; that is to say, not only has the Pen written, but it is permanently writing as things become manifested; in the first case, the Pen determines the possibilities of manifestation in the principial order, and in the second, it realizes them in the manifested order by its immediate act. It may be added that the two surfaces of the Tablet are symbolically equal to the "two seas" (*bahrayn*), that is to say, to the "upper Waters" and the "lower Waters", which are respectively formless—or supra-formal—possibilities and formal possibilities.

—— ·:· ——

use Hindu terms; Christ is the "Pen", and the Virgin the "Guarded Tablet"—returning to Islamic symbolism—whereas the Prophet comprises both aspects; his quality of "illiterateness" corresponds to the "purity" of the Virgin, and so to the attribute of "guarded" or "preserved" (*mahfūz*), which designates the protocosmic Tablet. Moreover, the "Immaculate Conception" is a necessary derivation from this pre-existential character of the Virgin.

The Throne (*'Arsh*), being the first "creation" after the Pen and the Tablet, and therefore the manifestation of the first word that is inscribed thereon—and which is "Mercy" (*Rahmah*)—corresponds to what the Hindu doctrine designates by the term *Buddhi* (or *Mahat*), which is the first of all manifestations, namely that of *Brahma* affirming Himself as universal Intellect; from this it will be apparent that the Pen and the Tablet, which precede the Throne "by fifty thousand years", coincide respectively with the two principles that the Hindu doctrine calls *Purusha* and *Prakriti*, the two unmanifested poles of every manifestation.[9]

A difficulty might seem to arise here owing to the fact that the Pen, the Tablet, and the Throne, which nonetheless belong, as we have seen, to incommensurably distinct degrees of reality, are said to be "created", or more precisely "created of Light"; however, the unitary perspective of Islam admits in God only the distinction of the "Essence" (*Dhāt*) and of the "Attributes" (*Sifāt*)[10] and has to consider as being "created" (*makhlūq*) that which could appear to be an "association" (*shirk*);[11] the Attributes are all aspects of Unity; while the sole point for being of the pair *Qalam-Lawh*—or *Purusha-Prakriti*—is its duality.

As for the "Light" (*Nūr*), which is simultaneously attributed—like the character of "creature"—to divine, and therefore unmanifested, Realities, and to cosmic, and therefore manifested, realities (or more precisely to realities belonging to formless manifestation), it must be appreciated that the cosmos comprises three fundamental degrees: firstly, "earth" (*tīn*), secondly "fire" (*nār*), and thirdly "light" (*nūr*); the

---

[9] According to a cosmological theory of Ibn Arabi—a theory that derives from a more analytical perspective than that of the *ahādīth* quoted, and which is founded on the terminology of Plotinus—the Guarded Tablet is identified with the "Universal Soul" (*An-Nafs al-kulliyah*), the ψυχή of the Plotinian system. In this case, the Guarded Tablet will only be the distinctive aspect of *Prakriti*; the latter, from the standpoint of its indifferentiation, will be identified with the "supreme Element" (*Al-'Unsur al-a'zam*).

[10] The apophatic theology of the Greek Church knows this distinction between the "Quiddity" and the "Energies".

[11] According to Ibn Arabi, the idea of creation (*khalq*) comprises two aspects: according to the first, creation signifies the essential determination (*ta'ayyun*) of possibilities in the state of non-manifestation; according to the second aspect, which must be limited to the divine Name, "The Producer" (*Al-Bāri'*), the creation is the "manifestation", that is to say, the production in distinctive mode, of the essential and immutable determinations (*Al-A'yān ath-thābitah*).

human body, like the whole sensory order (*'ālam al-mulk*, in Sanskrit *sthūla-sharīra*), is made of "earth", beings of the "subtle state" (*'ālam al-malakūt*, in Sanskrit *sukshma-sharīra*)—that is to say spirits (*jinn*)—are made of "fire", and the angels and the whole formless order (*'ālam al-jabbarūt*, in Sanskrit *vijnānamaya-kosha*) are made of "light". These three cosmic substances, if one can so call them, are static expressions of the qualities or tendencies inherent in the cosmos—the *guna*s of Hindu doctrine—in the sense that the "earth" (or more exactly the "clay" from which the body of Adam was made) or gross manifestation is obscurity or ignorance (*tamas*); "fire" or subtle manifestation is expansion or passion (*rajas*); and "light" or formless manifestation is the tendency towards Reality or conformity to Being (*sattva*). Now, if the summit of the cosmos is light by reason of its conformity to Being, Being itself will be *a fortiori* Light (*'ālam al-'izzah* or *'ālam al-ghayb*, in Sanskrit *ānandamaya-kosha*), for the luminosity of the heavens can derive its origin only from the Light of God; to say that the heavens are "created" of Light can therefore signify only one thing, namely that they are alone in being directly conformed to the divine Light, and consequently in being identified with this Light in the sense of an essential identity. God is necessarily the Archetype of all light: "*Allāh* is the Light of the heavens and of the earth" (Koran, *Sūrah* "Light" [24]:35).

Ibn Abi Hatim says in his commentary that "*Allāh* created the Throne of His Light, and the Footstool (*Kursī*) from the periphery adjoining the Throne; and round the Throne are four rivers: a river of sparkling light, a river of blazing fire, a river of white snow, and a river of water, and the angels stand upright in these rivers and glorify *Allāh*". "*Allāh* is 'seated' on the Throne" and his "Feet"—the one symbolizing "Glory" (*Jalāl*) or "Anger" (*Ghadab*) and the other "Beauty" (*Jamāl*) or "Mercy" (*Rahmah*)—are placed on the Footstool, which contains formal manifestation; the "Throne" itself constitutes formless manifestation, "made of Light", and that is why it is called "the Throne which encompasses" (*Al-'Arsh al-muhīt*), in conformity with the teaching of the Koran, since the formless cosmos in fact encompasses the formal cosmos. From the Footstool "Glory" and "Mercy" radiate as far as the earth, "Mercy" prevailing over "Glory" as it is proclaimed in the inscription on the Throne already quoted: "My Mercy precedeth My Wrath." Again according to Ibn Abi Hatim "*Allāh* created the Throne out of green emerald, and made for it four columns of red rubies; the distance which separates one column from another is that of a journey of eighty thousand years . . . and the columns are carried by eight angels, and it is like a dome above the angels and the world".[12]

The same exegetist gathered the following *hadīth*: "In truth, the Throne (which is here identified with *Ar-Rūh*, 'the Spirit') was on the water (cosmic possibilities), and when *Allāh* created the heavens, He placed it above the seven heavens, and placed the clouds (*sahāb* or *ghamām*)[13] as a sieve for the rain (the graces, whether spiritual or psychic or even physical, emanating from the Throne, of which the visible sky is the terrestrial image); were it not thus, the earth would be submerged (manifestation would be annihilated, or rather re-absorbed or re-integrated by the immensity of the divine Mercy, as if the Name *Rahīm* were replaced by the Name *Rahmān*)."[14] Ibn Abbas adds: "Rain water derives from a sea situated between heaven and earth, and this sea possesses a multitude of waters. . . . *Allāh* entrusted the rain to the angels, and not one drop descends without being accompanied by an angel who places it on the spot that *Allāh* has chosen, whether on the earth (the physical world), or in the sea (*al-bahr al-muhīt*, 'the sea which surrounds', that is to say the subtle world that surrounds the gross world as the formless world surrounds the formal world, and as *a fortiori* God surrounds the formless world and with it all the lower worlds); and when the angel thus places the drop on the earth, *Allāh* produces from it wheat and grasses (the indispensable gifts for

---

[12] See on this subject: "*Ar-Rūh*" and "Note sur l'angélologie de l'alphabet arabe", by René Guénon, in *Études traditionnelles*, August-September 1938. As for the Throne and the Footstool, we may note that Al-Ghazali compares the first to the heart and the second to the brain. According to the Koran (*Sūrah* "The Cow" [2]:255), "His Footstool (*Kursī*) extends over (*wasi'a*) (or 'encompasses') the heavens and the earth, and their conservation causes Him no labor; He is the Most High (*Al-'Alī*), the Immense (*Al-'Azīm*)". "Causes Him no labor" signifies that He remains unaffected by the creative act and the functions related to it.

[13] "Do they wait for *Allāh* to come to them in the shadow of a cloud and with the angels?" (Koran, *Sūrah* "The Cow" [2]:210). The clouds constitute the partition (*barzakh*) that separates two different cosmic degrees, without which the lower degree would be absorbed in the higher degree; such a *barzakh* always presents itself as a void.

[14] Bearing in mind the symbolism of the "Lower Waters", this sieve will be seen as the passage from Cause to effect; by this passage, the simultaneity of the possibilities of formal manifestation is translated into effective and successive mode. A simultaneous, instantaneous, or total manifestation would in fact be equivalent to a cataclysm.

physical life, for man on the one hand and for animals on the other).
And when the angel places the drop in the sea, *Allāh* creates of it
small and large pearls (gifts concerning the psychic and spiritual life,
or again, concerning respectively the 'Lesser Mysteries' and the 'Great
Mysteries')".

We have seen that *Al-'Arsh* is equivalent to *Buddhi*; this equivalence
emerges in a very explicit way from the following passage of the
Mānava Dharma Shāstra (1:12-15): "In the primordial Egg (*Hiranyagarbha*), the Lord (Brahmā) lived one divine year, then He caused
the Egg to divide into two parts; and from these two parts He formed
heaven and earth; between them He placed the atmosphere, the
eight celestial regions, and the permanent abyss of the waters. . . .
And, before the inner sense (*manas*) and individual consciousness
(*ahankāra*), He produced the great intellectual Principle (*Mahat,
Buddhi*). . .". These eight celestial regions correspond to the circumference of *Al-'Arsh*; they are constituted, like the latter, of the four
cardinal points and the other intermediary points; the eight "Gods"
(*Devas*) who preside there are exactly identical with the eight angels
who carry the Throne (*Al-Malā'ikatu hamalat al-'Arsh*) and who are
likewise placed at the cardinal points and at the intermediary points.
The "abyss of the waters" is situated beneath heaven as the "sea" is
situated beneath the Throne from which emanates the "rain"; finally,
Mahat is identified with heaven insofar as the latter is the first "region
of Light", and thus as it were the "abode" of *Mahat* into which He
penetrates and from which, as *Trimūrti*, He penetrates and rules all the
worlds; in the same way, the four archangels (Jibrail, Mikail, Israfil,
and Izrail) inhabit the heavens beneath the luminous vault of the
Throne, and they are identified with the latter insofar as it embraces
the totality of all the worlds, and insofar as they are so to speak the
functions of the "Throne which surrounds" (*Al-'Arsh al-muhīt*).
Ar-Rūh ("the Spirit"), which resides at the center of the Throne, is
none other than Brahmā who is born from the "golden Egg": "Then,
the Lord subsisting by Himself (*Svayambhū*), who is not visible,
appeared . . . rendering the Universe visible . . . and dissipated the
darkness (the *Fiat Lux* of Genesis). . . . He whom the Intellect alone

can perceive . . . having resolved to make the diverse creatures come forth from His Substance, produced first the waters; and He placed in them a seed.[15] The seed became an Egg shining like gold, flashing with a thousand rays, and in this Egg the Lord Himself was born as Brahmā, the Grandfather of all the worlds" (*Mānava Dharma Shāstra* 1:6-9).

According to the traditions (*ahādīth*), "the greatest of the angels is called *Ar-Rūh* ('The Spirit'); *Allāh* says (in the Koran): 'The day when the Spirit and the angels will raise themselves in ranks'—and also: '*Allāh*, Lord of the degrees (*ma'ārij*) by which the angels and the Spirit will mount towards Him'; or again: 'The angels and the Spirit have descended in it (in the night of the Revelation)'. In truth, this angel whose name is *Ar-Rūh* will on the Day of the Resurrection occupy one row by himself because of his immensity, and the totality of all the angels constitutes another row; and the Spirit has power over the angels by his immensity". As for the angels in general, it is said that "*Allāh* created the angels of radiant light, and they are ranked in different categories: there are those who resemble the sons of Adam by their constitution, and others who inhabit the heavens, and yet others who inhabit the earth, and lastly those to whom has been entrusted the task of guarding the sons of Adam; in addition there are the bearers of the Throne; and (above them all) there are *Ar-Rūh*, Jibrail, Mikail, Israfil, and Izrail". "*Allāh* created the four generous angels, and he placed in their hands the affairs of creatures and the governance of the whole Universe; He made of Jibrail the Lord of revelation and of message, of Mikail the Lord of rains and of crops, of Izrail the Lord of the carrying away of souls (death), and of Israfil the Lord of the trumpet (of the Last Judgment)."[16]

---

[15] The "Lord", the "waters", and the "seed" correspond respectively, in the symbolism of the Arabic alphabet, to the letters *alif* and *bā* and to the diacritical point under the *bā*. The Pen, the Guarded Tablet, and first drop of Ink that fell from the Pen signify the same realities; this first drop is the diacritical point of the *bā*—symbolically identical with the golden Egg—from which emanate the "letters" the totality of which will constitute the manifested universe. When using the term "archangels" to designate the quaternary polarization of the cosmic Spirit, it is in the ordinary meaning of the term, which simply establishes an elementary hierarchical distinction between angels and archangels, and not in the strictly Dionysian sense that places other angelic hierarchies above the archangels.

[16] According to Saint Dionysius the Areopagite, the first angelic order, that of the Thrones, Cherubim, and Seraphim, "makes a circle round the Divinity", which is another way of saying that it is the direct reflection of the latter in the cosmic Substance.

It is clear from these quotations that *Ar-Rūh* (or *Sayyidnā* Mitatrun) corresponds, as was said above, to the creative Principle, Brahmā; a correspondence which emerges very clearly from what is said of *Ar-Rūh* in Genesis: "The Spirit of God moved upon the face of the waters." *Sayyidnā* Israfil and *Sayyidnā* Mikail are identified by their respective functions with two fundamental and complementary aspects of Vishnu, for both affirm manifestation, the first in a "vertical sense" (or according to the principial dimension), namely by the resurrection of the dead at the end of the cycle, and the second in a "horizontal sense" (or according to the manifested dimension), by giving life and subsistence to beings. As for *Sayyidnā* Jibrail and *Sayyidnā* Izrail, they are identified by their respective functions with two fundamental and complementary aspects of Shiva: both remove, transform, or absorb manifestation, the first in a "vertical sense" or positively by leading manifestation back towards its Principle, and the second in a "horizontal sense" or negatively, namely by destruction (or rather by dissociation, separation, or decomposition).

On the other hand, the five archangels are reflected even in the corporeal order, where they are mirrored in the five elements that are at the basis, not of manifestation as such, but of the sensible world that symbolizes it integrally: thus Israfil gives life thanks to the force of the Principle (*bi-amri 'Llāh*), hence in a quasi-supernatural or miraculous manner, and not through a chain of causation of a purely physical or "horizontal" order, while Mikail gives it in a natural fashion, that is to say by means of ordinary causality; in like manner, there exists a completely analogous distinction between the air, a primordial and universal food in the framework of the terrestrial world, and water, a relatively secondary food compared to air. Again: Jibrail reduces manifestation to its Principle in principial mode, whereas Izrail reduces it to nothingness in manifested mode; in the same way fire reduces matter by a sort of direct essential integration, whereas the earth absorbs it by indirect material integration; finally, *Ar-Rūh* will here be represented by ether, which contains and penetrates the other elements, exactly as the Spirit contains and penetrates the archangels.

Ar-Rūh (or *An-Nūr*) is in the doctrine of the same saint "the simple Ray of Light in itself"; in fact, and whatever exoteric theology may say, it is really with the Holy Spirit that we are concerned here, envisaged not in its divine transcendence, but in its existential or cosmic manifestation.

According to Ibn Abbas, "Israfil requested *Allāh* that He should give him the strength of the seven heavens, and *Allāh* gave it to him; and (that He should give him) the strength of the seven earths, and *Allāh* gave it to him; and (that He should give him) the strength of the winds, and *Allāh* gave it to him; and (that He should give him) the strength of the mountains, and *Allāh* gave it to him; and (that He should give him) the strength of men and of *jinn* (literally: of 'the two heavy ones', that is to say those who are not created of Light like the angels, but of earth in the one case and of fire in the other, elements whose materiality is expressed by the idea of heaviness), and *Allāh* gave it to him; and (that He should give him) the strength of lions, and *Allāh* gave it to him". These requests signify the receptive predisposition of the angelic Intelligence; it is clearly the divine Strength that this archangel contemplates or realizes, and there is no manifestation of strength that does not derive from him, as indeed the account given above indicates, although in an inverse sense. But to continue: "And from the soles of his feet to his head, he has hairs and mouths and tongues over which are stretched veils; he glorifies *Allāh* with each tongue in a thousand languages, and *Allāh* creates from his breath a million angels who glorify *Allāh* until the Day of the Resurrection, and these are: the 'Near Ones' (*Al-Muqarrabūn*) who are close to *Allāh*, and the 'Bearers of the Throne' (*Al-Malā'ikatu hamalat al-'Arsh*), and the 'Magnanimous' (*Al-Kirām*), and the 'Scribes' (of destinies) (*Al-Kātibūn*); and they all have the aspect of Israfil. And Israfil looks each day and each night three times towards Hell and approaches without being seen and weeps; and he grows thin and becomes like a bowstring and weeps bitter tears".[17]

---

[17] This calls to mind Shiva devoting himself to austerities on the sacred Mount Kailasa. On the subject of *Sayyidnā* Israfil, there also exists the following description: "He is the angel who must sound the trumpet; and it is said that *Allāh* created Israfil five thousand years before Mikail and entrusted him with the horn. Tradition also recounts that the horn has the form of a beast's horn and it contains dwellings like the cells of a bee's honey comb, and it is in these that the souls (of the dead) repose. Its length is the distance that is between heaven and earth, and when the days here below are accomplished, *Allāh* orders him to sound the horn and the souls come out of these cells (which are the tombs), and they are in flames; and he sounds the horn three times: first the sound of terror, then the sound of a cry, and finally the sound of the resurrection. It is recounted also that Israfil possesses innumerable wings; and *Allāh* gives him more strength and greatness than the other angels."

"As for Mikail, *Allāh* created him five thousand years after Israfil; he has hairs of saffron from his head to his feet, and his wings are of green topaz; and on each hair he has a million faces, and in each face he has a million eyes, and he weeps from each eye, out of pity for the sinners among the believers; and in each face he has a million mouths, and in each mouth he has a million tongues; each tongue speaks a million languages, and each tongue asks forgiveness from *Allāh* for believers and sinners; and from each eye fall seventy thousand tears, and *Allāh* creates from each tear a single angel in the image of Mikail, and they glorify *Allāh* until the Day of Resurrection. Their name is Cherubim (*Kārūbiyyūn*); they are the helpers of Mikail and they lean down over the rain and the plants and the crops and the fruits; and there is nothing in the seas, nor fruits on the trees, nor plants on the earth, that are not under his domination and that he does not take care of".[18]

"As for Jibrail, *Allāh* created him five hundred years after Mikail; he has one thousand six hundred wings and he has hairs of saffron from his head to his feet; and the sun is between his eyes, and on each hair he has the brightness of the moon and of the stars; and each day he enters the Ocean of Light three hundred and seventy times. And when he comes forth, there falls from each wing a million drops and *Allāh* creates from each drop a single angel in the image of Jibrail, and they glorify *Allāh* until the Day of Resurrection; these are the 'Spiritual Beings' (*Rūhāniyyūn*)".[19]

---

[18] Another version: "It had been given into his care to provide for the subsistence of the sons of Adam, as well as to look after the birds and the animals (of the earth) and the rain and the clouds and the seas and the trees and all the plants. And as for his attributes, tradition recounts that he has a green plumage of the color of emerald; on each plume are a thousand faces, and in each face a thousand mouths and in each mouth a thousand tongues, which ask forgiveness of *Allāh* for the sinners of the community of Muhammad. And *Allāh* creates each day seventy thousand angels according to the attributes of Mikail, who have, like him, care of the subsistence of beings. And it is recounted that Mikail, since he caught sight of the fire (of Hell), laughs no more nor smiles for dread of what he had seen of the fire, and for fear of Him who governs with a terrible and irresistible power".

[19] Another version: "He has six thousand wings; and between each pair of wings is a distance (from one wing to another) of a journey of five hundred years; and he has plumage that goes from his head to his feet and which is of the color of saffron; and each plume resembles the light of the sun. And tradition recounts that he plunges each day three hundred and sixty times into the Ocean of Light, and when he comes forth

"And the appearance of the angel of death is like unto that of Israfil through the faces and tongues and wings and immensity and force, without any addition or omission." According to a tradition that goes back to the Prophet himself, "When *Allāh* created the angel of death, He veiled him before creatures with a million veils. His immensity is vaster than the heavens and the two earths (East and West); the eastern and western countries here below (in the terrestrial world) are between his hands like a tray on which all things were as if set, or like a man who had been put between his hands that he might eat him, and he eats of it what he wishes;[20] and thus the angel of death turns and turns over the world just as men turn their money in their hands. He is attached by seventy thousand chains; each chain has the length of a journey of a thousand years; and the angels do not approach him, and they do not know his whereabouts, and they do not hear his voice, and they do not know his state. And when *Allāh* created death, He gave it for master the angel of death; the latter said: 'Lord, what is death?' Then *Allāh* commanded the veils that they should uncover death so that the angel might see it and *Allāh* said to the angels: 'Stop and behold, this is death.' And all the angels remained upright and said: 'Our Lord, hast thou created a creation more terrible than this?' *Allāh* said: 'I have created it, and I am greater than it, and every creature shall taste of it.' And *Allāh* said then: 'O Izrail take it! I have subjected it to thee.' Izrail replied: 'O Divinity, by what strength shall I take it? For it is greater than I.' And *Allāh* gave him the strength; and Izrail took death, and it dwelt in his hand;[21] and death said: 'O Lord, allow

drops of Light fall from him, and *Allāh* creates from these drops angels in the image of Jibrail, who glorify *Allāh* until the Day of the Resurrection. And the meaning of the name Jibrail, which is Syriac, is in Arabic: servant of *Allāh* (*'Abdu 'Llāh*)." The archangel appearing to the Prophet is described in the following way: "His wings stretched from the East to the West. It is said that his feet were yellow, his wings green, and that he carried a necklace of red rubies, or according to others, of coral. His hair had the color of coral, his brow was clear, his face luminous; his teeth were of a radiant brightness; between his two eyes were written the words: 'There is no divinity but God, and Muhammad is the Prophet of God.'"

[20] This image corresponds exactly to that of Kali—or of Yama—devouring a human body; this does not symbolize solely death in the ordinary meaning of the word, but more generally time that engulfs everything that is situated in it. Time must here be understood in a sense that goes beyond the temporal condition: we are here concerned with universal transformation and not its physical mode alone.

[21] In Hindu terms, this would be expressed by saying death is the *Shakti* of the *Deva* Izrail.

me to call out in the heavens just once.' And *Allāh* allowed it; and he
called out loud: 'I am death who separates friends! I am death who
separates husband from wife! I am death who separates daughters
from mothers! I am death who separates the brother from his sisters!
I am death who destroys houses and palaces![22] I am death who fills
the tombs! I am death who seeks you and finds you, even though you
were "on high towers" (Koran, *Sūrah* "Women" [4]:80)! And there
remains no creature who does not taste me.' It is said also that Izrail
seized the souls of the sons of Adam and of other beings, such as the
birds and the animals of the earth, and all that possess a soul. Tradition recounts that his attributes are like those of Israfil, and that he is
seated on a throne in the sixth heaven; he has four wings which spread
from the East to the West; it is said again that the rest of his body is
covered with as many eyes as there are creatures, and that they look
towards all that possesses a soul; and when he seizes a soul, the eye
that had looked at it closes; and when all creatures are dead, all these
eyes that are on his body will be closed, and there will remain only
his eye (which concerns himself);[23] and he knows that only this eye
will remain to him (which will be extinguished in its turn at the end
of the Universe)."[24]

[22] This extension of death to inanimate things indicates that we are really concerned
here with the universal function of Shiva, which embraces all Manifestation.

[23] According to the cosmology of the Sioux, and of other North American Indians, at
the creation of the world a bison was placed in the North-West, in order to retain the
waters of the sea. Each year this bison loses a hair and when he has lost them all, our
world will have arrived at its term. Each of the feet of the bison corresponds to one
of the four ages of the terrestrial cycle; and the Sioux affirm that in our days the bison
is almost completely hairless, and that there remains to him only one foot. The bull
of the *Dharma*, in the Hindu tradition, is exactly the same symbol: at the end of each
of the four ages (*yugas*), this bull withdraws one of its feet from the earth. It may be
noted in passing that this remarkable analogy is an indication, amongst others, of the
hyperborean affinities that exist between the two traditional forms just mentioned.

[24] As-Suyuti recounts in his *Kitāb ad-durar al-hisān*: "It is said that the angel of death
has four faces: one face before him, and a face on his head, then a face behind his back,
and finally a face beneath his feet; and he seizes the souls of the Prophets and the angels
while looking at them with the face that is on his head, and the souls of the believers
while looking at them with the face that is before him, and the souls of the unbeliev-
ers while looking at them with the face that is behind his back, and finally the souls of
the demons while looking at them with the face that is beneath his feet. And it is said
also that the angel of death turns the world between his hands as a mortal turns his
money. And his body is covered with eyes to the number of the creatures, and when

All the ineffectualness that the descriptions quoted above have in their complexity, their abstruse intelligibility, as also their apparent monstrousness, merely reflect the impossibility of rendering celestial realities into human language; human thought, being unfitted to grasp a great diversity of aspects simultaneously, especially when their subtlety and complexity appear to imply contradictions and when subject also to ceaseless movement, can only contain a broken, frozen, simplified, and absurd image of the realities that surpass it; it is the very transcendence of what it has to contain that breaks as it were the natural bounds of expression. To describe a celestial reality is, to employ an analogy, to describe a melody, or more specifically a polyphonic melody, or again, to employ another image, it is to describe the infinitely differentiated and joint movements of the waves of the ocean to a blind man who has never heard of the sea. The sheer immensity of what has to be expressed by limited and feeble means gives to the images, on the one hand, the character of sketches, and on the other an imprint of horror, which clearly expresses the incompatibility between the celestial dimensions and terrestrial matter.

The essential identity between *Svayambhū* ("He who subsists by Himself") and Brahmā born from the golden Egg (*Hiranyagarbha*) enables us to understand this teaching of the Prophet: "*Allāh* was in a cloud (*ghamām*), and above Him there was no air, and below him

a creature dies here below, one eye is extinguished on the body of the angel. Tradition also teaches us that *Allāh* created under the Throne a tree whose leaves are of the number of the creatures, and which is called the 'Lote-tree of the extremity' (*sidrat al-muntahā*); and when a servant must die and there remain to him not more than forty days to live, a leaf of this tree falls on Izrail; the angels call this man dead, although he is still living on earth for forty days." This number forty, which is found in various traditional forms in connection with the posthumous states, constitutes the numerical value of the letter *mīm*, whose meaning amongst others is death (*al-mawt*). The texts quoted—which the author has drawn from various Arabic treatises of which he knows no translation—belong to a very complex descriptive symbolism, characteristic for Islam as for the Semitic mind in general; such a symbolism, which all told compensates for the absence of painted or sculptured images, would doubtless have less point in a civilization like that of the Hindus, for example, where sacred images (*pratīkas*) have become the predominant forms of symbolic language.

there was no air;[25] therefore He created His Throne on the water." Indeed, the "Spirit of God" (*Ruah Elohīm*) of Genesis, which "moved upon the face of the waters", is God, but it is also identified with "divine Manifestation", the "Throne on the water"; and in Hindu cosmogony, "He who walks on the waters" (*Nārāyana*) is not only Being polarizing itself into *Purusha* and *Prakriti*—the latter representing existential water—but also the divine Spirit manifested, Brahmā. It is said that *Nārāyana*, after having placed the golden Egg in the water, "was Himself born again as Brahmā" (who is the central and creative aspect of *Mahat*); however, Vishnu (who is the conserving aspect) has likewise the name of *Nārāyana*, because formless Himself, He moves on the waters of formal manifestation. Vishnu *Nārāyana*, or by extension *Mahat* (or *Buddhi*), is thus the direct and primordial manifestation of the supreme *Nārāyana*, as the formal Waters are the reflection of the formless Waters; this is what we must never lose sight of when encountering apparently divergent acceptations of the Arabic terms *'Arsh*, *Rūh*, and *Nūr*. In other words, *Al-'Arsh*, like *An-Nūr* and *Ar-Rūh*, is an essential or "vertical" reality which, as such, can be considered independently of the levels in which it affirms itself; it may therefore be said that the Throne in itself, and independently of the levels of reality, is the partition that separates the Principle from its refraction; but this partition is at the same time an opening, for not only does it hide the incommensurability of *Allāh*, but it expresses and transmits it through *Ar-Rūh*. The Throne and the water, on whatever level they are envisaged, are inseparable; the Throne would in fact have no reason for being without something in relation to which it supports the Divinity; and the water is conceivable only if it is separated from its transcendent Principle by a principial discontinuity, without which it would be identical with this Principle.

It is therefore quite permissible to define *Ar-Rūh* as the affirmation of Unity in all the degrees of universal Existence, which is equally true for *An-Nūr*, albeit in a slightly different relationship; *Ar-Rūh* is

---

[25] God, insofar as He prepares to create, is clearly identified with Being, in relation to which Non-Being is, symbolically speaking, nothingness, that is to say, "non-determination"; but there is in relation to Being also a lower non-determination, as the *hadīth* quoted indicates, and this is the symbolic nothingness from which God draws the world; it is in a certain sense the infinite distance that separates pure Being from the possibilities of manifestation; these possibilities, indeed, can in no wise be conceived as parts of Being.

most often figured as a center, a ray, a descent, a presence or immanence, whereas the nature of *An-Nūr* can be rendered by an expression such as "divine Substance", with all the reservations that such a
formulation requires; as for *Al-'Arsh*, it has more an aspect of totality
and of integration; it is the circumference of which *Ar-Rūh* will be the
center and *An-Nūr* the matter.

A last point that deserves to be mentioned is the following:
according to a *hadīth*, Christ is called *Rūhu 'Llāh*; it is said also, having
regard solely to the human nature of Christ, that "Jesus (*Sayyidnā* Isa)
is equal, before *Allāh*, to Adam; He created him of earth, then He said
to him: 'Be!' And he was" (*Sūrah* "Family of Imran" [3]:59). Indeed,
Jesus, like Adam, had no human father: each one is *Rūhu 'Llāh*; and
this enables a better understanding of the meaning of the adoration
of Adam by the angels (Koran, *Sūrah* "The Cow" [2]:32), who themselves are peripheral beings—albeit luminous—and who by this fact
are subordinate to *Ar-Rūh*, with which must also be included its functions, the four archangels. *Ar-Rūh* might be symbolized by the numeral
1, the angels by the numeral 2, and Adam by the numeral 3; now the
numeral 2 is nearer Unity than the numeral 3, but the latter reflects
unity in an integral and adequate, and not "fragmentary", manner as
does the numeral 2; and thus the angels, although superior to Adam
by their substance, which is *Nūr*, "Light", are nonetheless made in the
image only of aspects of God, in the sense that each angel reflects only
a single one of these aspects or Names and is ignorant of the others,
while Adam, although lower than the angels by his substance, which
is "hardened earth" (*tīn lāzib*), is made directly in the image of God
and reflects God in His integral Unity. The angels are situated in the
proximity of the Throne, since they are made of its luminous substance; but they remain in its periphery, the center being occupied by
Ar-Rūh; now *Sayyidnā* Adam, in his earthly existence, is far off from
the Throne, but he is situated in the central ray emanating therefrom,
at the end of the vertical axis that is the locus of prophetic Revelation.

Nirvāna

According to an error widespread in the West, the spiritual "extinction" Buddhism has in view represents a "nothingness", as if it were possible to realize something that is nothing. Now either *Nirvāna* is nothingness, in which case it is unrealizable; or else it is realizable, in which case it must correspond to something real. It is too easily forgotten that Paradise—not to mention uncreated Beatitude,[1] which is none other than the positive content of *Nirvāna*—can also be regarded as an annihilation, the relationship between formal and non-formal manifestation being analogous to that between manifestation as such and non-manifestation.[2] On the other hand, since Paradise is necessarily

---

[1] According to Saint Macarius of Egypt, "the crowns and diadems that Christians will receive are uncreated". Western theologians tend to ascribe a merely poetical meaning to such expressions, which is absurd, for the Fathers did not write literature; this attitude is explainable, however, by the viewpoint Western theology adopts regarding grace, which, in the final analysis, it views only as something created, whereas Eastern— that is, Palamite, Areopagitic, Patristic theology, which is metaphysically complete— recognizes the "divine Essence" in grace and its modes, therefore its uncreated or divine character. It is true that Latin theology is not altogether wrong in attributing a created character to grace, and Greek theology therefore is not entirely right in condemning the Western point of view: the Latin considers things according to a properly cosmological and hence "horizontal" and distinctive perspective, whereas the Patristic views them according to a metaphysical and hence "vertical", essential, and synthetic perspective; in the first sense, grace is created, which is to say it constitutes an interference of non-formal manifestation within the formal; in the second sense, grace is uncreated for it is none other than the mysterious interference of God in manifestation as such.

[2] If between one level of reality and another there is a parallel analogy with respect to positive contents, there is on the other hand an inverse analogy with respect to relationships: for example, there is a parallel analogy between earthly and heavenly Beauty, but there is an inverse analogy as regards their respective situations, in the sense that earthly beauty is "outward" and divine Beauty "inward"; or again, to illustrate this law by symbols: according to certain Sufi teachings, earthly trees are reflections of heavenly trees, and earthly women are reflections of heavenly women (parallel analogy); but heavenly trees have their roots above and heavenly women are naked (inverse analogy—that which is situated below becoming situated above, and that which is inward becoming outward). The three great degrees of reality are: formal manifestation (comprising the gross, corporeal, sensible plane and the subtle, psychic plane), non-formal manifestation (constituted by the universal Spirit, the supreme Angels), and non-manifestation (God, in His Essence as well as in His Word).

a reflection of divine Beatitude—lest it be bad and even non-existent[3]—
it cannot but represent, in each of its aspects, a "less" in relation to its
divine Prototype, in the same way that the earthly world in which we
live is necessarily a "less" in relation to Paradise, which is its heavenly
Prototype; were it not so, the earthly world would be indistinguishable
purely and simply from the heavenly world, just as that world, were it
not a "less" in relation to God, would be indistinguishable from God
Himself.[4] Therefore, if the reabsorption of a being in God is viewed
as an annihilation,[5] then logically the reabsorption of the earthly being
into paradisial existence must also be viewed as a passage from the
real to nothingness; and conversely, if Paradise is regarded as an intensification or exaltation of all that is perfect and lovable in this lower
world, then the state of supreme Extinction must also be regarded as
an intensification or exaltation of what is positive and perfect, not only
in the earthly world but in the entire universe. It follows that a higher
level of reality—that of non-formal manifestation or, beyond the universe, that of non-manifestation—can be regarded either with respect
to the negative aspect that it necessarily presents from the standpoint
of the lower plane on which one is situated and whose limitations it
negates, or else it can be regarded with respect to the positive aspect it

---

[3] It cannot be validly objected that evil, since it exists, is also a reflection of God for,
firstly, it is not a reflection inasmuch as it is evil, but solely by virtue of its reality,
however relative that may be; and, secondly, the fact that evil, by its mere existence,
is such a reflection in no way prevents it from not being so with respect to its content.
Hence evil is a reflection of God in only one respect, that of existence or container,
whereas the good—Paradise, for example—is such a reflection in two respects at once,
namely with respect to "that which exists", or content, as well as *a fortiori* that of existence, or container. Thus there is a respect in which evil is in no way a reflection of
the Divine. That which is not a reflection in any respect is that which does not exist.

[4] This is an application of the *Shahādah*, the Islamic testimony of faith: "There is no
divinity if not The Divinity" (*Lā ilāha illā 'Llāh*). In other words, there is no reality, if
not the only Reality; or again: there is no perfection if not the sole Perfection. Christ's
saying: "Why callest thou me good? God alone is good", has the same meaning and
thus lends itself to the same cosmological and metaphysical applications.

[5] The distinction between *Nirvāna* and *Parinirvāna* does not apply from the standpoint
taken here; it will suffice to recall that *Nirvāna* is extinction in relation to the cosmos,
and *Parinirvāna* in relation to Being; *Nirvāna* is thus identified with Being, according
to a conception that is more initiatic than properly metaphysical, since a "principle"
is here represented as a "state"; and *Parinirvāna* is identified with Beyond-Being, that
is to say with the divine Quiddity, which, according to Greek theology, "envelops"
Being, or which, according to Sufism, "erases all predicates" (*munqat al-ishārat*).

Amitayus
Irradiation of the Buddha Amitabha
Tibetan *tanka*

contains in itself and thus also—and *a fortiori*—in relation to the lower plane under consideration. When Christ says that "in Heaven there is no marrying or giving in marriage", He refers to the negative aspect presented by the higher reality when seen from the lower plane; by contrast, when the Koran speaks of the houris and other delights of Paradise, it refers to the positive aspect of the same higher reality, as does every mythological symbolism, Hindu symbolism for example; and this makes it easy to understand that it is pointless to deny the existence of the *hūris* (the Hindu *apsarās* and the Buddhist *dākinīs*) and other delights of Paradise, since the existence of analogous delights in this lower world—which precisely allow the symbolism in question to be established—proves the existence of the heavenly delights, just as a mirage proves the existence of the object reflected.

What has been said above should help us see that whenever confronted with a teaching which, in regard to the summit of all spiritual realization, seems to maintain the insuperable distinction between the creature and God, one is not yet entitled to conclude—in the absence of other criteria—that one is dealing with a limited point of view, namely one that does not go beyond such a distinction; for like every possible distinction, this one has its immutable prototype in the divine Order itself, namely in the distinction—absolutely fundamental in pure metaphysics—between Being and Beyond-Being, or, to use the language of Eastern theology, in the distinction between the revelatory Energies, or Processions (πρόοδοι), and the impenetrable Substratum (ὕπαρξις); or again, expressed in Sufi terms, the same distinction is made between the Qualities (*Sifāt*) or Names (*Asmā'*) of God—which alone can be known distinctively—and the Quiddity (*Dhāt*), which eludes all penetration by an individualized intelligence, and thereby eludes all definition; or in other terms, it is the distinction—always in ascending order—between Unicity (*Al-Wāhidiyyah*) and Unity (*Al-Ahadiyyah*), the second term symbolically expressing Non-Otherness (the *Advaita* of Hindu doctrine).[6]

---

[6] Islam, being pre-eminently the doctrine of Unity, in the sense that it has to insist as expressly and exclusively as possible on Unity, could not designate supreme Reality by a term that would seem to deny Unity, as does for example the Hindu term *Advaita*, "Non-duality"; it must of necessity give this supreme meaning to the term "Unity" and to no other, and it does so by a transposition that confers upon this term the meaning of "Absolute". Moreover, the expression "Non-duality" does have its equivalent in Muslim language, namely in the formula "He hath no associate" (*lā sharīka lahu*) which, depending on one's vantage point, can be applied to Beyond-Being as well as to Being.

If the creature can indirectly contemplate an aspect of God, this is because within God Himself, who is the totality of the Processions and Attributes, the Word eternally contemplates its Essence or, expressed differently, because the Son eternally contemplates the Father—although it goes without saying that there is no common measure between the relationship of the creature to the Creator and that of the Son to the Father. Be that as it may, if it is legitimate to identify the Angels—who are none other than the direct and consequently non-formal, or supra-formal, reflections of the divine aspects or Names—with different Paradises or states of Bliss, then it is *a fortiori* legitimate to identify these aspects or divine Names themselves with states or places of Bliss, and hence with Paradises—whence the expression *Jannat adh-Dhāt*, "Garden (Paradise) of the Essence", used to designate the supreme spiritual realization.

To discuss the question of whether the delivered saints are annihilated in God or whether they remain separate within Him is pointless, since it amounts to knowing whether the divine Names are distinct or indistinct in God; now every divine Name is God, but none is any of the others and, above all, God is not reducible to any of them. The man who "enters" into God can obviously add nothing to Him nor modify anything in Him, God being immutable Plenitude; however, even the being who has realized *Parinirvāna*, that is, who is no longer limited by any exclusive divine aspect, but has become "identified" with the divine Essence,[7] such a being is still and always—or rather "eternally"—"himself", for, quite obviously, the divine Qualities cannot not be inherent in the Essence in some way;[8] they may be extinguished therein, but not lost. In a word, the saints "pre-exist" eternally in God, and their spiritual realization is but a return to themselves; and in an analogous way, every quality, every earthly pleasure is

---

[7] The feeble resources of human language—and we would even say of human thought as such—do not allow the translation of transcendent truths without altering them partially by contradictions that cannot be avoided.

[8] Were it otherwise, it would have to be admitted that the "Son" knows things that the "Father" does not, which is absurd.

but a finite reflection of an infinite Perfection or Beatitude. Nothing, therefore, can be lost; the simple fact that we enjoy something proves that this enjoyment exists infinitely in God. The Koran (*Sūrah* "The Cow" [2]:25) expresses this in these words: "Every time they (the blessed) receive fruits (of Paradise), they say: 'We have tasted of this beforehand'", which is to say: we become aware of what we have tasted (near God or in God) from all eternity.

According to a saying of the Prophet Muhammad, "the world is the prison of the believer and the Paradise of the infidel",[9] and according to another, "Paradise is peopled with the ignorant". It is in an analogous sense that the Sufi Muadh Ar-Razi could say that "the Paradise of the believer is the prison of the sage", which shows clearly that if metaphysical Deliverance implies the "extinction" (*fanā'*)[10] of every created thing, it does not at all mean that the state of the "extinct" being is a kind of nothingness; exactly the reverse is true, since every created thing—be it heavenly or earthly—is a nothingness in relation to the divine Bliss, or let us say in relation to God without attribute. After extinction, or rather correlatively with it, comes permanence (*baqā'*): this is the reintegration of the saint into his eternal Prototype, a given divine Name, and thereby into God; the term "permanence" shows that the state of a being reintegrated into God is as positive as possible, that is, positive without limits; which is why Christ could say that He is the "Life". There is between two levels of Reality not only a relationship of analogy, but also one of inversion, as we have seen: if Paradise is a life because its divine Prototype is Life, and if for the same reason, the earth also comprises a certain mode of life—a mode whose Prototype is heavenly life and still more so divine Life—the inverse is equally true: the earthly state, like the Heaven of which it is a pale glimmer, is also a death, first that of the terrestrial state in relation to Heaven, and then both earth and Heaven in relation to God; for if God is "the Living" (*Al-Hayy*), no one else but He can be so.

— ·:· —

---

[9] The word "infidel" (*kāfir*) has here the meaning of "profane" or "worldly" and not that of "pagan".

[10] Literally, "disappearance".

Given that the question of *Nirvāna* represents a passage from the world to the Divine Reality, or from manifestation to the Principle, it raises the problem[11] of the continuity—or discontinuity—between the relative and the Absolute; pantheism, a Western philosophical conception, admits this continuity—"from below", of course—in such a way that in fact it amounts to a kind of atheism adorning the world with the name "God"; howbeit, a pantheism that includes a kind of vague theism also exists among "liberal" theologians, as well as among Westernized Hindus, who deduce crude simplifications from the symbolism of their Scriptures. This supposed continuity between God and the world, such as they conceive of it, does not correspond to any reality, needless to say; otherwise there could be no discontinuity in the world itself; now the discontinuity that one can observe everywhere can only be the reflection of the discontinuity separating manifestation from the Principle, or the world from God, and that can be abolished only by the ontological—or spiritual—reduction of the first to the second, or by the supernatural radiation of the Principle into the manifested order. In reality, there is simultaneously discontinuity and continuity between the relative and the Absolute; which is to say that there is continuity in discontinuity and, in another respect, discontinuity in continuity. It goes without saying that discontinuity is conceivable only from the standpoint of illusion—the standpoint of every creature as such—since there is nothing in Reality that could be discontinuous in relation to It; consequently, discontinuity is the product of manifestation itself, and is identified with it in a certain sense.

As for continuity in discontinuity, it is none other than the presence of the Principle in manifestation, according to the appropriate modes, for "*Brahman* is not in the world"; this means that It is not present as *Brahman*, but as reflection, either as *Sattva* and *Buddhi* (existential and intellectual manifestations of the "Holy Spirit")— terms that correspond respectively to *An-Nūr* and *Ar-Rūh* in Sufism— and their particular manifestations, such as the *Avatāras* and *Yogins*, or as spiritual Influences quite generally, such as the eucharistic Presence for instance. These realities, while necessarily pertaining to the cosmic order, are nonetheless *Brahman*—or *Allāh*—with respect to essential identity. Light is not the sun, but it is essentially identified

---

[11] By "problem" we mean a question that cannot be resolved in the absence of sufficient information deriving from Revelation or Intellection.

with it and represents the presence of the sun on earth; here too there is simultaneously discontinuity and continuity; however, the essential continuity can never abolish the discontinuity between Principle and manifestation, for this discontinuity subsists independently of the continuity in view, whereas continuity presupposes the exteriorization of God and hence discontinuity. The sun can exist without the earth, but light cannot exist without the sun; Reality is independent from illusion, but the fact that illusion is integrally linked to Reality in no way modifies the absolute transcendence of the latter.

"In the Absolute", said Ramakrishna, "I am not, and you are not, and *Brahman* (in Its personal determination) is not, for It (the Absolute) is beyond all speech and all thought. Yet as long as there still remains something outside myself (that is, so long as I am still on the plane of individual consciousness), I must adore *Brahman* within the limits of my reason, as something outside myself." The fact that a spiritual man who has attained *Nirvāna* can return to his individual modality, and even remain in it parallel with his state of supreme Identity,[12] proves precisely that *Nirvāna*, if it is an extinction, is not an annihilation, for nothing that is can cease to be.

It is sometimes asked how the sensible appearance or the activity on earth of a being possessing supreme sanctity—the Holy Virgin, for example—is compatible with her posthumous state, which, being divine, is thereby beyond all individual determination and hence beyond all form. To this it must be replied that sanctity is effacement in a universal Prototype: being holy, the Virgin cannot but be identified with a divine Model of which she is as the reflection on earth. This divine Model is first of all an aspect or Name of God, and it can therefore be said that in her supreme reality or knowledge the Virgin is this divine aspect itself; but this aspect necessarily has a first reflection in the cosmic or created order: this is the "Spirit", the *Metatron*

---

[12] If *Nirvāna* were a nothingness, how could it be explained that a being such as the Buddha not only returned to his human consciousness after purely contemplative states, but could even manifestly maintain this wholly nirvanic state in a permanent manner, hence even in the state of earthly consciousness?

of the Kabbalah, *Ar-Rūh* or the supreme angels in Islamic doctrine, and also the Hindu *Trimūrti,* or more precisely—since it is the Virgin who is being considered—the feminine and beneficent aspect of the *Trimūrti,* hence Lakshmi who, at the summit of all worlds, is the immediate imprint of divine Goodness and Beauty; from this imprint all created beauty and goodness are derived or, in other words, it is through this imprint that God communicates His Beauty and His Goodness to the world.

Thus the Virgin Mary—regarding what may be termed her posthumous state with reference to her human existence—is at once created and uncreated; whatever self-imposed limitations exoteric theology is forced to assume here for reasons of expediency, we need not take account of them since our point of view is esoteric. Be that as it may, even if exoterism cannot recognize Mary's divine reality without entering into insoluble contradictions—although it admits this reality implicitly at least when, for example, it defines the Virgin as "Co-Redemptress", "Mother of God", "Spouse of the Holy Spirit"—it is nonetheless able, without running the risk of ill-sounding formulations, to recognize that the Virgin is created before Creation; and this amounts to identifying her with the universal Spirit envisaged more particularly in its feminine, maternal, and beneficent function.

This divine imprint in supra-formal or luminous manifestation also comprises, by cosmic repercussion, a psychic imprint—or rather a psycho-physical one, since the corporeal can always issue from and be reabsorbed into the psychic plane of which it is, in the final analysis, merely a mode—and it is this psychic imprint that is Mary in her human form; this is why the universal Prototypes, when they manifest themselves in that portion of humanity for which Mary lived on earth, do so by way of the psychic,[13] hence individual and human, form of

---

[13] In other sectors of earthly humanity, the same Prototype—at once divine and angelic—takes the form appropriate to the respective ambiences; it appears most often in the form of a beautiful woman, as is the case in the apparitions of the *Shekhinah* in Judaism, of Durga, "the Mother", in Hinduism, or of Kwan-Yin or Tara in the Far East; similarly, in the Sioux Indian tradition, the Sacred Pipe—the pre-eminent sacred instrument—was brought from Heaven by Pté-San-Win, a marvelously beautiful celestial maiden, dressed in white. But the merciful Principle can also take on—when there is inverse and not parallel analogy—a masculine form, for example that of Krishna or that of the *Bodhisattva* Avalokiteshvara—likened moreover to Kwan-Yin, "Goddess of Grace", in Chinese and Japanese Buddhism—or again, in Islam, the form of the Prophet, one of whose names is precisely "Key of Mercy" (*Miftah ar-Rahmah*). Let us

the Virgin; this form can always be reabsorbed into its Prototypes,[14] as the body can be reabsorbed into the soul, and as the created Prototype—the "Spirit" in its function of Mercy—can be reabsorbed into the uncreated Prototype, which is the infinite Beauty, Beatitude, and Mercy of God.

not forget to add that these manifestations of Mercy sometimes have a terrible aspect, closely related with that of purity. Concerning the Blessed Virgin, the following can be said: she is co-eternally in God—otherwise there would be perfections in the world lacking in the Creator—in two ways: firstly as "existential Substance" or *Materia Prima* (the divine *Prakriti* of Hindu doctrine), and secondly as "divine Quality" (thus an aspect of *Purusha*, the male Principle of the creative act) or as "divine Name"; thus she is the Beauty, the Purity, the Mercy of God; but in being such, she is also, and *a fortiori*, present in the manifested or created divine Spirit, of which she is the merciful Beauty as well as the forbidding Purity; finally, she is incarnated as Mary—and in other human forms, for the Unique becomes of necessity multiple once it manifests itself on the formal plane, barring which it would annihilate this plane—and, owing to her individual and psychic form, she can even appear on the corporeal plane.

[14] We use the plural because all perfection derives from two principal Prototypes, one cosmic or angelic, and the other divine.

The Posthumous States

The point of view specific to the religions of Semitic origin is characterized, among other things, by its tendency to deny all that does not concern man as such: accordingly, it will deny the immortality of the animal soul and also, what in a certain respect amounts to the same thing, the transmigration of the soul through non-human existences; however, one can speak here of denial only in an altogether outward and quite relative manner, for there are no errors in the Revelations, and what is in question in the present case is rather a very synthetic and simplified conception of the posthumous states, whose totality is reduced to two "eternal"[1] states, namely Heaven and Hell.[2] If in this conception the animal soul is denied, that is because, not being human, it cannot participate directly[3] in the means of salvation and hence cannot be saved on the basis of its own state. Analogously, any posthumous state that does not correspond to the human state will be assimilated, implicitly if not explicitly, to the infernal states or the "limbos", depending on the case. It goes without saying that if the non-human states—we are not of course speaking of angelic states—can be assimilated to Hell because they do not constitute salvation, these same states can on the other hand, and with no less reason, be assimilated to limbo since they do not constitute damnation;[4] conse-

---

[1] "Eternity" is an absolute quality—the relative absence of which is precisely the cause of time—and for this reason can be attributed only to God, unless when using purely symbolic language.

[2] The fact that neither the Orthodox Church nor Islam explicitly admits purgatory does not mean that they deny the thing itself, as is shown for example by this teaching of the Prophet: "Those who have deserved Paradise will go there; the condemned will go to Hell. Then God shall say: Let all those come forth from Hell in whose hearts there is faith, be it no more than the weight of a mustard seed! Then they will be made to go forth even though they are already burnt; and then they will be plunged into the river of rainwater (the rain signifying Grace)—or into the river of life (that is, of Bliss which, being beyond suffering and death, is identified with pure Life)—and at once they shall be reborn."

[3] This reservation is necessary because in sacrificial rites such as they exist in Judaism and Islam, the soul of the sacrificed animal also benefits from the rite, perhaps by being reborn into a central or free state like our own.

[4] If this were not so, animals, for instance, would be in Hell. It is true that the state of

quently, when "pagans" and "heretics" are declared to be excluded from salvation—and to the extent that this is so—this could not mean, esoterically speaking, that they must enter the infernal abodes. On the other hand, the equation of non-human—or sub-human states, if one prefers—with infernal states is further justified by the fact that transmigration implies suffering, or more precisely the alternation between happy and unhappy states, from which a being is delivered only in Paradise; but this argument is obviously reversible and can equally serve to show that transmigration, inasmuch as its sufferings are ephemeral, is not infernal in the absolute sense that the theological point of view gives this word.

It seems inevitable to reply here to an objection too often formulated and which moreover glaringly throws light on the provisional and consequently vulnerable elements involved in the specifically theological point of view owing to its very anthropomorphism: this is the objection—amply exploited by atheists, but necessarily poorly refuted by exoterism—that there is no common measure between an act, no matter how evil, and an eternal punishment, or in other words,

the lower species can often recall an infernal state, all the more so in that in all probability it is the entire species that here constitutes an individual; such a state would then come to an end only through the exhaustion of the species, which would very well symbolize the perpetuity of Hell. It is perhaps this multiple aspect of a single individual that the Law of Manu has in mind when it speaks of a great number of rebirths in the body of a lower animal. The reverse is the case of the angels where each "individual", if one may say so, is the equivalent in himself alone of an entire species. It must not be forgotten that cosmic "quality" is more or less independent of cosmic "degree", otherwise there would be no vile men or noble animals; which is to say that an animal, in relation to man, is not necessarily an inferior individual, and can even be the opposite, according to case; but its cosmic state will nonetheless be inferior in relation to the human state; a distinction must therefore be made between "individual" and "state". As regards the angels, a distinction must be made on the one hand, between those that are the highest of the peripheral or passive beings, and on the other, those that are aspects or functions of the "Spirit" and are therefore pre-eminently central and active states; they constitute the "created" aspects of the "Holy Spirit", and hence of God, a fact that ordinary theology obviously cannot admit in this form. In Hindu doctrine, these angels are the *Devas* of the *Trimūrti*; Islamic doctrine for its part teaches that the "Spirit" (*Ar-Rūh*, and in Sanskrit *Buddhi*)—whose aspects or functions constitute precisely the "supreme angels" (*Al-Malā al-aʿlā* or *Al-Malāʾikat al-kirām*)—did not have to prostrate before Adam like the angels, and that, according to a spatial symbolism, it surpasses in immensity all the ordinary angels taken together, which amounts to saying moreover that, in the universal order, by virtue of inverse analogy, the center is "greater" than the periphery.

that a limited cause cannot have an unlimited effect; this objection contains an undeniable truth, and even shows that Heaven and Hell cannot be "eternal" in the proper meaning of the word;[5] yet, if the objection is true in itself, it is not, however, in the least to the detriment of what religious Revelation really has in view, for apart from the fact that it is perfectly legitimate, in human language, to say that a deed is "rewarded" or "punished" by God, it is not the particular deed that is punished, but a particular basic and consequently irremediable attitude or tendency;[6] the sinful deed thus represents only a manifestation or symbol of this attitude or tendency. In other words, only those go to Hell who, if God brought them out, would do all they could to return; the perpetuity of Hell thus inheres less in the rigor

[5] This "eternity" can only be a "perpetuity", hence an indefinite duration; moreover, neither the Christian expression *in saecula saeculorum* nor the Koranic words *khalada*, *khālid*, *khuld* (referring to perpetuity or immortality) signify eternity. According to Saint Thomas Aquinas, "Hell is termed eternal only owing to its invincibility. . . . For this reason there is in Hell no true eternity, but rather time. . .". Heaven and Hell are "eternal" because they are relatively immutable in relation to our earthly life, and this in various degrees. It is important to point out here that ordinary theology cannot constitute a closed system in relation to pure metaphysics, and that it cannot without impunity pose as such; this appears very clearly in certain theological propositions of which the least that can be said is that they are fragmentary and that their only way of making up for their apparent unintelligibility is by vague references to an "unfathomable" divine Wisdom. We have in mind here particularly the theory concerning "infinite Goodness" and "infinite Justice", and explaining man's creation by the former and his damnation by the latter; or again, the idea of "eternal punishment", deserved owing to an almost infinite offense against God's dignity, an idea that implies the absence of compassion among the elect with regard to the damned; all these propositions clearly have a meaning and are therefore justifiable, but only metaphysically, not by anthropomorphic reasonings. Thus it follows from exoterism itself that it cannot be really complete without esoterism, and that it contains fissures which only sacred science can fill or else the powers of darkness will intrude. Esoterism alone possesses sufficient lights to face all possible objections and to give a positive explanation of religion; but this supposes that it explains by the same token all of religion, and thereby all religions; in short, either one upholds both exoterism and esoterism—the form and the essence—against the "wisdom after the flesh", or else one upholds nothing whatsoever.

[6] According to Islamic doctrine, he is damned who bears the "rejection of Truth" (*kufr*) in his very essence (*dhāt*), and not he who bears it only in his "attributes" (*sifāt*), the latter being conceived of as accidents. A *hadīth* recounts that a man entered Paradise for having given water to a dog; it is obvious that this one deed could not of itself have such an effect, but all becomes understandable when the deed is understood as a particularly characteristic—as it were culminating—manifestation of the basic and fundamentally good tendency of the soul in question.

of the Judgment than in the nature of the damned. God is not subject to time and, for Him, "punishment"—as well as "reward"—marks an essential aspect of a particular being, just as the actions or attitudes that, from the human point of view, seem to have provoked the corresponding retribution. The individual is what he must be according to his possibility, which is to say that he is a necessary expression of All-Possibility; particular possibilities have no other explanation than the infinity of universal Possibility, and cannot be explained by moral considerations.

According to a Hindu expression, "the human condition is hard to obtain", which means that for the being in transmigration, the chances of entering a central state, such as the human one, precisely—or to remain in it after death if already in it—are immeasurably less than those of falling into a peripheral state, such as that of animals, plants, or even minerals. This disproportion is most clearly expressed in the geometrical symbolism from which we have borrowed our terms: even when replacing the geometric point by a visible point—hence by a circumference as scaled-down as possible, that is, right up to the limit of visibility—the extent of this center will always be infinitesimal compared to that of the circumference. Let us imagine rain watering a field whose center is marked by a pebble: the chances are infinitely greater that the drops of water will fall on the ground than on the stone; and this picture, suitably transposed, enables us to understand why the human condition is "hard to obtain", but also why this condition—or the analogous condition in any other world—represents God "on earth"; indeed it is solely by starting from this condition that a being can realize God and consequently leave transmigration (*saṁsāra*). The sufficient reason of the human state, its existential law (*dharma*), is to be a bridge between earth and Heaven, hence to "realize God" to some degree or other[7]—or what amounts to the same thing, to leave

---

[7] The Hindus express this truth in the following way: just as it is the *dharma* of water to flow and of fire to burn, or of birds to fly and of fish to swim, so is it man's *dharma* to realize *Brahma* and, in consequence to be freed from *saṁsāra*. In the same sense also, Christian theology teaches that man was created to know, to love, and to serve God, and by this means to acquire eternal Life.

the cosmos, at any rate the formal cosmos.[8] This explains moreover why all sacred morality insists upon the importance of procreation in marriage and sees in marriage no other end: procreation, indeed, enables souls wandering in peripheral and passive states—analogous to, but not identical with, the animal, plant, and mineral species of our earthly world—to enter into a central, active, free state—the human state—and there to win salvation or deliverance; the woman, if she can guarantee the means of salvation to her children, as is the case within traditional civilizations, thus performs an infinitely charitable work by her maternal function; the mother is thus a sacred door to deliverance.

There is no contradiction in the fact that Christian morality simultaneously demands both procreation and chastity, and even the latter before all else, for these two functions are alike in having meaning only in relation to God: chastity in a direct, inward, "vertical", and mystical way, and procreation in an indirect, outward, "horizontal", and social way; in other words, the former is qualitative and the other quantitative, at least in a certain sense. Far from contradicting the function of procreation, chastity thus corresponds—not in itself, but in virtue of the effective role it plays in a particular spiritual path— to that which constitutes the sufficient reason of the human state; viewed from this perspective, it can be said that without chastity, life has no meaning; but without procreation, there would be no one to be chaste; therefore a point of view must be adopted that reconciles these two demands. The procreative man must, in fact, realize chastity in appropriate modes; and likewise, but conversely, the chaste man must procreate in accordance with modes required by his function: that is, the married man must be chaste firstly in relation to women other than those allowed to him by religious law, and then also to a certain extent in relation to his own wife, and finally towards his own soul, whose position in relation to the spirit is feminine. As regards the man who has made a vow of chastity, he in turn must procreate, but

---

[8] The formal cosmos constitutes the cosmic periphery, the cosmic center being Paradise in the ordinary sense of the word. This reservation is useful because in esoteric doctrines, Paradise often means what could be called, for want of a better term, the "divine State", hence realization of God. If we speak here of Paradise in the singular, it is not, of course, in order to exclude the plurality of Paradises, attested by all Revelations, but because this word can in fact designate the paradisal worlds as a whole, or again, in God Himself, all His Names taken together.

spiritually, and he does so on the one hand by the transmission of spiritual truths and graces, and on the other by the radiance of his sanctity. What we have just said implies that chastity according to the flesh does not constitute an absolute demand since it is in itself a strictly human attitude; as regards spiritual chastity, of which carnal chastity is but one support among others equally possible, it is required unconditionally, for without it there is no exit from the illusory world of forms. But this spiritual chastity can take different names depending on the spiritual path: thus in Islam it becomes "poverty", so that the functions of procreation and chastity can be combined, here and now, even on the carnal plane.

After this digression, let us return to the question of the possibility that the human state—and, in other worlds, analogous states—offers of leaving the indefinite cosmic round: in order to be able to realize this liberation, man must already possess a certain eminently superior freedom[9] in his very nature, and this freedom is the free will that raises man above passive beings such as animals. But it is also this freedom that, by a tragic paradox—inherent moreover in creation as such—allows man not to take into account his existential or innate law, or let us say, the meaning of his life; in this case he is man only accidentally or almost by chance,[10] and not so necessarily or by essential definition.[11]

---

[9] It goes without saying that animals and the lower beings also reflect divine Freedom and, as a result, are necessarily free, at least in a certain respect, precisely that of their participation in God's Freedom; but their participation is, to an eminent degree, less direct than man's, so that it is perfectly legitimate, from the human point of view, to deny animal freedom, just as it is legitimate from the "divine point of view" to deny human freedom.

[10] Strictly speaking, there is no chance; if, nonetheless, we use the word here, it is in a wholly relative and provisional sense in order to indicate a certain absence of necessity.

[11] This is what the Hindu language expresses symbolically by saying that the man who is unfaithful to his own sufficient reason—to the human *dharma*—is *shūdra* or even "outcaste", and not "twice-born" (*dvija*), that is, consecrated or initiated. Christian baptism also has the meaning of an integration of the accidentally human being into the essentially human state, in the sense that it confers the virtuality of the primordial or Edenic state. Caste is founded on psychic heredity, and this is an undeniable fact, even though here, as everywhere in the cosmic order, there are "exceptions that prove the rule"; the Hindu system takes this fully into account, since no one would ask a wandering hermit (*parivrājaka*) what his caste had been previously; human differences are effaced in sanctity, and even simply in the social—or rather extra-social—state that corresponds to it.

It follows from our exposition that the sufficient reason of every form of Revelation consists in realizing, in the fullest possible way, that which constitutes the reason for being of our very existence; we mean that religion must address every aptitude, even the most modest, by making use, as do the angels, of spiritual languages that differ but always conform to the fundamental Idea; religion thus supplies to whoever by nature answers to the definition "man", the means of realizing his final end—to be perfectly man is "to become God"[12]—and also, to those who are men somehow in spite of themselves, a means, not in the first place to go to God, but to wish to go, hence, above all, to become fully men.[13]

[12] According to Saint Basil, "man is a creature that has received the order to become God"; in the same sense, Saint Cyril of Alexandria said: "If God has become man, man has become God." Hindu doctrine would say that it is necessary to "become That which we are", namely That which alone "is".

[13] It is these truths that materialism wants to ignore at all costs; by the logic of things, its outcome is egalitarianism, hence that which is most contrary to human nature. Indeed, if we are all equal in terms of matter, that is, in our material needs and in obedience to physical laws, this has nothing whatever to do with our quality as men; now, this quality is our reason for being, or in other words, it is this alone that distinguishes us from animals. Thus materialism amounts to reducing man to the animal, and even to the lowest animal, since this animal is the most collective; this explains the materialists' hatred for all that is supra-terrestrial, transcendent, spiritual, for it is precisely by the spiritual that man is not animal. To deny the spiritual is to deny the human: the moral and legal distinction between man and animal then becomes purely arbitrary, like any other tyranny; it means that by his abdication man loses all his rights over the life of animals, they having the same rights as man, since their material needs are the same; obviously it is possible to invoke the right of might, but then there is no longer any question of equality, and this right will also apply to men between themselves. Finally, there is one more thing that the materialists take no account of, namely the fact that a normal man suffers from being in the flesh: the shame that he feels for his physiological existence is a sufficient indication of the fact that he is a stranger and an exile in matter; the possible "transfiguration" of the flesh by human beauty in no way alters the humiliating laws of physical existence.

Part II

Forms of the Spirit

Christianity and Buddhism

Christianity and Buddhism present certain remarkable analogies which are all the more striking given that in other respects these two traditional forms appear as very different from each other, to the extent that Buddhism has even been qualified as an "atheistic religion"—an absurd definition, but understandable on the part of people whose idea of God is almost exclusively anthropomorphic. In reality, the Divinity takes on a concrete form in the Buddha just as it does in the person of Christ: indeed, both appear in an expressly superhuman, transcendent, divine mode; the "kingdom" of the Buddha, like that of Christ, "is not of this world"; contrary to the case of other *Avatāra*s,[1] Christ and the Buddha are neither legislators nor warriors but wandering preachers; Christ frequents "sinners" and the Buddha "kings", but they do so as strangers and without involving themselves organically in the life of men. Their respective doctrines are characterized—notwithstanding the universality they imply, which contains no limitation—by an exclusive spirit of renunciation, a monastic or eremitical spirit one might say, and hence an asocial one in a certain sense, if one leaves aside the question of charity that here seems to replace all law, but which in reality cannot compensate in practice for the absence of a legislation properly so-called. In one word, these doctrines never consider the here-below as capable of serving as a positive support for the spiritual path, but reject it as an obstacle; which is to say that they consider it, not in relation to its symbolism, which connects all things essentially, qualitatively, or vertically to the divine Prototype, but solely in relation to its character of manifestation, creation, hence of non-divinity, imperfection, corruptibility, suffering, and death.

Another striking analogy consists in the fact that each of the two religions springs from another, which it abolishes for its own purpose

---

[1] We have in mind here Sri Rama and Sri Krishna, both great warriors who outwardly lived the life of the world; and also, as regards the Semitic world, Abraham, Moses, and Muhammad. The universality of holiness implies that it can be clothed in the most varied of modes.

and in relation to which it will therefore appear as heterodox.[2] Need-less to say, this does not prevent it from being orthodox from the standpoint of its intrinsic truth; for Christianity as well as for Bud-dhism, the previous religion serves the symbolic role of the "dead letter"—whence in Christianity the rejection of the Mosaic Law, and in Buddhism, the rejection of the *Veda*. The subjectivism of these negations is to be explained by the evident and necessary opportunism of every specifically initiatic perspective, which is therefore above all methodical. In Christianity the negation has a mystical stamp, whereas in Buddhism it assumes a rational appearance, which however does not imply any rationalist character in the slightest, but on the contrary demonstrates, in its own way, the spontaneity and independence of the Intellect in relation to forms. The new *Avatāra*, far from passing unnoticed in the mother civilization, leaves a deep albeit more or less external mark on it: the imprint left by Christ on the Jewish civiliza-tion is particularly important since Judaism henceforth lost its center and thus an essential aspect of its cohesion; likewise, the advent of the Buddha marks a turning point in the history of Hindu civilization, although this was not at all detrimental to its spiritual or traditional continuity.

But the most profound analogy between these two forms of uni-versal Revelation lies in the fact that each possesses—in principle and *grosso modo*—an integrally initiatic character, not one that is *a priori* exo-esoteric like Judaism and Islam. Yet, and however paradoxical this may seem at first sight, it is in this common characteristic that there also lies the greatest divergence between the Christian and Bud-dhist religions,[3] in the sense that if their intrinsic nature is similar in the aspect we have considered above, the extrinsic consequences of

[2] The great Shankara sees in Buddhism only its extrinsically heterodox aspect; as the providential and inspired spokesman of Hinduism, he was not obliged—any more than the Hindu tradition itself—to take account of the intrinsic orthodoxy of a doctrine for which he had no need. In an altogether general way, it is always illogical to demand of a traditional authority a scientifically objective knowledge of a foreign religion, since the latter assumes in such a case only a symbolic value; it is therefore legitimate to agree with Sri Shankara while at the same time accepting Buddhism in itself.

[3] We are excluding here the doctrinal divergence that results from the different con-ceptions of the Absolute, Christianity conceiving it as a "Being" and Buddhism as a "State"; both terms have here, needless to say, only a wholly provisional sense, for "God"—in the apophatic sense—is beyond Being, and *Parinirvāna* is no longer a "state" since there is no individuality left.

that nature differ totally, somewhat like the solutions to one and the same difficulty can vary according to circumstances. The difficulty here lies in the fact that while Buddhism and Christianity are initiatic in their structure, they had to meet not only the spiritual needs of an elite but the manifold demands of a total human collectivity, and thus of a society containing the most diverse of minds and aptitudes;[4] if there is a contradiction here, it was nonetheless unavoidable, and it is precisely this contradiction that constitutes the particularity of the two religions. Both of them had to reconcile their character of spiritual path with the demands of a collective equilibrium: Christianity, for its part, had no choice but to veil the esoteric nature of its dogmas and sacraments by declaring them to be "unfathomable" and by qualifying them as "mysteries"; but the difficulty was only apparently resolved, because in reality all that was done was to avoid its implications; the reaction of the "swine" and the "dogs" was bound to occur sooner or later, and in fact the "wisdom according to the flesh" ended up invading everything, triumphing in the form of that unearthed paganism called the "Renaissance" and culminating over time, via a series of secondary subversions, in the extreme negation of all that is "mystery".[5] As for Buddhism, it was able to avoid a similar fate thanks to the rational—and not mystical—appearance of its doctrine; this appearance was eminently suited to neutralizing *a priori* and as it were in the bud, the above mentioned reaction, which—seeing that Buddhism possesses no exoterism properly so-called—would have inevitably occurred without this anticipation. We have said "rational appearance", for it goes without saying that Buddhist "reasoning", just as the Christian "mystery", is in itself not a form of mental elaboration but a symbol meant to act as the vehicle of a wisdom "according to the Spirit"; such a wisdom is never bound by the contingencies of the human mind, but transcends and annihilates them in the absolute plenitude of pure Truth.

---

[4] This is why the Buddha could say: "Three things shine forth openly: they are the sun, the moon, and the doctrine of the Perfect One." This saying also refers to the rational form mentioned above.

[5] There is a prefiguration of this destiny of Christianity in the fact that Christ himself gave Judas the piece of bread intended to designate the traitor; this indicates the necessary and providential character of what in Christianity might appear as an accidental deficiency.

—— .:. ——

Christianity and Buddhism, we have said, had to reject the religions from which they respectively issued; but they made the spiritual store of these religions accessible to many foreign peoples, precisely owing to this rejection—if such a paradoxical formulation is permissible. What had closed monotheism to non-Jewish humanity—we are speaking only of those peoples that were destined by nature to adopt it—was a sacred legislation which, ordered according to the needs of the Jewish people alone, lost its reason for being in other ethnic settings and therefore could not act as the vessel of universal Monotheism; now, neither the monotheist idea nor messianism could remain tied solely to the people of Israel.[6] Likewise, neither could the idea of liberation through Knowledge, nor that of transmigration, which depends on it, remain the prerogative of the Hindu world alone, for they answered too well the needs of peoples outside India; these peoples, however, had no need of the caste system, which was suited to the particular conditions of Hindu humanity,[7] but which was useless and inapplicable to the yellow races, and above all superfluous in the early Buddhist community itself whose character was, as mentioned above, initiatic and not social.

It will perhaps be objected that this function of the universalization of an idea hitherto confined to a form not lending itself to expansion, is not particular to Buddhism and Christianity, that it is notably incumbent on Islam as well; yet the case of Islam is different, for if on the one hand it is true that Islam also universalizes an idea which without its intervention, would not have known the full expansion it is capable of, it does not however present itself at all as

[6] We know what Saint Paul says of circumcision "in the spirit", which he opposes to the one "in the flesh". The Buddha's rejection of castes "in the flesh" and their replacement by castes "in the spirit" has the same significance; similarly, Islam replaces the "baptism of men" by that "of God" (*sibghatu 'Llāh*). Heterodoxies often adopt an analogous attitude, out of a need for compensation and due to hypocrisy, but without being able to justify it by any intrinsic truth and spiritual strength; heresies, in fact, always depend negatively on the truths they deny; error is but a shadow, and a shadow has no independent existence.

[7] Other civilizations possessed a caste system, but here in fact it is only the castes of Hinduism that are under consideration.

an initiatic extraction of the religions to which it is related, but much more as an exo-esoteric synthesis, or a sort of Christian Abrahamism, as it were. Consequently, Islam is distinguished from Christianity and from Buddhism—apart from other differences not applicable here— by the fact that it possesses an exoterism revealed as such and not merely adapted *a posteriori*; but it is also distinguished by the fact that it was revealed parallel to the forms it synthesizes in its own way, and not outside these forms as is the case with Christianity and Buddhism, whose Founders were respectively Jewish and Hindu.

As we were saying earlier, pity or charity, or rather a particular manner of stressing this quality, is another feature that brings Buddhism closer to Christianity. One must beware, however, of confusing this charity with a vague and flabby attitude; in other words, charity is not a sentimentalism that causes one to be blind to the objective differences of phenomena, nor is it equatable with a "psychologism" that reduces all culpability to nothing. Indeed, it is one thing not to know how to tell a wolf from a lamb and quite another to recognize their distinction on the plane of contingencies even while perceiving the ontological unity of opposites, and refraining from entering into the impasses of passional illusions and in the mechanism of concordant actions and reactions. As in the case of Christ's Law—requiring that one love one's enemy and turn the other cheek—so also for a Buddhist, it comes down finally to a question of transcending the plane of affective contrasts, and this in view of a reality—or of Reality as such—that contains all things and is situated beyond all things; a Christian would say: "for the love of God". It is a pernicious error to believe that serenity is blind and egalitarian; on the contrary, it is serenity's very lucidity that gives it all of its value: not to "resist the evil one" makes sense only on condition that we remain aware, on a certain plane which concerns us unquestionably as living beings, that an evil person is something other than a good one. Few things are more suffocatingly intolerable than the sentimentalist's attempts "to see only the good everywhere" or "to see evil only in oneself", at the expense of the truth and to the detriment of human equilibrium; for just as generosity has value only if one is strong, so the perception of unity has meaning only for he who is capable of discerning diversity. Charity, in the sense intended here, is to seek to discover in those whom we have to judge the qualities they really possess, and not blindly to attribute to them qualities foreign to their nature or which in no way counterbalance their defects; for charity has no value, in fact, apart from its contents; without the truth it is nothing. It is an outrage to intelligence to want to abolish our capacity for judgment for the sole pleasure of persuading ourselves that we are charitable; now, it is true that such behavior may have a certain ascetic meaning, depending on circumstances, but in that case it is not devoid of a certain selfishness.

And this is important: an outward attitude, whatever may be its usefulness, is never more than an approximation, not a totality; it has a value as a symbol and as a key, not that of a strict adequation, otherwise hypocrisy would not be possible: the moral exteriorization of the letter of the law must not be taken "word for word" anymore than scriptural symbolism, for here too "the letter killeth, but the spirit giveth life". Buddhist charity is above all a spiritual perspective, therefore it is transcendent with respect to its possible forms.[8] The *Tathāgata* has no vices, assuredly, but he is likewise above virtues.[9]

To love all beings without distinction is to love that Being which is indistinct in all things—it is therefore to love the Divine or the Void whence every creature springs and it is to love, in the creature, the center where it ceases to be itself and where there is no longer anything but "Oneself", without either virtue or vice, or any other determination. However, it is proper to distinguish cleanly between a unitive vision of all beings due to a spiritual realization, and a mental attitude that seeks to anticipate this realization through sentimentalities and mirages.

While we are on the subject, it will not be inopportune briefly to sum up the monotheistic doctrine[10] concerning human charity,

---

[8] Proof of this is that Buddhists never had the idea of abolishing the death penalty—a demented and criminal idea, born moreover from contemporary "psychologism", which forgets not only the charity owed society but also, in the last analysis, the charity owed the condemned person himself.

[9] Virtues, that is to say inasmuch as they are distinctive properties and illusorily conscious. The satanic imitation of this wisdom would be to declare oneself independent of virtues we do not possess.

[10] And universal if one sets aside a certain type of terminology, while taking account of circumstances that actualize the problem.

since this doctrine has become blurred in the consciousness of the majority of people, being replaced by social concepts having no connection whatsoever with traditional truth:[11] what counts in the sight of the Absolute and regarding our last ends is a charity practiced in virtue of the "love of God" and which is accepted for the sake of that same love; for human life has no other meaning, either for him who gives or for him who receives.[12] It can however happen that charity is exercised out of love of God, but on behalf of someone who fails to profit from it in view of God, just as it may happen that someone exercises charity without loving God, but on behalf of another who does profit from it spiritually; in both cases the gain is one-sided, and the other party will have served only as an instrument of destiny. Can one infer from this that charity should be practiced only towards those who are supposed to profit thereby in view of their last ends? If such an alternative is encountered, then yes; otherwise no; but even in a case where a choice is possible, one practices charity towards an "unbeliever" when it seems that this might somehow help to heal his soul and on condition that the "believer" in need is not thereby harmed with respect to a vital interest; and the same holds good when the need of the "unbeliever" is of a more important order than that of the "believer" and when this charity is not harmful in the end to those who exercise it.

One additional point to be noted is the following: poverty, no more than illness or any other misery, does not carry with it in the sight of God any "right" to impiety, displeasing as this may be for religious demagogues who, under pressure of a materialistic and atheistic environment, accept this kind of blackmail; love of the Divine is a "categorical imperative" which, coming from Heaven, cannot fail to take account of the limits of our nature or of our responsibilities and which, consequently, could not depend *de jure* on any social or economic condition. The requirement of recognizing the Absolute is itself absolute, it concerns man as such and not man under a given

---

[11] In fact, this kind of confusion occurs everywhere, in the East as well as in the West.

[12] Likewise for work: far from constituting a merit in itself, work become meritorious only on condition that it is carried out for the love of God, which implies that it be done as well as possible and that its content—when it is a question of a work of art—transmits something of the truth, of the spirit, of that which gives meaning to life.

condition;[13] it is even a fundamental aspect of human dignity—and above all of the intelligence that makes up man—that we accept Truth because it is true and for no other reason.

There is still another analogy we wish to point out, namely the fact that neither Christianity nor Buddhism possesses a sacred and hence unique language, which again is a result of the particular and to some degree exceptional nature of these two religions; in fact, they are founded much less upon a revealed Book than on a more direct or more concrete, a more immediately tangible mode: namely the very Body of the God-Man, which offers an as it were consubstantial participation in the Word. In Christianity, this sacred Body has taken the form of the Eucharist, and in Buddhism the form of the sacramental image of the Blessed One, which image is derived from the very shadow of the Buddha,[14] and was left by him as a "remembrance"[15] for his spiritual

---

[13] What renders religion implausible—notwithstanding the absence of the desire to understand it—is not this or that "standard of living", but the scientistic and machine-driven ambience that has made poverty more odious than ever and removes from work any quality of art, all intelligibility, all human character, and as a result all satisfaction. It has to be acknowledged that the abnormal and antihuman nature of industrialism provides some excuse for the materialism of the victims—whether poor or rich—of this state of affairs, but this excuse can never be more than very relative, man being what he is.

[14] The *Chitralakshana*, the Indo-Tibetan canon of pictorial art, attributes the origin of painting to the Buddha, which is quite significant; it will be recalled that the sacred art of Christianity, that of icons, goes back to Saint Luke and the angels. Buddhist tradition tells also of a sandalwood statue, which King Prasenajit of Shravasti (or Udayana of Kaushambi) had made during the lifetime of the Buddha, a statue of which the Greek statues of Gandhara may have been superficial and decadent copies; be that as it may, the spiritual source of the sacramental statues of the Blessed One is the same as that of the paintings, and in any case the symbolic rigor of the forms and proportions of Buddhist sacred sculpture exclude the hypothesis of a Greek influence for this art, although it is not impossible that the Greeks supplied some formal elements of a secondary order.

[15] There comes to mind here the words of Christ on the occasion of the institution of the Eucharistic sacrament: "Go and do this in remembrance of me." In Sufism, the "eucharistic" invocation of a holy Name, under whatever form, is called "remembrance" (*dhikr*); in Buddhism too, to invoke the Buddha is called "to remember the Buddha" (*Buddhānusmriti*).

posterity, hence as a means of grace; as a result, the bodily appearance of the Buddha is said to be a teaching no less than is his doctrine,[16] which explains the central position of the sacred image in the Buddhist system: contemplation of the revealed image of the Buddha is indeed, like Christian communion, an absorption of the sacred Body of the manifested God.[17] Needless to say, one should not look for a strict analogy between this Image and the Eucharist, for the points of view remain nonetheless very different since in the Eucharist it is the aspect of Presence that outweighs the aspect of Symbol, whereas in the image of the Buddha it is essentially through the symbolic form that the real Presence is transmitted. But to return to the liturgical languages of the two religions: what matters almost exclusively in Buddhist and Christian texts is the meaning of the text and not the language that conveys it, since this language does not constitute the sacred materiality of the Revelation. Moreover, the part played in Christianity by the "gift of tongues" suggests that the diversity of liturgical languages, already affirmed by the three inscriptions—Hebrew, Greek, and Latin—on the Cross, has a positive significance in the sense that it denotes in its own fashion the universality of the New Alliance. By contrast, in all the other traditional forms—excepting Buddhism—the language of the Revelation is like the sacred flesh of the divine Word; it is thus the "Body of the Buddha" as well as the "Word made flesh"; and if a book like the Koran may not be read in a language other than that of the Revelation, it is for a reason analogous to that which forbids making the Eucharistic Species from materials other than those prescribed by the Church, or making the sacramental images of the Buddha otherwise than according to strictly established rules.

—— ⋅⋮⋅ ——

---

[16] Tao-Cho, in his work entitled *An-le-tsi* (*The Book of Peace and Happiness*), one of the chief sources of the Pure Land doctrine, says, quoting a *sūtra*: "All the Buddhas save human beings in four ways: 1. By the oral teaching of Buddhism as it is set out in the twelve categories of Buddhist Scriptures. 2. By their physical traits of supernatural beauty. 3. By their marvelous powers, their properties, and their transformation. 4. By their names, which when uttered by beings remove all obstacles and assure rebirth in the presence of the Buddha" (Daisetz Teitaro Suzuki, *Essays on Zen Buddhism*).

[17] Hindu *darshan*—the contemplation of saintly persons—is of the same order.

The four divine gifts bequeathed by the Buddha are: the doctrine of Deliverance, the visible symbol of the Blessed One, his ever-present spiritual Power—or his Blessing—and finally his saving Name. These gifts will be found with Christ in the following forms: the Doctrine of Redemption and of Love, the Eucharist, the Paraclete, and finally the salvific Name of Jesus, as it is invoked in Hesychasm. According to Buddhist teaching, these four gifts proceed from "all the Buddhas", and are to be found in appropriate forms in every divine Messenger.[18]

To conclude, we shall sum up the function or role of Buddhism and that of Christianity in the following terms: each had to reject outwardly the form—with respect to its formal expression, not of Revelation[19]—from which it issued; each presents itself as the spiritual or specifically initiatic essence of the preceding religion, which had become more or less literalist or pharisaical, at least in a transitory and in fact providential manner; finally, each adapted the said essence to the needs of an autonomous and hence integral religious existence, thus making possible an expansion and radiation of certain spiritual treasures far exceeding the possibilities of their original frameworks.

---

[18] The "celestial" Name of Muhammad is *Ahmad*; when the letter *m* (*mīm*) is removed, which is that of death (*mawt*), what remains is the divine Name *Ahad*, "One". The Prophet expressed his identity with God through the following *ahādīth*: "I am *Ahmad* without *mīm*"; "I am an Arab without 'ayn"; and "Whoso hath seen me hath seen God" (*Al-Haqq*, "the Truth"). In the second *hadīth*, the word "Arab" ('*arabī*) becomes "my Lord" (*Rabbī*) by the suppression of the letter 'ayn, which is that of "servitude" ('*ubūdiyyah*, from '*abd*, "servant"), that is, of cosmic, relative, unreal existence. The Prophet also said: "Whoso knoweth his soul, knoweth his Lord"; in this *hadīth*, the truth expressed in the three others becomes a general truth and thereby a spiritual rule of cardinal importance, concerning the realization of "God within us".

[19] A Revelation, as such, comes from God alone; however, just as a man, although he is not the creation of his parents, borrows from them the constituent elements of his earthly form, so a tradition, although it is never the creation of a human ambience, must nevertheless borrow from it certain elements of a formal order.

The Mystery of the *Bodhisattva*

There is a side of Buddhism in which it resembles not only Christianity, but also the Semitic religions in general—paradoxically so, considering its non-theistic character—in the sense that its starting point depends on a human point of view rather than on the metaphysical nature of things; indeed, when it is said that Existence is but suffering and that the Absolute is the cessation of suffering, and further that human perfection lies in "compassion for all living beings", this opens up a perspective that corresponds to our human situation and to our ultimate interests, no doubt, but it does not offer from the outset the most direct possible definition of "that which is", if it may be expressed thus when considering both the manifested Universe and that which transcends it. Such an observation is not, however, of a kind that need logically disturb Buddhists,[1] and this for two reasons: firstly, because they are not unaware of the fact that the doctrines of the Buddhas are only "celestial mirages" intended to catch, as in a golden net, the greatest possible number of creatures plunged in ignorance, suffering, and transmigration, and that it is therefore the benefit of creatures and not the suchness of the Universe that determines the necessarily contingent form of the Message; and secondly, because Buddhism, within the framework of its own wisdom, goes beyond the formal "mythology" or the "letter" and ultimately transcends all possible human formulations, thus realizing an unsurpassable contemplative disinterestedness as do the *Vedānta*, Taoism, and analogous doctrines.

Hence the question that Shakyamuni might have asked himself—had he needed to ask one—was: "Which is the most effective way of conveying the saving Truth to men—or to certain men—in these Latter Times?" and not "Which is the most adequate—or least inadequate—formulation of the metaphysical nature of things?" Neither the *Vedānta* nor Neoplatonism include the possibility of addressing all men usefully and of serving as the vehicle of an integral tradition, nor indeed is this their purpose; but Buddhism wishes to and has to include this possibility, and cannot therefore not offer itself first of

---

[1] No more so than the anthropomorphism of the Semitic Scriptures need disturb Kabbalists, Gnostics, or Sufis.

all as an *upāya*, a "provisional means", with an aim that is above all charitable, in the broadest and most complete sense of that word. Buddhists, it must be stressed, find it all the easier to recognize this in that they are—especially in Zen—far from claiming that the nirvanic Truth can be enclosed definitively within the mold of any dialectic. Nevertheless, there results from this general situation—apart from any fluctuations of terminology—a certain difficulty in speaking of Knowledge in such a way as to satisfy at one and the same time the metaphysical Truth and the voluntaristic and emotional side of Buddhism.

Original Buddhism distinguishes extrinsically between a *Samyaksam-Buddha* and a *Pratyeka-Buddha*; the former corresponds to what Hindus would call a major *Avatāra*, having by definition the function of founder of a religion, and the latter to a *Jīvan-Mukta*—a man "delivered in this life"—who has neither the quality of a major or plenary *Avatāra* nor consequently the function attaching to such a one; and not having had a Buddha as master, neither does he have disciples.[2] After this comes the *Shrāvaka*, who is a disciple—or the disciple of a disciple—of the Buddha; like the *Pratyeka-Buddha*, he is an *Arahant* or perfected saint, but in some fashion owing to the direct influence of the Master. Finally there is the *Bodhisattva* who, in principle, is a saint on the way to becoming a Buddha.

Now, when it is stated, as in the *Mahāyāna* writings, that the state of a *Pratyeka-Buddha* is inferior to that of a *Bodhisattva* because the realization of the former is "selfish" and lacks compassion for crea-

---

[2] It could be that the *Pratyeka-Buddhas* are in fact identified to the Hindu *Yogins* and *Avatāra*s, of whom nascent Buddhism could obviously not be unaware and whom it needed to "situate" in one manner or another. The saints of Brahmanism indeed "have no master" in the sense that they do not follow the Buddha, and they "have no disciples" because they do not teach Buddhism and do not address the Buddha's followers; but it might also be admitted—and one thing need not exclude the other—that the *Pratyeka-Buddhas* correspond to the category of saints whom the Sufis call "solitaries" (*afrad*, from *fard*) and who likewise have neither masters nor disciples. Be that as it may, the *Sūtra* of the Rhinoceros (*Khaggavisāna Sutta*), where Shakyamuni has a *Pratyeka-Buddha* speak, seems to indicate that this type of sainthood is based essentially on the mystery of solitude, which calls to mind an inscription we once saw in a medieval hermitage: O *beata solitudo, o sola beatitudo.*

tures, it seems to be forgotten—or at least this logical objection comes to mind *a priori*—that *Nirvāna* implies by definition the abolition of all egoism and the realization of total charity. This is an objection that the *Mahāyāna* itself raises in its own way and in its sapiential dimension, without really contradicting itself since it recognizes two truths, the one being relative and provisional and the other absolute and definitive, and since its doctrinal form is essentially apophatic and antinomic. In other words, when it is said that the *Mahāyāna* is "great" (*mahā*) for the sole reason that its aim is the salvation of "all sentient beings"—thanks to the sacrificial ideal of the *Bodhisattva*—and not the salvation of a single individual as is the case with the *Hīnayāna*, then it is proper to object, in accordance with the higher teaching of the selfsame *Mahāyāna*, that the reason adduced carries no weight with respect to *Nirvāna* or, what amounts to the same thing, with respect to Knowledge; not to mention the fact that this world of ignorance and suffering—this *Samsāra*—is metaphysically necessary and need not be considered solely from a volitional and emotional angle.

Be that as it may, the sapiential *Mahāyāna* intends to support the heroic ideal of the *Bodhisattva*, but does so by bringing it back to a strictly metaphysical perspective: it specifies that compassion is a dimension of Knowledge, then it adds that the neighbor is non-real, and that charity must therefore be exercised "quietly when the occasion arises" and without slipping into the dualist and objectivist illusion for, it says, there is no one whom our charity could concern, anymore than there is a charity that could be "ours". Thus, on the very basis of the bhaktic interpretation of the *Bodhisattva*, Mahayanic *gnosis* rejoins as if by a roundabout way the most rigorous and hence the most objective or most disinterested metaphysical positions.

To be as precise as possible, Buddhism can be said to present itself under the following fundamental aspects: first of all, original Buddhism; then *Theravāda* Buddhism, which is its continuation as to form if not to all its content; finally, *Mahāyāna* ("Great Vehicle"), which characterizes the preceding as *Hīnayāna* ("Lesser Vehicle") and which in its general form exalts the heroic ideal of the *Bodhisattva*; then, within the framework itself of the *Mahāyāna*, a sapiential perspective that corrects and counterbalances the specifically bhaktic elements in the Mahayanic ideal; and parallel with this perspective there is another that is devotional and centered above all on the cult of the Buddha Amitabha. Therefore, if we acknowledge the greatness of the "Great Vehicle", this is not because of the altruistic ideal that appears as its mythological mantle and its elementary thesis, but because of the two quintessences just mentioned—the one sapiential and the other devotional—the ultimate crystallizations of which are, in Japan, Zen and *Jōdo*.[3]

While sharing the sacrificial ideal of Buddhism's foundational doctrine, but without following it into what is too literal and too human in its interpretations, sapiential *Mahāyāna* adopts the terminology of this doctrine and projects its own certitudes into it: consequently it will say, not that *Nirvāna* requires charity, but that the state of the *Pratyeka-Buddha* is not *Nirvāna* in the fullest sense, or that it is a *Nirvāna* on a transitory level, comparable no doubt to the *Brahma-Loka* of the Hindu *Krama-Mukta*; in this case, the use of the designation "Buddha" seems to prove that there has been a change of terminology, for it is *a priori* unusual to call a man "Buddha" when he is placed lower than a *Bodhisattva*; it is, however, possible to justify such a designation seeing that it refers to a state that is already nirvanic, when there is extinction at least in relation to the formal world, and that owing to this fact alone there is no obligatory return to the round of births and deaths.[4]

These considerations bring up the matter of the authenticity of the Mahayanic *sūtras*, since these supposedly report the discourses of the Buddha, just as do the texts in Pali. Now, it is not the authenticity itself that is in question, but the mode of authenticity: that is to say, these texts, or certain of them, while certainly based on the teachings of Shakyamuni—for otherwise they would not assert this[5]—seem to present developments or commentaries rather than the sermons themselves, and they do so availing themselves of the terminology

---

[3] This juxtaposition may well appear paradoxical to many of the faithful of these two schools, even though both were recommended by the great Nagarjuna himself, and even though Honen, the illustrious spokesman of *Jōdo*, expressly admitted all the forms of traditional Buddhism.

[4] The Mahayanist polemic against the *Pratyeka-Buddhas* should not astonish us unduly on the part of a perspective of sacrificial idealism; the Vishnuite *bhakta* too readily represents the Shivaite *jnānin* as a sterile and dreary rationalist, lacking what is essential until, touched by Grace, he discovers devotional love—as if the latter were not eminently comprised in *jnāna*.

[5] This argument will surprise those scholars who have no idea either of the nature of spiritual inspiration or of the organic laws governing—and guaranteeing—the Tradition.

in use in the environment where they were composed.[6] However, whether it is a question of the Buddha himself or of his inspired commentators, it is well not to lose sight of a principle to which we have already alluded and which finds an application in all sacred Scriptures, namely the distinction between two kinds of truth, the one relative or provisional and the other absolute and definitive,[7] at least inasmuch as there can be anything definitive on the plane of verbal crystallizations;[8] or again, from a more contingent point of view: the Buddha, in his long career, could have presented diverse perspectives to audiences of unequal levels, and could even have used varying terminologies.[9]

As far as the Mahayanic ideal of the *Bodhisattva* is concerned—an ideal of sacrificial compassion in the heroic *Mahāyāna* and a symbol of spiritual totality in the sapiential doctrine—account must be taken of the following fundamental situation: Buddhism unfolds as it were between the empirical notions of suffering and cessation of suffering; now, the notion of compassion springs from this very fact: it is an inevitable or necessary link in what might be called the spiritual mythology of Buddhism. He who speaks of suffering and cessation of suffering speaks of compassion, given that he is not alone on earth; and this is where the *Bodhisattva* intervenes: he embodies the element compassion—this quasi-ontological link between pain and Bliss—just as the Buddha embodies Bliss and just as ordinary beings embody

---

[6] On the other hand, it is not out of the question—or is even probable—that certain particularly homogeneous and concise texts, such as the *Mahā Prajnā Pāramitā Hridaya* or the *Vajracchedikā*, render faithfully, and without development or commentary, the sacred discourse word for word.

[7] When Christ strikes the Temple merchants, he manifests a partial and conditional truth, namely that there are phenomena—of the hypocritical or blasphemous type—that by their nature authorize or call for violence; but when he enjoins us to turn the left cheek to him who smites us on the right, he is teaching a total and unconditional truth concerning, as such, our inner attitude and hence also our general tendency, which means that holy anger and holy patience can and must be combined, the levels being different. The Scholastic distinction between a truth *secundum fidem* and another *secundum rationem* stops halfway between belief and intellection; it is more like a syncretism than a synthesis.

[8] This reservation brings into question, not the immutability of intellectual evidences or of sacred formulations, but the absoluteness of concepts as such from the standpoint of the Divine Selfhood and in the context of direct Knowledge.

[9] For example, in presenting the *Shrāvaka*, the *Pratyeka-Buddha*, the *Arahant*, and the *Bodhisattva*, in the latter sermons, as so many different degrees of realization.

suffering; he must be present in the cosmos as long as there is both a *Samsāra* and a *Nirvāna*, this presence being expressed by the statement that the *Bodhisattva* wishes to save "all beings".[10]

From a more contingent point of view, it could also be pointed out that concern for personal deliverance, while irreproachable in itself, does involve a certain danger of egoism once it becomes the sole motive of a tradition carried by a large collectivity whose tendencies are bound to be exoteric; from this point of view, the intervention of the *Mahāyāna* appears to be providential. At the time when it first asserted itself, the Buddhist tradition had doubtless given rise to all kinds of narrow and pharisaical perspectives; the same had been the case with Brahmanism in the Buddha's time, as also with Judaism at the time of Christ, which does not mean that these crises involved either of these traditions in their entirety or in their subsequent existence; thus there is no need of taking up the polemic of the early Mahayanists against the Theravadins of Ceylon and Indo-China. Or again, in a more fundamental sense concerning religion as such: the very necessity of an emotional element—in the absence of a theism properly so-called and given the conditions of the "Latter Times"[11]—explains the opportune-

[10] The Buddhist adage, "May all beings be happy", or the will of the *Bodhisattvas* to save "all sentient beings", has its equivalent in the Islamic "Blessing on the Prophet" (*Salāt 'alā 'n-Nabī*), which proceeds from above to below in the sense that Muhammad, who is mentioned first, is the center of the cosmos, upon which all other creatures depend, these being designated—in descending order—by the terms "Family" (*āl*) and "Companions" (*sahb*). But even if it were not specified that the blessing extends to the "Family" and the "Companions", the graces would reach the totality—or a totality—of mankind by virtue of the avataric character of the name *Muhammad*, which includes all human beings while at the same time indicating their summit; he is at once summit and circumference. In the Buddhist perspective, the blessing—actualized, among others, by the prayer wheels—concerns all sentient beings without exception.

[11] According to the *Nirvāna Sūtra*: "Those who despise the *Dharma* will then be like the volume of earth of the ten directions, and those who remain faithful to it will be like the crumb of earth that can be put on a fingernail." And similarly according to the *Saddharma Pundarīka Sūtra*: "At the horrible time of the end, men will be malevolent, false, evil, and obtuse and they will imagine they have reached perfection when it will be nothing of the sort." According to the caliph Ali, "The inhabitants of the here-below are nothing but barking dogs and ferocious beasts howling at one another; the strong devour the weak and the great subjugate the small. . .". Under such circumstances, a spiritual treasure can no longer take hold collectively except by means of a sentimental, even a passional, element, which alone is capable of acting effectively in a milieu of this kind.

ness of the cult of the *Bodhisattva* in its connection with the path of works and the path of love; in this respect, the difference between the Buddhism of the North and that of the South is no more than one of style and mythology, without prejudice of course to their supra-formal essences. Be that as it may, it can be admitted that if in the climate of the *Mahāyāna* the Buddha Amitabha is the object of a special cult, this is *a priori* because, as *Bodhisattva*, he was able to accumulate the merits capable of creating a "Buddha-field" and a "Pure Land"; but, quite obviously, it is also possible that this retrospective motive need not concern contemplation, whether devotional or other, especially since the same causal sequence may also be conceived in the reverse direction: in other words, the prime mover is not a contingency like the merit accumulated by an individual, or by a "karmic nexus" if one prefers, but a principle of Mercy that creates simultaneously both the merit itself and the saint who accumulates the merit. The principle of Mercy results from the very nature of the *Ādi-Buddha*, namely the Absolute who is at once Knowledge and Love.

The doctrine of Shinran presents a wonderful synthesis between the devotional and the sapiential paths: to start with, it envisages the "Pure Land", the *Sukhāvatī* Paradise, in its aspect of transcendence, hence of identity with *Nirvāna*; similarly, it reminds us that death, by virtue of universal analogies, can serve to rend the veil of *Māyā*, and hence can be an occasion for Enlightenment and Deliverance,[12] provided we are in a spiritual situation that enables this junction or actualizes this analogy, and this precisely is made possible by the Grace of Amitabha and our trust in it. The whole emphasis is placed here on the element "faith"—partly evoking, *mutatis mutandis*, the *satori* of Zen[13]—and this faith is an attitude of trust which, by its quality, coincides with the forgetting of the ego. The Absolute—which has revealed itself under the particular name of *Amitābha*—is essentially

---

[12] This is the case with the Hindu *Videha-Mukta.*

[13] This comment permits the following remark: it has been possible to say in Zen: "If you meet the Buddha, slay him"; this means, paraphrasing the first sentence of the *Tao Te Ching* ("The Tao that can be grasped is not the real Tao"): the Buddha whom you can meet is not the real Buddha. This is the point of view of the absolute Subject, hence infinitely transpersonal, namely the point of view of perfect non-objectification. It is encountered also in Western *gnosis*, for example when it is said that God could not "live a single instant" without us: what then is meant by "God" is only the mental objectification—hence the relativization—of the Ineffable, which, Itself, is beyond all polarity.

Wisdom and Compassion, Knowledge and Mercy; that is to say, in the symbolism of the Buddha Amitabha, the "original vow" to enter *Nirvāna* only on condition that all those who invoke the sacred Name with faith be saved, is in fact the Absolute's aspect of Mercy; it is as if the Absolute were saying, to paraphrase the vow: "I would not wish to possess Beatitude if there existed between Me and contingent beings an insurmountable barrier preventing them from drinking deeply of my Beatitude"; or again: "I would not be the Absolute were I not blessed and merciful."[14]

But this path of Amitabha of which Shinran, after Honen, was the last great spokesman, likewise includes, at a lower degree than the nirvanic miracle of which we have just spoken, a properly human finality: it leads to the *Sukhāvatī* Paradise where the faithful will await *Nirvāna* till the end of the cycle. This Paradise—which Hinduism, analogically speaking, also knows since that is the condition of the *Krama-Mukta*—is of quite a different order from the ones comprised in the round of transmigration; it is the exact equivalent of the Paradise of the Semitic religions, in which "eternity" means precisely this nirvanic conclusion and the ceasing of *Samsāra*.[15]

A distinction must be made between the personal *Bodhisattva* who is transmigrating and the celestial or universal *Bodhisattva* endowed with ubiquity; the former, if he is not simply a manifestation of the latter, accumulates merits by his virtues and actions;[16] the latter,

---

[14] In Christianity, the Name of the Virgin, which signifies Mercy, is joined with that of Christ, which is an indirect Name of the Absolute. In Islam, the Name of the Absolute—*Allāh*—is followed immediately by the Names of Mercy, *Rahmān* and *Rahīm*—the one intrinsic and the other extrinsic—in the formula of consecration at the beginning of every Revelation and every rite.

[15] If in the Semitic monotheisms there is no place for the concept of the *Bodhisattva*, it is because these perspectives take into consideration neither what is before birth nor what may be situated outside the human Paradise. The function of the celestial and compassionate *Bodhisattva* is nonetheless represented, in the West, by the "apotropaic" saints or "Holy Helpers" (in German *Nothelfer*), not to mention the guardian or protecting angels.

[16] "A hundred beatitudes of the *Gandharvas* are as one beatitude of the *Devas* who

namely the universal *Bodhisattva*, is the cosmic emanation of a Buddha, or—in Western terms—he is the Archangel who manifests a given divine Quality; his reintegration into *Nirvāna* coincides with the *Mahāpralaya*, the Apocatastasis, which brings about the return of each and every manifestation to the Principle, or the return of all contingency to the Absolute.[17] The human *Bodhisattva* is—to use now Hindu terminology—either a *bhakta* or a *jnānin:* in the former case the path alternates between devotion and compassion—devotion towards the Buddhas and celestial *Bodhisattva*s and compassion towards the creatures wandering in the *Samsāra*—whereas in the latter case, that of the *Bodhisattva* who is a *jnānin*, it is *gnosis* that takes precedence over everything else: compassion is not something added sentimentally to an imperfect mode of knowledge but, on the contrary, this compassion is the secondary dimension or internal complement of a knowledge that is virtually or effectively perfect, because it is situated on the axis of Buddhahood or is identified with Buddhahood itself.[18]

have attained to their divinity by the accumulation of meritorious works, and a hundred beatitudes of the *Deva*s by merit are as one beatitude of the *Deva*s by birth . . ." (*Brihadāranyaka Upanishad*, IV, 3, 33). The samsaric situation of the personal *Bodhisattva*s places them in the category of *Deva*s by merit; these have less beatitude than the *Deva*s by origin because merit can always be exhausted and cannot be maintained save by means of new merits. As to the *Gandharva*s, they are "celestial musicians", creatures that are more or less "peripheral", and perhaps comparable to our terrestrial birds in certain respects or, on the contrary, incomparable in relation to the things of this world.

[17] Saint Gregory of Nyssa alludes to the Apocatastasis in speaking of the demons: "And these, it is said, the Apostle accounts as subterranean beings, wishing to indicate by this turn of phrase that no creature will remain excluded from the Kingdom of the Good when, after long periods of centuries, all evil shall be destroyed . . ." (*Conversation with Macrina*, IX:2).

[18] A Buddhist has rightly pointed out to the author that the merits, compassion, and knowledge of the *Bodhisattva* correspond respectively to *karma*, *bhakti*, and *jnāna* and consequently are addressed to those who follow those ways; for each of them the *Bodhisattva* reveals himself under this or that aspect; to use Buddhist terminology, these are the three aspects respectively termed *upekshā* (impassivity), *maitrī* (love of one's neighbor), and *prajnā* (knowledge). In the framework of *gnosis*, however, compassion changes its mode: Jacques Bacot was correct in declaring, in his introduction to *Le Poète tibétain Milarepa*, that "Buddhist pity has no relationship with sensibility. It is entirely objective, cool, and connected with a metaphysical conception. It is not spontaneous, but the outcome of long meditations. The idealism that tends no longer to differentiate between 'me' and 'not-me' is the generator of this pity for all that lives and is the victim of illusion." It is the compassion comprised in *prajnā*.

Some will no doubt object that the *gnosis* of the *Bodhisattva* is not that of the Buddha: namely that the Buddha's compassion is intrinsic in the sense that he carries all things in himself—but at that degree the *Samsāra* cannot oppose *Nirvāna* or be associated with it in any manner whatsoever, which means that the opposition "existence-Void" only becomes meaningful at the degree of existence and is resolved in the principial Void—whereas the universal pity of the *Bodhisattva* is extrinsic and therefore still situated under the sign of duality; but this would not do full justice to the nature of the great *Bodhisattvas*, for the sacrificial sojourn in the world necessarily combines with *Nirvāna*; it is a way of realizing *Nirvāna* in a certain sense also "outwardly", within the samsaric condition itself.[19] This must needs be so, for the simple reason that a being cannot deprive himself, from life to life, of that which constitutes the very meaning and end of all his efforts, all his virtues, and all his merits; it is neither possible to persist in an exclusively negative situation, on the one hand, nor, on the other, to consider the ultimate Wisdom merely as a means of coming to another's aid, which would amount to making a means of the end or a contingency of the Absolute; Knowledge as such cannot be an instrument designed for charity any more than the Real can be subordinate to the illusory.[20] The condition of the gnostic *Bodhisattva* would be neither conceivable nor tolerable if it were not a manner of contemplating the Absolute at once in the heart and in the world; and above all it must be stressed that Knowledge, by definition, has no connection with the quantity of merits or the number of incarnations.[21] Only a bhaktism with an exoteric bias could imagine perfect

---

[19] This brings to mind the Arabic divine Names "the Inward" and "the Outward" (*Al-Bātin* and *Az-Zāhir*) and the mystery of the Divine "outwardness" in connection with the concepts of the "metaphysical transparency of phenomena" and the "relatively absolute".

[20] In the opinion of the Tibetan *Arahant* Milarepa, "One should not show oneself rash and hasty in the intention to serve others as long as one has not realized the Truth oneself; otherwise one risks being a blind man leading the blind."

[21] This is what *Dhyāna*—Zen—teaches in the most explicit manner. Texts like the *Diamond Sūtra* or the Chinese *Sūtra of Huang-Po* formulate the decisive truth in the most explicit possible fashion and thereby express—in terms of doctrine—the very quintessence of Buddhism. In the same vein of thought, the *Lankāvatāra Sūtra* and other texts establish a distinction between a progressive realization and a realization that is immediate, the progressive concerning the rooting out of vices and illusions and the immediate the assimilation of nirvanic Light; according to this distinction, there are two kinds of saints or, within the same being, two degrees of sanctity, or two stages.

Knowledge as being the fruit of a process of accumulating elements of one kind or another, even be they sublime from the human point of view;[22] in short there is nothing either quantitative or moral about the Spirit. At the same time, the following should also be emphasized: *Nirvāna* seen or experienced from the standpoint of a formal condition—as is the case with the Hindu *Jīvan-Mukta* and the Buddhist *Arahant*—is not absolutely the same as the *Nirvāna* experienced beyond all form; thus the refusal on the part of the great *Bodhisattvas* to enter *Nirvāna*—and here we have in mind not only their celestial prototypes, where the matter is self-evident—is not a refusal, in itself impossible, of total Knowledge, but a merciful hesitation to cast off one last veil or to leave the formal Universe definitively.[23]

Here one has to insist on the difference between *Nirvāna* and *Parinirvāna*: only death allows of a total reintegration—for those who in their lifetime have realized "Extinction"—in that "supreme Extinction", which is none other than the Vedantic "Self". Living beings, whatever their degree of spirituality, remain of necessity linked with Being, which belongs to the realm of *Nirvāna*, since it represents a perfect transcendence in relation to all manifestation and to the whole cosmic sequence of cause and effect, but which, being still of the realm of *Māyā* whereof it is the summit or quintessence, is not yet the Self. If in a certain respect death brings no change for one who has realized *Nirvāna*—the Hindu *Jīvan-Mukta* or the Buddhist *Arahant*—yet in another respect it nonetheless produces a considerable change, so much so that it can be said that death for the "living liberated one" is neither a modification nor a non-modification, or that it is both at once. However: if we say that the Buddha, in dying, entered *Parinirvāna*, this is again only an earthly way of speaking: in reality, he was always there as *Dharmakāya*, "body of the *Dharma*"; similarly he did not cease to dwell in Heaven in his manifestation as *Sambhogakāya*, "body of Bliss", even while manifesting himself

---

[22] According to the *Lankāvatāra Sūtra*, the *Bodhisattvas*, while holding back from entering into *Nirvāna*, are there already in fact, "for in their love and compassion there is no cause for illusory distinction and consequently no intervention of such a distinction". The *Diamond Sūtra* mentions this saying of the Buddha: "A *Bodhisattva* who would say: 'I will deliver all beings'—do not call him a *Bodhisattva*."

[23] The attitude of the great Hindu *bhakta* Sri Chaitanya rejoins the ideal of the *Bodhisattva*: "Lord, I desire neither riches, nor servants, nor a beautiful damsel, nor the poetic muse. Let me, O Lord, from birth to birth, have only devotion to Thee—a devotion which seeks nothing in return" (*Shrī Shrī Shiksāstakam*).

among mortals by virtue of *Nirmānakāya*, the "body of supernatural metamorphosis". In monotheistic terms, we would say that to every Prophet or *Avatāra* there corresponds an Archangel and, beyond creation, a divine Name, and that each divine Name reflects in its own way the whole Divinity.

A question that might be asked about the supreme *Bodhisattvas*—given the virtually divine cult surrounding them—is the following: are they no more than archangels, that is to say, do they remain at the summit of the cosmos, thus below Being, or can they be situated at the summit of *Māyā*, thus at the degree of Being but below Beyond-Being? The response has to be negative with respect to the latter part of this question, despite certain hyperboles or verbal syntheses that could suggest the contrary; for the "divine Names" or Qualities of Being are represented, in Buddhism, by the different Buddhas—notably the "*Dhyāni-Buddhas*"—or in other words, by absolute Buddhahood envisaged under the aspect of differentiation, which—being already contingent—is specific to *Māyā*. Let us add that for the celestial *Bodhisattva*, who even while becoming "incarnate" does not leave his Paradise, "to become incarnate" may also mean "to delegate a power", and it is in this sense that a particular saint or great lama may be described as an "incarnation" of Avalokiteshvara or of Manjushri.[24]

Another question that may be asked is this: whence originates the initiative for the coming into being of a *Bodhisattva* and *a fortiori* of a Buddha? Does it come from man or from the heavenly *Logos*? The two things coincide: once the human support is ready, namely once it has attained a degree of perfection, the *Logos* descends upon it and settles in him, just as light automatically settles on a clear and smooth surface; but precisely, the ripening of the human support is in its turn and by anticipation an effect of the *Logos*—which is at once Wisdom and Mercy, Knowledge and Love, light and warmth—so that we are obliged to admit that the original initiative comes from Heaven and that the support was brought forth in the realm of the cosmic play solely in view of the manifestation of the *Logos* and by the *Logos* itself. It is in an analogous sense that it has been paradoxically affirmed, in

---

[24] The terrestrial charity exercised by the celestial *Bodhisattvas* brings to mind a Saint Theresa of Lisieux wanting "to spend her time in Heaven doing good on earth"—symbolized by the "shower of roses"—although in this case the intention is situated in the context of an altogether different eschatology.

the language of various traditions, that the world has been created for the Prophet or *Avatāra* or for the sake of his manifestation.

An important point touching the mystery of the "virtual Buddha" is understanding the nirvanic essence of the *Samsāra*: just as we have written upon other occasions that the finite is a sort of internal dimension of the Infinite—an indispensably necessary dimension, obviously, by reason of infinity itself or the intrinsic character of infinity—so too we could define the *Samsāra* here as a sort of dimension of *Nirvāna*, or as an "ignorant" manner (in the sense of the term *avidyā*) of envisaging it, the factor "ignorance" occurring as a result of the very infinity of the divine "Void". The actual substance of this reality in reverse is constituted by those countless "grains of sand" that are the *dharmas*—the elementary qualities—these being like the segmented, innumerable, and "inverted" crystallizations of the Void or of the pure nirvanic Substance. The impermanence of things is none other than their own relativity.

To summarize what has just been explained and at the same time to complete it, it is necessary to distinguish between three *Nirvānas*—or three degrees of Extinction—two of which are still in the order of *Māyā* or contingency, whereas the third, *Parinirvāna*, is the Absolute; if another *Nirvāna* were the Absolute there could not be a question of a *Parinirvāna*. The first *Nirvāna* is ontologically that of the *Bodhisattva*: it is extinction in relation to formal manifestation and corresponds to the degree of the Archangels, Heaven, Existence; we say "ontologically" because the *Bodhisattva* "lives" at this level even if he has already realized the second *Nirvāna*, the one which coincides with the state of the terrestrial Buddha, namely the extinction in regard to universal manifestation, which corresponds to the degree of Being. The third *Nirvāna*, beyond *Māyā*, is that of the celestial or absolute Buddha: this is *Parinirvāna*, extinction in relation to Being or to *Māyā* and which corresponds to the supreme Self of the Vedantists.[25] Now

---

[25] The lowermost tip of what could be called the "nirvanic axis" is the heart or the pure Intellect, or again the mind in a state of perfect truth and purity, or the *mantram*, the *nembutsu*. In monotheistic, or simply theistic, language we would speak of the "heavenly" or "divine axis".

to say that the *Bodhisattva* renounces *Nirvāna* is to say that he intends to remain, not in formal manifestation alone, but in transmigration, whatever the degree of extinction he may inwardly have attained. What the *Bodhisattva* desires is not a divine perfection but a cosmic one, one which will result in the obtaining of a divine message; now this function—that of the *Samyaksam-Buddha*—requires a perfection of cosmic Knowledge that the *Pratyeka-Buddha* does not possess and that moreover is—like the fact of Revelation itself—insignificant with regard to absolute Knowledge;[26] in Islamic terminology, we would say that the Prophet is sublime, not by virtue of his prophetic mission (*nubuwwah*), but by virtue of his perfect sanctity (*wilāyah*), which has led certain people to claim that saints are superior to Prophets, whereas in reality prophecy, without being in itself a degree of sanctity, requires or implies total sanctity.[27] But the *Bodhisattva* can "renounce" *Nirvāna* only on condition of having attained it in the mode accessible within formal existence, and it is only then that his decision to become a *Samyaksam-Buddha* has any meaning; prior to that, his desire even to "become a Buddha" or "to save all sentient beings" is at the same time a stimulus and an obstacle, depending on whether his path is primarily related to *bhakti* or *jnāna*. On attaining *Nirvāna* he will know whether the *Ādi-Buddha*—the supreme Buddhahood, identified with the nirvanic Infinite—has chosen him or not; or in other words whether the universal economy, or the equilibrium or rhythm of the Cosmos, has decided whether he is to be a Messenger or whether he is finally to be integrated—until the exhaustion of the "life of Brahmā"—into the state of an Archangel, such as Avalokiteshvara or Manjushri. All that has just been pointed out implies that the specific Knowledge of the *Samyaksam-Buddha* is "neither superior nor inferior", but simply "other"—although in a certain sense more "ample"—than the Knowledge of the *Arahant*; it is a kind of existential penetration into worlds and creatures, a dilation in the direction of the *Samsāra*, which is as a projected shadow, so to speak, of his

---

[26] Sri Shankara realized this Knowledge without having produced the *Veda*; and in an analogous sense, Mary Magdalene was perfectly holy without possessing the cosmic and quasi-divine greatness of the Holy Virgin.

[27] A further distinction must be made between minor Prophets (*nabī*, plural *anbiyā'*), who have a limited mission within a given tradition, and major Prophets, the "Messengers" (*rasūl, rusul*) who have a universal mission and are founders of a religion.

dilation in *Nirvāna* or *Parinirvāna;* and this is doubtless connected with the "remembrance of former births", for the penetration in question embraces both "time" and "space" simultaneously, symbolically speaking.

The Enlightenment that occurred in the lifetime of Shakyamuni beneath the *Bodhi* tree is none other than what in more or less Western parlance would be called "Revelation", namely the reception of the Message or of the prophetic function:[28] just as the soul descends suddenly on the embryo once it is sufficiently formed—neither before nor after—so *Bodhi* descends on the *Bodhisattva* who has acquired, alongside his Knowledge and his *Nirvāna,* the cosmic perfections required for the prophetic radiation.

At the risk of repetition, it is necessary to return here to a particularly important point: if there is in the *Mahāyāna* an element that may be open to question from the metaphysical point of view, it is not the path of the *Bodhisattva* quite obviously but, what is quite different, the ideal of the *Bodhisattva* insofar as it is polemically opposed to the "non-altruistic" spirituality of the pure contemplative, as if, firstly, all true spirituality did not include charity and, secondly, as if the consideration of some contingency or other could rival pure and total Knowledge. But if the wish to deliver all beings, as expressed under this elementary and even sentimental form, is of necessity opposed to Knowledge—since it is here a question of "interested disinterestedness"[29]—one may well ask what, from the point of view of tradition, can be the profound meaning or the alchemical function of a desire objectively so disproportionate and subjectively so contingent? The answer is that this is a means of channeling certain mentalities towards Virtue and Truth; it is this idealism of heroic abnegation, this heroism at once karmic and bhaktic—and nothing else—which will attract their goodwill and kindle it, and this is a factor that tradition must take into account in its multi-faceted formulation. As for

---

[28] This Revelation is summed up in the highly elliptical formula of the *Bodhi* of Shakyamuni: "This being, that becomes, from the becoming of that which becomes; this non-becoming, which does not become, from the cessation of that which ceases." Here is the commentary on it by one of the Buddha's disciples: "Of those things that proceed from a cause the *Tathāgata* has explained the origin, and likewise their cessation he has explained. This is the doctrine of the great *Shramana*."

[29] In a parallel and reverse manner, the non-acting solitude of the contemplative could be described as "disinterested interest", at least from a certain point of view.

the *Bodhisattva* himself, his refusal of *Nirvāna*—not of the "nirvanic axis" that passes through him, but of the repose in Extinction—is simply the will to be reborn despite the possibility of no longer having to be reborn; since this possibility exists and presents itself to him, he is entitled to it according to his vocation and destiny.[30] What the *Bodhisattva* then lacks is not the formless, nor even the supra-existential, *Nirvāna*—that which the terrestrial Buddha enjoys—but solely the prophetic mandate that would make him a *Samyaksam-Buddha*, and the retirement into unmanifest, hence extra-samsaric, Reality; the absence of such a mandate is of course involuntary, whereas sojourn in transmigration is vocational and aims either expressly at obtaining the mandate or mission, or else at a state of beneficent and angelic presence in the *Samsāra*. It is this and this alone that is meant by the refusal to enter into *Nirvāna*, for it goes without saying that no-one can prevent—or could wish to prevent—the flowering forth of Knowledge.

Humanly speaking, the *Bodhisattva* is an altogether extraordinary being owing to the acuteness, amplitude, and scope of his faculties, something which, on this scale, cannot be the case with the *Pratyeka-Buddha*, who, while "delivered in this life" and possessing supreme Knowledge to the extent that it can be imparted to one still bound to the earthly or formal condition, may only be endowed with individual faculties that—apart from intellectuality and contemplativity—do not really go beyond the general norm, as seen by the example of a Ramakrishna or of a Ramana Maharshi; when leaving aside their inner realization, their human breadth—which is the sole consideration here—is obviously less than that of a Rama or a Krishna, or of the young prince Siddhartha, the future Buddha; there is here no common measure, and even the mightiest genius disappears next to this order of greatness—speaking uniquely from the point of view of human constitution and without taking account of any posthumous spiritual destiny. Or let us take the example of the Mother of Jesus: tradition tells us that in a natural—or "supernaturally natural"—manner she possessed every virtue and all knowledge in the fullest possible degree of unfolding; this supereminent perfection was indispensable for her role as "Co-Redemptress", but this is a case of

---

[30] We may recall here the text of Chaitanya, already cited, according to which the saint has one sole desire, to "have only devotion to Thee, from birth to birth".

providential configuration or cosmic prodigality which, while necessarily combined at a certain point with Knowledge, is nonetheless not the prerequisite for it, otherwise it would be pointless to speak of *gnosis* and to teach it to mere mortals. The "superhumanly human" perfection of the *Bodhisattva* is necessary, not for Knowledge as such and hence for departing from this world, but for the earthly manifestation of the Divine Principle, of the liberating Truth, of *Nirvāna*—which is an altogether different matter; far from being exclusively directed towards the unmanifest, the properly angelic human nature of the virtual Buddha on the contrary radiates into the cosmos, as the sun illuminates the night. This, we repeat, is what renders his nature capable of transmitting that crystallization of the Infinite—or that Truth "become flesh"—which is Revelation, the seed and nourishment of a universal and millenary tradition.

To the question of whether this perfection, combined with the *Bodhi* for which it is the predisposed receptacle, constitutes a degree of Knowledge, the answer is both yes and no; in a sense, it is as if one were to ask whether the *Samsāra* is real; the answer can be affirmative or negative, depending on the viewpoint, so long as the absolute truth be acknowledged. "Each thing is *Ātmā*", certainly, but "the world is false, *Brahma* is true", and "there is no divinity save the one Divinity"; what the problem comes down to is that of the "divine nature" of *Māyā*, or the nature of *Māyā* as "modality", "play", "unveiling", or "aspect" of the ineffable Self, of *Paramātmā*. The supreme Knowledge attributed to the *Samyaksam-Buddha* comprises essentially three factors: the unimaginable cosmic unfolding of the perfection of the *Bodhisattva*, then the *Nirvāna* comprised in that perfection, and finally the "celestial weight" of Revelation, of the *Dharma*. As for knowing whether extra-nirvanic factors, however incomparable they may be at their respective levels, add something to *Nirvāna* or constitute an element of principial Knowledge, this seems to us to be a question that metaphysically answers itself.

There is nonetheless a factor that allows one to accept, with the appropriate reservations, the interpretation of the specific Enlightenment of the *Samyaksam-Buddha* as a degree—or as the supreme degree—of Knowledge, and it is the following: in the *Bodhisattva* ready to receive it, Revelation coincides with the "recollection" of the Wisdom "previously" acquired, but temporarily "forgotten" owing to the fact of incarnation. This "forgetting" or this initial perplexity occurs for the simple reason that it is not in this new world of forms that the *Bodhisattva* had acquired his Wisdom. The temporary obscuration in question is moreover comparable, in the natural order, to childhood, which also transitorily veils faculties that are nonetheless pre-existent. Under the *Bodhi* tree there was therefore a twofold Enlightenment: on the one hand the "recollection", which was bound to occur after the inevitably fumbling efforts to find one's way around in a new body and in a new space, and on the other hand the Revelation accompanied by the samsaric Knowledge that characterizes the *Samyaksam-Buddha*. If we admit that the term *Buddha* can have two or more meanings, as the *Mahāyāna* obliges us to do, we must equally admit two or more kinds of *Bodhi*; there is one *Bodhi* that belongs to every Buddha, whether externally a *Bodhisattva* or not, and there is another that concerns solely the Buddha as Revealer and in which an extrinsic dimension is combined with the intrinsic *Bodhi*.[31]

As we have remarked, the *Bodhisattva* who has become Buddha possesses absolute Knowledge not by virtue of his quality of *Samyaksam-Buddha*, but by virtue of his quality of *Arahant* or fully perfected saint, that is to say he can be—but does not have to be—a *Samyaksam-Buddha* because he possesses this Knowledge; we also pointed out that the altogether illusory opposition *Samsāra-Nirvāna* exists only from the point of view of the world and is resolved in and by *Nirvāna* and not otherwise, for there is here no possibility of any reciprocity or symmetry, so that the particular Knowledge of the Buddha in his capacity of Revealer could add nothing whatever to nirvanic Knowledge. Now it must not be lost sight of—and we have already alluded to this—that it is possible to consider the *Samsāra* under its aspect of indirect "Nirvanahood", in other words as an internal dimension of the Void or of the Infinite, and in that case one could, if need be—while observing the proper precautions, which are necessary, albeit relatively so—speak of a supreme Knowledge belonging to the *Samyaksam-Buddha* alone.[32] We will say no more

[31] A distinction is made, moreover, between the unconditional *Bodhi* of the Absolute and its heavenly and earthly reflections, the three levels belonging to every Buddha, according to the theory of the three "bodies" of the "Awakened".

[32] *Samyak* means "upright", "perfect", or "whole", whereas the prefix *sam*—as in the Latin words *summum* and *summa* or the German words *samt, zusammen, sammeln*—expresses the related ideas of "summit" and "totality". The scholarly transcription attaches this prefix to the following word, which renders the familiar terms of *Buddha*

of this, if only for the simple reason that it is impossible to speak adequately of the dimensions of space in planimetric terms.

The Buddha wished at first to keep the Revelation—or the corresponding Knowledge—to himself, and it was only after the thrice repeated insistence of the gods[33] that he decided to communicate it; this initial hesitation is deeply symbolic, for it manifests an aspect of the very process of Revelation, rather like the breaking of the first Tables of the Law by Moses on Sinai. Later, the Buddha declared that he had hidden nothing, but had on the contrary made the Truth radiate as the daylight that illuminates everything; these words, far from contradicting the gradated plurality of meanings in the sacred teaching, as some imagine, really affirm the universality and totality of the *Dharma*: even the most subtle aspects of the Truth have been expressed with a clarity sufficient for "those who have ears to hear"; the Teaching has yielded all the necessary keys, be it only in the form of a flower in the hand of the *Tathāgata*.[34] Moreover, no truth is esoteric in itself; it is so only in relation to a particular degree of understanding; now the source of incomprehension resides more often in the will than in the intelligence, which is to say the obstacles are above all of a passional order, taken in the broadest sense; and this brings us back, all told, to the distinction between two kinds of limitations, those which are fundamental and those which are accidental, and to the problem of their entanglement within human nature, or again, and in other words, to the question of knowing to what extent an apparent substance is accidental or whether an appearance of accidentality indicates on the contrary a substance.

When we say that the Buddha's Revelation is accompanied by a concrete and penetrating consciousness of the rhythms of the *Samsāra*—of the world as an indefinite chain of causes and effects—it

and *Bodhi* somewhat indistinct visually speaking. A term such as *Sambodhi* brings out well the "synthetic" character—both supreme and non-supreme—of the Enlightenment of the Founding Buddha.

[33] The *Deva*s, who correspond to the angels of monotheism.

[34] "He who has thus gone", a name of the Buddha.

must be clearly understood that the kind or style of this knowledge depends on the style of the Revelation that it accompanies: whatever the Revelation enunciates is something the *Avatāra* knows immediately without its being always possible to assign a priority, in the avataric soul, either to the Knowledge itself, or else to the "divine fact" of the Revelation. As for the question of spiritual style, it is for example possible to know space in various ways, starting from different symbolisms or by applying different measures: it can be known in terms of a circle, a cross, a star, or a spiral and it is thus that the *Samsāra* can be known according to diverse perspectives, analogically speaking; but this science will never have anything more than a character of "relative absoluteness", like every reflection of the absolute in the contingent.

Monotheism seems to teach that the world has a beginning and not an end, whereas Buddhism seems to assert, no less paradoxically, that the world has an end, but does not have a beginning. This remark, made by a Buddhist to the writer, calls for the following comment: the answer to both difficulties is contained in the idea of Apocatastasis, which satisfies the demands of both the above metaphysics by bringing creation to an end—but without annihilation, quite the contrary—and by realizing the humanly impossible ideal of the *Bodhisattva*s. When Buddhists admit that the *Samsāra* will come to an end thanks to the *Bodhisattva*s and Buddhas who will have saved "all sentient beings" down to the last one, they implicitly attribute the final reintegration to the *Ādi-Buddha*, the universal or divine Buddha whose Act is in effect identified with the transmutative *Logos*; in other words, the Apocatastasis or *Mahāpralaya* is the *Bodhi*—the passage to the state of Buddha—of all celestial *Bodhisattva*s, such as Avalokiteshvara, Manjushri, Kshitigarbha, Akashagarbha; the nirvanic light that submerges, penetrates, transmutes, and devours the *Samsāra* is their Enlightenment saving the Universe, and in fact it is through the celestial Essences that this Light will act, before reabsorbing them in their turn in its infinite Silence.

In Buddhism, which is averse to speculations of a cerebral literalism, language seeks to communicate or provoke a state of "being" rather than of "thinking": understanding and being tend to merge as far as this is possible, whence the wide use of *upāya*s, "concepts as means", the justification of which is not so much a truth conceived in the abstract as an inward transformation and a kind of existential intuition, if such a paradox is permissible. Thus the idea of the *Bodhisattva* has for its aim above all to destroy egotism, and then the ego itself; perhaps the *Mahāyāna* at bottom reproaches its Southern opponents less with an imperfection of doctrine than with one of method, that is to say, it considers that the ideal of *Bodhi* is in practice unrealizable without the ideal of the *Bodhisattva*, who alone is capable of cutting the Gordian knot of egoity. Other views can assuredly be held on this point, but however that may be, if the *Bodhisattva* is supposed to save all sentient beings, this indicates above all a total gift of self, hence a perfect victory over the ego. Compassion then appears as the criterion of authenticity of Knowledge, as is the case with love in Christian *gnosis*,[35] for which wisdom without love is but "sounding brass, or a tinkling cymbal". Love is that which enables "understanding" to pass into "being", or that which attaches us ontologically to Truth and thus opens us to the transforming magic of the Symbol.

By way of conclusion, let us return to these fundamental ideas by specifying them further: the *Bodhisattva* could not accumulate innumerable merits and thereby an inexhaustible *karma* if he were not inwardly a Buddha, that is to say freed, as such, from transgression; it is because he can no longer fall into sin or passion that the *Bodhisattva* gains continuous merits and realizes sublime perfections; the sacrificial actions attributed to him symbolize both his perfections—the *Pāramitās*—and the sacrifice his very samsaric condition represents. What distinguishes the *Bodhisattva* from the Buddha is not necessarily an inferior knowledge—as we have said—but the fact of being in the *Samsāra*, or more precisely of finding himself there in a certain fashion and as a matter of principle; the terrestrial Buddha, for his part, is distinguished from the *Bodhisattva*s by the fact that a celestial Word has become "incarnate" in him and that he has thus obtained the function to found a religion—to speak in Western terms—and to exit transmigration thereafter; moreover, the one does not go without the other, for he who has effected an "exit" out of this world must henceforth

---

[35] We specify that here it is a question of *gnosis*, since for the way of love, which more often than not coincides with a relative exoterism, this is self-evident.

keep watch over this path and has no further function to exercise with regard to "sentient beings".[36]

There are, finally, four "realities" to be considered: *Samsāra*, *Nirvāna*, the *Bodhisattva*, and the Buddha; the latter is, in a certain sense and in his capacity of *Tathāgata*, "*Samsāra* having entered into *Nirvāna*", whereas the *Bodhisattva* is on the contrary and in principle "*Nirvāna* present in *Samsāra*"; it has also been said that the Buddha represents the contemplative aspect and the *Bodhisattva* the active aspect of *Nirvāna*, or that the former is turned towards the Absolute and the latter towards contingency. The Buddha is a ray emanating from the Center and returning to it, and the *Bodhisattva* is a circle projecting the Center into the periphery; the Buddha enlightens or saves by radiation, while the *Bodhisattva* saves by a spiraling movement. Or again: the Buddha transmits Light or Knowledge "vertically", whereas the *Bodhisattva* manifests "horizontally" Warmth, Compassion, Mercy.

The Buddha manifests the truth that "*Samsāra* is *Nirvāna*", and the *Bodhisattva* the truth that "*Nirvāna* is *Samsāra*"; but it could also be said that each manifests both truths in his own way, according to the aspect or function that predominates in each case. This amounts to saying that *Bodhisattva* and Buddha alike are manifestations at once free and necessary of the *Ādi-Buddha* or of Mahavairochana.

---

[36] The *Mahāyāna* is sometimes presented as being the doctrine, not of the earthly Buddha—hence in the *Nirmānakāya*—as is the case with the *Hīnayāna*, but of the "divine Buddha", in the *Dharmakāya*. What is absolutely certain is that in no case could the Mahayanic *sūtra*s be of human origin and reflect an "evolution" of any kind, whatever their dialectical means may be.

Elementary Remarks on the Enigma of the *Kōan*

Anyone who has taken however minimal an interest in Zen Buddhism knows that the *kōan* is a formula rendered absurd by design because intended to provoke a kind of liberating rupture in the mind of the person meditating on it—the mind being considered in this instance with regard to its hardness and blindness. All too frequently, however, the *kōan* has been represented in a rather regrettable manner: people like to pretend, not without a hint of relish with regard to common sense in general or to allegedly "Western" logic in particular, that *kōan*s are there to confer a new vision of the world and life, an aim completely devoid of interest as such; or else they make out that Zen is an integral part of a practical type of life of the most everyday sort, a view that takes no account of spiritual values. We do not say that such assertions or praise are totally groundless, we are simply emphasizing that they do not constitute definitions and that if they did they would not be of the kind to convey a lofty idea of Zen spirituality.

Obviously it is quite inadequate to declare that the purpose of the *kōan* is to produce a particular mental change of some kind or another, and that this is achieved by its very absurdity; such an opinion fails to explain why one *kōan* differs from another, nor does it account for the trouble taken to assemble a collection of *kōan*s—a traditional work deriving all its canonical authority from the fact that the *kōan*s were given by the greatest masters. Were it enough for a *kōan* to be absurd so as to provoke in the end a state of enlightenment, one could simply declare that two and two make five, and there would be no need to resort either to a traditional *kōan* or to one *kōan* rather than another.

The fact that *kōan*s do not deliberately contain an insight into metaphysical doctrine and that it is impossible to explain their meaning verbally does not imply that they have no meaning at all: people are not made century after century to meditate on absurdities pure and simple; and the traditional character of the *kōan* as well as its enlightening result prove that this formula is not just anything. But if the *kōan* possesses no intentional doctrinal content, what can its content be? Both the specific character of Zen itself and the replies of the masters provide us with the meaning: the *kōan* expresses the spiritual experience of a given master in a symbolical—and intentionally paradoxical—form, the significance of which is only verifiable by undergoing the selfsame experience. At the moment of the rupture that is *satori*[1] or enlightenment, the *kōan* is suddenly "understood", its contents are identified; and if one *kōan* differs from another this is not because the effect of *satori* is multiple but because its aspects are such. No doubt a *kōan* is bound to have a metaphysical meaning if it has any meaning at all, or since it has a meaning; but its justification lies precisely in its referring to the inexpressible aspect of the experience of Awakening. The objection could be raised that in such a case the *kōan* has no right to exist, having no place in language since language implies intelligibility; this objection is in itself pertinent, but exceptions must be allowed their due, given that paradox can have a catalytic function in the economy of *Māyā*.

The above observations call for some further remarks on the intentions and means of Zen in general. What Zen wants is the supernatural recovery of the perception of things *sub specie aeternitatis* or in the "Eternal Present"; the mind, having neither the ability nor the need to step outside relativity, finds itself henceforth rooted in the Absolute, both intellectually and existentially. But Zen also comprises another dimension, complementary to the first: this is its aspect of "simplicity" or "equilibrium", a returning to primordial nature. The complement of lightning and of rupture, or *satori*, is found in the peace that dwells in the nature of things, as revealed in the stillness of a pond reflecting the moon, or in the contemplative grace, one might say, of the water lily, or yet again, in the calm and precise elegance of the tea ceremony. The nature-loving and somewhat iconoclastic sobriety of Zen is no mere luxury: whoever wishes to bring the human mind back to that "intuition of Eternity" for which it is made, but which it has lost

---

[1] *Satori* is not absolute enlightenment; it amounts already to a degree of *bodhi*, but is not yet the *Samyaksambodhi* of the Buddha. If the profane state is separated from that of the Awakened as the circle is separated from its center, *satori* would be the sudden realization of the ray which, without itself being identical with the center, is as it were a prolongation of it. In relation to the profane state one may say that *satori* "is" Enlightenment in itself; distinctions between degrees of Enlightenment only have a meaning on the spiritual plane, not in relation to the world.

through its decadence—its scattering curiosity and its compressing passion—must also bring the soul and body back to their primordial simplicity by freeing them from the artificial superstructures of civilization.[2] The one thing does not go without the other: there is no content without an adequate container; the lightning's perfection calls for that of the lotus. In this second dimension, Zen was able to profit from the ground prepared by Shinto, just as, with regard to its first dimension, it had been helped by the presence of Taoism. This, however, must not make us lose sight of the fact that all was given from the beginning: by the Buddha's gesture, his smile, and by the flower he held in his hand.

When one starts from the very basic idea—targeting only a certain effectiveness—that the world is impermanent and nothing else, that it is composed of impermanent and ever-shifting "categories" or "atoms" and that *Nirvāna* alone possesses permanence, one oddly forgets—unless one deems it superfluous to consider it—that escape from impermanence, or even the mere conception of the idea of impermanence and deliverance, would be impossible if no trace of permanence existed within the impermanent, or of absoluteness within the relative. Conversely and *a priori*, there must be an element of relativity in the Absolute, otherwise the relative would not exist, let alone the notion of relativity and escape from the relative; the *yin-yang* symbol represents this in its own particular way, as we have often pointed out on other occasions.

Now this element of absoluteness or of permanence at the very heart of the contingent, or of the impermanent, is precisely our own essence, our "Buddha nature"; to rediscover our own true nature is to realize Permanence and to escape from the "round of existence". It is by basing itself on this idea of immanence that Zen sets out to detach itself, not from tradition of course, since it is Buddhist, but

---

[2] The posture in Zen meditation, *zazen*, is revealing in this respect: erectness and motionlessness; balance between effort and naturalness. Zen has developed an "art of gesture" extending to various crafts, including the profession of arms and all kinds of decorative and more or less feminine activities, and which is poles apart from the fake sincerity of the sloppy casualness and false "naturalness" of our times.

from concepts as such: its very foundation is the fact that everything Revelation offers is to be found principially within ourselves. Zen teaches its disciples, by means of various signs and attitudes, to perceive and to become everything that constitutes the reason for being of words, ideas, and tradition.

We are not Aristotelian, but it goes without saying that Aristotle is a thousand times preferable to a falsified Zen, one divorced from its roots and thus deprived of its justification and its effectiveness; if this point is stressed here, this is because modernistic Zen all too readily overlooks the fact that Zen is "neither with nor without forms" and that, besides rigorous introspection and what may be termed the cult of voidness, it includes an attitude of devotion, of humility, and gratitude, at least *a priori*,[3] which it shares in common with all spirituality worthy of the name.[4] Be that as it may, a spiritual method is not something that is freely available: to the very extent that it is subtle or esoteric it turns to poison when not practiced within the framework of canonical rules, hence "in the name of God", as one would say in the West; in the case of Zen, this framework is above all the triad "Buddha-Law-Community" (*Buddha-Dharma-Sangha*). Zen depends on everything implied by this triad, or else it is nothing.[5]

---

[3] This reservation implies that the devotional virtues are supposed to become absorbed ultimately in an inward extinction that transcends them but without being opposed to them; from another point of view one may also say that in Zen divergent attitudes are found side by side, everything being set in its proper place.

[4] Zen monks recite the *Sūtras* every morning, which proves they are far from scorning texts; they also repeat the prayer of Ta-Hui, which contains a series of spiritual and material demands and is addressed to "all the Buddhas and *Bodhisattva-Mahāsattvas* of the past, present, and future in the ten quarters (of the Universe), and to *Mahāprajnāpāramitā*", the *Shakti* of the *Ādi-Buddha*—Vajradhara—with whom she is sometimes identified. One should also note that every meal is accompanied with prayers and that the main building of the monastery contains an image of Shakyamuni.

[5] Thus there is nothing in common between Zen and the theories of men like Jung or Krishnamurti, or any other type of psychologism.

Īmān, Islām, Ihsān

The Islamic religion, and more specifically the quality of *muslim*, comprises three elements or fundamental states: first, *al-īmān*, faith, the seat of which is the heart; second, *al-islām*, abandon or submission to the divine Will, an attitude that encompasses the whole individual, including his corporeal limit and more particularly his faculties of sensation and action;[1] and third, *al-ihsān*, right-acting (the Arabic word containing both a meaning of "action" and of "beauty"), which consists in the qualitative progression of the two preceding elements. *Al-īmān* and *al-islām* are, *a priori* and according to the usual interpretation made in the *sharī'ah*, the "way" or, in other words, the outer Law; as for *ihsān*, it is identified, in the language of the Sufis, to *tasawwuf* (esoterism) itself: it is as the life of the two other states, which it penetrates and deepens; in that case, however, they are envisaged in a way that no longer pertains to the exoteric domain[2] since the possibilities of this domain are limited to the individual order. Exoterism, although insisting fully on faith and submission, which are its pillars as well as its content, has for *ihsān* no more than an outward definition[3] and without being able to account for its nature. It is here that Sufism comes into play for, apart from its metaphysical doctrine as a theory and a spiritual method, it is the very science of *ihsān*; the latter is thus the point of junction between common religion and realizational wisdom.

Before returning to *ihsān*, it is worth considering what the deeper meaning is of *īmān* and *islām*: the first of these terms was just defined

---

[1] The *jawārih* which are: the hands, the feet, sight, hearing, the tongue, the stomach, and the sexual organs.

[2] Any element belonging to this domain can be transposed into the esoteric domain, whereas the converse is not always possible. The ternary *īmān-islām-ihsān* is that of the *dīn*, a term designating not only religion in general, but also esoterism. *Tasawwuf* (Sufism) is not separable from the *dīn*, but only from the *sharī'ah*, which is the outward aspect of religion.

[3] The exoteric definition of *ihsān* is reduced to the literal meaning of the following *hadīth*: "*Ihsān* is that thou shouldst worship *Allāh* as if thou sawest Him, and if thou seest Him not, He nonetheless seeth thee" (*Al-ihsānu huwa an ta'buda 'Llāha ka'annaka tarāhu fa-in lam takun tarāhu fa-innahū yarāk*).

as "faith" and the second as "submission". Faith is to consent to an idea; now the commitment to a religious doctrine must be something achievable by all the individuals that are part of a total collectivity, and this commitment will be partly intuitive, partly rational, and partly emotional and imaginative, which is as much as to say that it will be relatively passive as the collectivity is so itself. *Īmān*, in its purely spiritual meaning, is no longer an indirect and merely symbolic consciousness of the Divine, but is on the contrary a kind of immediate and active participation in it; in which case, it is no longer a question of mere belief in God, but truly of a share of divine Knowledge itself, if such a formulation is permissible.

On the other hand, if faith in the standard meaning of the term is considered as a virtue, which shows that it is not something intellectual, then it goes without saying that the certitude implied by one kind of knowledge or another could not be meritorious anymore than could any evidence acquired by the sensible faculties, for this certitude carries its fruit within itself; however, this does not take away from Knowledge its "paracletic", purifying, and truly "redemptive" quality, an idea moreover that is contained in the conception of "saving faith". Be that as it may, the exoteric perspective, being essentially moral, cannot but see a kind of merit in faith, apart from any question of grace; and what confers on faith its meritorious character and its moral value is precisely the presupposition of the absence of a sufficient objective reason, for it is virtuous to believe in that which one does not see,[4] whereas knowledge, on the contrary, carries its own reason for being within itself. This does not mean that knowledge is always direct in every respect, for it is clear that it contains degrees, since if this were not so, nothing would distinguish it from its ultimate essence; in fact, the existence of different "initiatic degrees" (*tartīb at-tasawwuf*) is well known. Yet if knowledge can in certain respects be indirect, such as is the case for theoretical knowledge, it is so in an altogether different manner than faith, at least inasmuch as faith is considered in its standard and psychic aspect: any knowledge is by definition static and objective, whereas faith, which is an intellectual function of love, will always be subjective and dynamic.

---

[4] The words from the Gospel, "Blessed are they that have not seen, and yet have believed", refer to the fundamental disposition of the contemplative soul to admit *a priori* the supernatural.

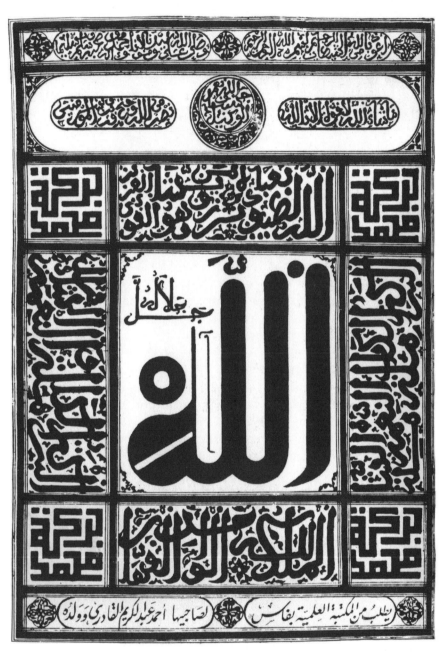

Divine Name
Moroccan woodcut print

91

It might seem surprising that the Muslim religion took its name from the term *islām* and not that of *īmān*; however, it is to be noted that if in principle the idea is greater than its application, this is no longer the case when seen from the point of view of manifestation where, on the contrary, it is the application that so to speak envelops the idea. Three degrees can be distinguished in the state of *islām*: first natural *islām*, which is the necessary, passive, and unconscious conformity of things to their ontological Cause, and by virtue of which every contingent being is *muslim*, "submitted"; second, the *islām* that is intentional, willed, and free, which is translated by a ritual and moral conformity to sacred legislation and which concerns those who have "submitted" (*muslimūn*)[5] of their own will; these are the Muslims or, to apply this idea outside the Islamic form, these are men inasmuch as they belong to their respective religion; and finally, in the third instance, there is the spiritual *islām* that, for its part, no longer embraces a whole collectivity as such since those who realize it are united in divine Love; they are "submitted" as a result of their spiritual realization and not by a will operating more or less separately from them, which is why they are their own Law unto themselves. The Sufi, who is *muslim* in plenitude of understanding and with his whole being, realizes universal *islām*, which is comparable in its perfection to natural *islām*, but actively and consciously so[6] and comprising to an eminent degree all possible modes of conformity. All told, this state proceeds from the fusion or the interpenetration of the *islām* willed by the individual and the natural *islām* belonging to all things: the soul extends out to the totality of manifestation and as it were infuses itself in it, and conversely, the totality of manifestation enters so to speak into the soul and becomes its *islām*. In other words, the natural or cosmic *islām* is penetrated and rendered symbolically conscious by the spiritual *islām* of the Sufi; thus the world seems to depend on the Sufi who, being his own Law, is the Law of the world; on the other

---

[5] Although the term *muslim* is normally used to designate those who have "submitted", namely the Muslims, the term of *mu'min*, "believer", designating a more inward aspect, is also encountered; everyone must be *muslim*, but none has the right to pretend to be *mu'min*, and even less so *muhsin*. Sufis consider themselves to be Muslims *par excellence*; the words "catholic" and "orthodox", like all traditional epithets of this kind, allow of the same universal application as the terms *muslim* and *islām*.

[6] In the same way that the passive perfection of the earth could, by its immobility, serve as a comparison with the active Intelligence of the immutable.

hand, the Sufi is penetrated by cosmic *islām* in such a way that his own *islām* is identified with the profound necessity of things.

It now remains for us to discuss the third state, *ihsān*, "virtue", which we can do with the help of the following ternary: *sharī'āh*, *tarīqah*, and *haqīqah*; the *sharī'ah*, "the way", contains *īmān* and *islām* as religious and social elements, that is to say with all that they imply in the dogmatic, ritual, and legislative orders; the second element of the ternary, *tarīqah*, "the path", is identical with *ihsān*; finally, *haqīqah*, "the Truth", is the reason for being and the supreme end of the ternary; consequently, the two latter elements of the ternary belong to the domain of esoterism. The *sharī'ah*, "the way", is the indirect participation with the *haqīqah*; the *tarīqah*, "the path", leads from the one to the other and does so by means of "Knowledge". *Ihsān* is thus the "Path" and the "Truth", "Knowledge" and "Love".

The relationship between these elements can be outlined as follows:

1. *Īmān*
   Faith   1. *Sharī'ah*
2. *Islām*   "the Way" (exoterism)
   Law

                                               Ma'rifah
                                               Knowledge
3. *Ihsān*   2. *Tarīqah*   *Mahabbah*
   Virtue   "the Path" (esoterism)   Love

                3. *Haqīqah*
                "the Truth"

In considering now the two modes of *ihsān*, Knowledge and Love, it will be seen that they can serve respectively as a kind of translation for the terms *īmān* and *islām*: indeed, *ma'rifah* or "Knowledge" is a "vivified" *īmān* that has gone beyond the "letter" and become "spirit"; and in an analogous sense *mahabbah*, "Love", is a "vivified" *islām*: the static "submission" has become a dynamic "participation", for "God is Love". Relative knowledge is cut off from relative love, as *īmān* is cut off from *islām*; but absolute Knowledge is identified with absolute Love; Knowledge and Love are then the two aspects of a same Reality, just as Truth and Perfection are one.

In the human microcosm, the Intellect holds the role of Principle and the individual that of the manifested; now *ihsān* is the conscious, active, immediate realization of the relationships that exist between the Principle and manifestation: *ihsān* is on the one hand the sanctification of the created and, on the other, its reabsorption into the Immutable.

Intellectuality and Civilization

True intellectuality, while being as "exact" as possible—that is, as adequate as a reflection can be in regard to what it reflects—is totally independent of what is commonly called "exact science", and is even in no way incompatible with ideas that run counter to this science. "Scientific errors" that are due to a collective subjectivity—for example, that of the human species, which sees the sun travel around the earth—convey an adequate symbolism, and hence "truths", even though remaining independent of the simple facts that serve, quite provisionally, as their vehicle; subjective experience, such as the example just mentioned, is obviously not fortuitous, otherwise it would not occur for an entire species. Hence it is legitimate for man to maintain that the earth is flat, since such it is empirically; however, it is completely useless to know that it is round, since this knowledge adds nothing to the symbolism of appearances and instead destroys it needlessly so as to replace it by another symbolism that can merely express the same—or analogous—truths, while at the same time comprising the disadvantage of running counter to immediate and general human experience. The knowledge of facts for their own sake, aside from practical applications that are always of limited interest, has no value. In other words, either one's standpoint is absolute Truth, in which case facts do not count, or else one's standpoint is on the plane of facts, and then one remains in any case in ignorance. Aside from this, it has to be repeated that the destruction of the natural and immediate symbolism of facts—for example, the "abolition" of the flatness of the earth or of the circular movement of the sun—entails serious disadvantages for the civilization in which it takes place, as the example of modern western civilization abundantly demonstrates.

This leads us to say something concerning the very relative values by which this civilization lives—or rather, dies. This is a subject that at first glance seems to have very little to do with the general content of our book; but since we live in said civilization, and since more-over no fact is cut off from total Truth, it will not be superfluous to dwell briefly on the contingencies in question, from which doubtless no man of our times can escape completely. In order to situate the question properly, we must begin with the following definition: what constitutes the very essence of the ancient civilizations—and we speak of civilizations as such, that is, viewed solely from the angle of their human, social, and historical existence—is that they are called upon to realize the most perfect equilibrium possible and thereby a maximum of stability; profoundly realistic, they conform to the possibilities of their plane of existence, necessarily sacrificing the exception to the general and the secondary to the essential. Modern civilization, on the contrary, does not take into account the distinction between what is possible and what is not, and replaces ineluctable principles by all-too-human aspirations which, of course, do not in the least modify the nature of things, that is, the cosmic laws that govern us; moreover, it matters little to appeal to an "idealism" or a "realism", since the first will always be above collective human possibilities, and the second, taken as such, below them; in a word, these "ideals" run counter to what is real, and it could not be otherwise since, all told, they correspond to desires and not to intellections. This rejection of normal principles is the inevitable consequence of the rejection of tradition, which alone can give a human group the framework that conforms to its possibilities; once this framework—indispensable guarantor of equilibrium and stability—is broken, every individual and individualistic aspiration, no matter how chimerical, can henceforth give itself free rein and make a ruling—"ideally" or not—on the merits of human, earthly, and cosmic possibility. Certainly, it is not difficult to notice the faults, abuses, and deleterious outgrowths inevitably found within the ancient civilizations, for as the Gospel says, "God alone is good"; it is more difficult to say how these miseries could have been avoided in fact, that is, "really" and not "ideally". Modernists can be reproached, not for having noted the various types of decay and hardening that took place within traditional civilizations—for no one can be blamed for seeing something visible—but for inferring about the overall inferiority of those civilizations. To have the right to judge thus, the modern world would above all have to possess the spiritual values that are the basis of all normal civilization, and it would have to demonstrate how it is possible for the human mind to focus all its attention at once on the most divergent domains, or again, how in practice a civilization can reconcile modern advances—fruits of such intense efforts strictly determined by an idolatrous overestimation of earthly things—with a contemplative spirit, hence turned away from these very things because turned towards eternal Realities.

For the entire question comes down to the following alternative: either the modern world as such possesses the spiritual values of normal civilizations, in which case it can hold up as an example some, at least, of its advances, namely those that can offer the individual certain real advantages; or else the modern world does not possess such values, but then it lacks that which alone gives meaning to life and makes it worth living; in which case, even its real advances are reduced to nothing, since there is no common measure between man's final ends and his earthly and animal well-being, something the modern world achieves moreover only provisionally and in any case quite precariously. In the eyes of a man who is aware of this abyss, scientific progress, for example, has no value unless it be the fruit of a civilization inspired by spiritual realities and turned towards them, and also only on condition that such progress not be neutralized, not to say annulled, either by some other "progress", albeit contrary to man's "well-being", or by a calamity due to the fact that in constructing a "new world" and destroying an ancient one, no account has been taken of what is possible; thus, if advances, even those most incontestable when considered in isolation, necessarily go hand in hand, firstly with the forgetting and disparagement of the real values of human existence, secondly, with negative "advances" that neutralize the positive ones, and thirdly with calamities that are the inevitable cosmic reactions to undertakings that are finally impossible, then it is plain to see that the advances in question cannot rightly be considered as criteria of superiority for the civilization that has conceived them. At all events, the decisive criterion against the so-called "advances" consists in the fact that it is impossible to realize them without for the most part sacrificing "the one thing needful", namely that which alone gives meaning to life.

In sum therefore, there are only two possibilities: an integral, spiritual civilization, implying abuses and superstitions, and a fragmentary, materialistic, progressivist civilization, implying—quite provisionally—certain earthly advantages, but excluding that which constitutes the sufficient reason and final end of all human existence. History proves that there is no other choice; the rest is rhetoric and chimera.

Part III

Spiritual Life

Modes of Spiritual Realization

It has been said that there are as many paths to God as there are human souls. But, since there is no complexity that cannot finally be reduced to syntheses and, consequently, to simple formulas—provided that these result from the nature of things and not from some philosophical artifice—the diversity of souls and paths comes down, in the last analysis, to three fundamental positions that may be designated respectively by the terms "knowledge", "love", and "action".

It is of action, the most outward attitude, that we shall speak first. Contrary to what occurs in the case of love and especially knowledge, action does not have its sufficient reason within itself; this means that the path of action, on pain of being restricted to exoterism, must be related to one of the two higher paths, which will give it its full meaning. This eminently dependent character of the way of action becomes clear when one has recourse to analogies in the sensible order, for example, when one considers the pair "light-heat", light representing knowledge and heat love, while action is not represented by anything, unless it be in the form of an extrinsic quality, such as the devouring power of fire, the manifestation of which depends on the presence of a combustible material; action is therefore not the equivalent of either love or knowledge. The latter two transcend and abolish the narrow determinism of works; it is faith that saves, just as it is knowledge that sets free.

The path of action (the Hindu *karma-mārga*) refers to the Divinity's aspect of Rigor, whence the connection between this path and "fear" (the *makhāfah* of Sufism); this aspect is manifested for us by the indefiniteness and ineluctability of cosmic vicissitudes; the goal of the path of action is liberation from these vicissitudes, and not from Existence itself, as is the case for the path of knowledge. But this liberation through action is nonetheless a deliverance, namely, from the cosmos of suffering;[1] and if it is action that here plays the part

---

[1] It would be wrong to conclude that Buddhism, for the simple reason that it is founded on the consideration of suffering, comprises only a cosmic path. Suffering being a subjective aspect of relativity, it can serve perfectly well as the negative starting point for liberation by knowledge, the positive starting point being the idea of *Nirvāna*; in conformity with its initiatic subjectivism, Buddhist doctrine envisages the supreme Reality, not in its aspect of "Principle", but in its aspect of "State".

of a support, this is because it is by action that we situate ourselves in time which, as the destroyer of beings and things, is precisely a manifestation of the divine Rigor. The connection that exists, on the one hand between Kali, the Hindu Divinity of destruction or transformation, and *kāla*, time, and on the other hand between *kāla* and *karma*, time and action, will help us to understand in what sense we must relate "fear" to *karma-mārga*. What confers on action its liberating quality, is its sacrificial character:[2] action must be envisaged as the accomplishment of the *dharma*, or "moral duty", which results from the very nature of the individual, and it must consequently be accomplished, not only to perfection, but also without attachment to its fruits (*nishkāma-karma*).

The most direct form of disinterested action is that which most visibly implies forgetfulness of self and which for this reason abolishes the barrier between "self" and "others". In the work of charity, the neighbor becomes the quasi-methodic support of the Divinity, for: "Whatsoever ye have done to the least of these, ye have done it unto Me." The ego is as it were absorbed by the "other", who becomes "God", so that the disinterestedness here lies in the very nature of things; nevertheless, the purely cosmic finality of this path is easily discernible in the fact that everything occurs at the creaturely level, and therefore in the outward and objective world. It follows from what we have just said that the way of action is inevitable to the extent that action itself is: in other words, even he who follows a purely contemplative path must, to the extent that action is unavoidable by dint of circumstances, act according to *karma-mārga*, that is to say, by careful conformity to the constituent elements of action,[3] hence to its symbolism, and always without attachment to the fruits of works.

[2] It is this path of liberation through sacrificial action that served as the basis of the warrior civilizations; we put this in the past tense because, with the exception of Shintoism and the almost extinct religion of the American Indians, no such civilizations seem to survive in our day.

[3] It is well known that great saints, far from disdaining the humblest aspects of daily life, insisted on the contrary that everything be done in the most logical and practical way possible. This means that nothing be done halfway; a thing must either be done perfectly or not at all. If the way of action is the one which, from the exoteric point of view, is of fundamental importance, this is because, on the one hand, it is sufficient for reaching the ends proposed by the common religion, namely the escape from the cosmic periphery and its sufferings, and on the other hand, because action alone is accessible to all men without distinction and is even strictly necessary for them.

This allows us to understand why the great spiritual methods, even those that most expressly insist on the excellence of an eremitical life, have never excluded the possibility of a path that is pursued in the midst of worldly occupations. The question that we now propose to address is how it is possible to reconcile an intense spiritual life with material and social obligations, and even to integrate them to a certain extent into the inward life; for if our daily work, whether professional or domestic, is not an obstacle to the path, this implies that it must play the part of a positive element in it, or more precisely, the part of a secondary support of spiritual realization.

Such an integration of work into spirituality depends on three fundamental conditions, which we shall designate respectively as "necessity", "sanctification", and "perfection". The first of these conditions implies that the activity to be spiritualized correspond to a necessity and not to a whim: one can sanctify, that is offer to God, every normal activity necessitated by the demands of life itself, but not just any occupation lacking in sufficient reason or being even reprehensible in nature; this amounts to saying that every necessary activity possesses a nature that predisposes it to being a support for the spiritual; every necessary activity has indeed a certain universality that makes it eminently symbolic. The second of the three conditions is that the activity thus defined be effectively offered to God, that is to say, accomplished out of love for God and without rebelling against destiny; this is the meaning of the prayers used in most, if not all, religions to consecrate work, which is thereby ritualized, and which in other words becomes a "natural sacrament", a sort of shadow or secondary counterpart of the "supernatural sacrament" that is the rite in the strict sense. The third condition implies the logical perfection of the work, for it is obvious that one cannot offer to God something imperfect, nor consecrate to Him an unworthy object; apart from this, the perfection of the act is self-evident like the perfection of existence itself, in the sense that every act necessarily retraces the divine Act as well as a modality of it. This perfection of the action comprises three aspects, which refer respectively to the activity as such, then to the means, and finally to the end: the activity as such must be objectively and subjectively perfect, which implies that it must be in conformity with or proportionate to the goal to be achieved; the means must also be in conformity with or proportionate to the goal in view, which implies that the instrument of work must be well chosen and then wielded with skill, that is to say, in perfect conformity with the nature of the work; finally, the result of the work must be perfect, in other words, it must respond exactly to the need that gave rise to it.

If these conditions, which constitute what one might call the internal and external logic of the activity, are well fulfilled, the work will not only no longer be an obstacle to the inward path, but will even be a help to it. Conversely, a badly accomplished piece of work will always be an impediment to the path, for it does not correspond to any divine Possibility; God is Perfection, and man, in order to approach God, must be perfect in action as well as in non-acting contemplation.

In the path of love (the Hindu *bhakti-mārga*, the *mahabbah* of Sufism), speculative activity—which by definition is of the intellectual order—does not play a preponderant part, as is the case in the way of knowledge (*jnāna-mārga*, *ma'rifah*); the "lover"—the *bhakta*—must obtain everything by means of love and by divine Grace;[4] doctrinal considerations, paradoxical as it may seem given the initiatic character of *bhakti*, do not have in this way the crucial importance that they have in *jnāna*,[5] and this explains why the *bhakta*s were able to reject with impunity Shankarian advaitism. One might say that bhaktic doctrine, as exemplified by Ramanuja, represents far more a sort of background for the spiritual work than a disinterested and perfectly adequate expression of Truth; in order to love, one must limit, or rather, one must direct one's attention to one sole aspect of Reality, the consideration of integral Truth being more or less incompatible with the subjectivism of an exclusivistic love. The way of love is comparable to a rhythm or a melody, not to an act of reasoning; it is a path of "beauty", not of "wisdom", if one may so express it at the risk of seeming to say

---

[4] For example, in order to understand that gold is but clay, as the Hindu Scriptures teach, Ramakrishna, having difficulty in understanding this satisfactorily, prayed to the Divinity to reveal it to him—until "I heard like the trumpeting of more than ten thousand elephants that clamored in my ears: clay and gold are but one for you!"

[5] According to Ramakrishna, "it is unimportant whether or not we believe that Radha and Krishna are *Avatāras*. . . . But we must all have that intense devotion (*anurāga*) which is the one thing needful."

that beauty is without wisdom and wisdom without beauty; in short, the perspective of the *bhakta* comprises inevitable limitations due to the subjective and emotional character of the "bhaktic" method.

In matters of doctrine, the *bhakta* has nothing to resolve by means of the intelligence alone, it is the entire religion that "thinks" for him, by means of all the symbols, scriptural and others, it possesses. This allows us to understand why the normal unfolding of *bhakti* is conditioned by a homogeneous religious framework that constitutes as it were an external skeleton as well as a protection against foreign and unassimilable influences; the deviations of *bhakti* have in fact often been caused when there has been contact with a foreign civilization.[6]

A comparison of the "bhaktic" doctrine of a Ramanuja with the "jnanic" doctrine of a Shankara shows what the essential limitations of doctrinal *bhakti* consist of; however, to recognize these limitations does not amount to seeking to explain *bhakti* as such as a mere lack in relation to *jñāna*—this would be as absurd as seeking to reduce femininity to a mere lack of virility—for it goes without saying that it is not enough to be lacking in *jñāna* in order to be a *bhakta; bhakti*, while being a less direct mode of knowledge than *jñāna*, nevertheless represents in itself a positive reality. But if it is incontestable that the doctrine of a Ramanuja is providential in the highest sense of the term, that it is thus directly "willed by God", and that in short it represents a fundamental mode of spirituality, it is no less true that its negative attitude towards Shankarian doctrine contains a shortcoming impossible to conceal.

We must not omit to mention here that the Islamic term *mahabbah* is not in every respect synonymous with the term *bhakti*, for it does not, like the latter, signify exclusively a way of love, but has

[6] The case of Vivekananda is particularly eloquent in this connection. To those who would reproach his master Ramakrishna for a lack of "discernment of spirits", we would reply with the Buddhist monk who converted King Menander (Milinda)—the latter having asked him if a perfect man, such as the Buddha, could be mistaken and commit errors—that "the perfect man may be uninformed in secondary things he has no experience of, but he cannot make mistakes regarding things that his perspicacity has already revealed to him. He is perfect here and now. He understands the entire mystery, the Essence of the Universe, but he may not know the simply outward variations by which this Essence is manifested in time and space. He knows clay, but he has not acquired knowledge of all the forms it can be given. The perfect man knows the soul, but he does not know all the forms and all the combinations whereby it can be manifested."

also a significance pertaining to the way of knowledge, and this is why all Muslim initiates use it, whatever be their personal path; it must be added that in Islam "love" and "knowledge" do not appear, as is the case in Hinduism, as two clearly separate paths, but rather, depending on the individuals involved, there is predominance of one over the other, as seems also to have been the case in Christianity. The use, in the different esoterisms, of the term "love" to designate an intellectual reality is moreover explained by the fact that sentiment, while being inferior to reason because of its emotional subjectivity, is nevertheless symbolically comparable to what is superior to reason, namely the Intellect; it is so because sentiment, like the Intellect at the antipodes of which it stands in some way, is not discursive, but direct, simple, spontaneous, unlimited; compared with reason, sentiment appears free from form and fallibility, and this is why the divine Intelligence can be called "Love" and really is so, in a transposed sense, in relation to paltry human intelligence; there is here a simultaneous application of "parallel" and "inverse" analogies that both link and separate the divine and cosmic orders.

One could define *bhakti* as a "path of beauty"; on this subject, it is worth noting that the aspect of beauty, like that of knowledge, is misunderstood and neglected in the perspective of merit, inasmuch as the latter confers on spirituality an essentially moral structure; such a perspective cannot but be ignorant of the fact that beauty is eminently a support for intellection, and with the methodical and blind mistrust that characterizes it, it will regard beauty above all as a temptation and thus a road towards sin, all the more so since the perspective of merit is *a priori* ignorant of the nature, value, and role of pure intelligence. Beauty, when it is associated with a contemplative attitude, is as pleasing to God as a sacrifice. Christ—the Wisdom of God—was borne by Beauty—the Virgin.

The third and last mode of spirituality, in ascending order, is the path of knowledge (the Hindu *jñāna-mārga*, the *ma'rifah* of Sufism); its dependence with regard to doctrine is the closest possible, in the sense that doctrine is an integral part of this path in an immediate manner, whereas in *bhakti* doctrine can be reduced to very simple syntheses and is practically situated as it were outside the path; on the other hand, *jnāna* is completely independent of any doctrinal formulation, and this precisely insofar as it realizes the "spirit" which, while necessarily expressing itself by means of the "letter", always remains transcendent and incommensurable in relation to its symbols. There is a saying from Meister Eckhart that expresses admirably the general attitude of the *jnānin*: "Truth is so noble that, if God wished to turn away from it, I would remain with Truth and leave God; but God Himself is Truth."

The speculative faculty, which constitutes an essential qualification and a *sine qua non* for *jnāna-mārga*, is the "natural" ability to contemplate transcendent Realities; we call this ability "natural" because the one who possesses it makes use of it more or less like any other faculty, that is to say, without the intervention of a "supernatural" state: thus, the *jnānin* has in his state of ordinary consciousness the knowledge that the *bhakta* gains in a "state of grace". It may perhaps be objected that intellectual intuition is no more natural than ecstasy and that the latter is no more supernatural than the former, to which we would reply that we have used these words here in an entirely provisional manner, and moreover in a sense that is easy to understand—unless it is preferred that we speak of the "naturally supernatural" or the "supernaturally natural", which while offering certain advantages, would complicate our terminology. We could also describe the speculative faculty here in question in the following terms: only he who possesses the truth in an active manner is really intellectual, and not he who accepts it passively; the first case is that of a man who, having learned a metaphysical truth, recognizes himself in it in a certain fashion and is capable of formulating it spontaneously, and thus in an original and inspired manner, while projecting the light of his knowledge onto the most diverse contingencies, thanks to a direct vision of the realities concerned and not by means of reasoning; the second case, on the other hand, is that of a man who, having heard the same truth, senses its evidence, but is incapable of expressing it other than by repeating the doctrinal statement that communicated it to him.

That which was intensity in the way of love will be certitude in the way of knowledge. In *bhakti*, the mental process is the ideal projection, in the Platonic sense of the word, of the limited beatitudes of this world—such as beauty or goodness, for example—into the limitless Beatitude of Being; the appearances of this world are on the one hand used as a foretaste of this Beatitude, and on the other hand rejected owing to their limitations, namely of what illusorily separates them from divine Beatitude or Beauty. *Jnāna*, on the contrary, instead of taking its starting point in the experience of earthly things, proceeds so to speak by abstraction, in the sense that its vehicle, knowledge— and the evidence it implies—is by definition "not of this world"; things apparently external, including the soul which, needless to say, is also conceived as outward, appear here as illustrations or traces of intellectual, and thus "paracletic", knowledge.[7] This exteriorization of the microcosm is accompanied by an interiorization of the macrocosm, and this is why, according to Sri Shankaracharya, "the *Yogin*, whose intellect is perfect, contemplates everything as dwelling within himself, and thus, by the eye of knowledge, sees that every thing is *Ātmā*".

Some very profane moralists who prefer man to God, if indeed they do not replace God by man, are surprised or indignant over the indifference that the saints—both western and eastern—have sometimes seemed to show towards the human miseries in the world where they lived. Now, there is a twofold reason for this attitude: firstly, many of the miseries in the body of a traditional world must be regarded as "lesser evils", that is to say, as the necessary channels for calamities in themselves inevitable, but capable of being reduced to a minimum; this is a point of view that moderns have never understood, for they do not even know that there are in the cosmos things that cannot be avoided at any price, and of which the apparent and artificial suppression only causes even more "massive" cosmic reactions;[8] secondly, the indifference of spiritual people with regard to these contingencies is explained by their desire to deal with evil at its root, and to help the

---

[7] It is thus false to maintain that *nihil est in intellectu quod non prius fuerit in sensu*. From the point of view of *jnāna*, which is that of the total Truth, it is the exact opposite that must be said.

[8] Nothing has meaning outside of truth; there is an idealism that is stupid and criminal. As for "altruism", we may recall that Christ said: "Love thy neighbor as thyself"; he did not say: more than thyself, nor: do not love thyself; yet his words are interpreted thus by a certain hypocritical and impotent morality.

world, not by dissipating energies in fragmentary and finally illusory efforts, but by returning directly to the very source of Good. The abuses one finds in all traditional civilizations are often more or less unavoidable, because evil, being implied in Existence itself, is inherent in everything and cannot but manifest itself in one way or another; these abuses, those for example that have become encrusted in the Hindu caste system, might well be capable of being eliminated—and action to this end has already been taken—but on condition that one takes as one's starting point the inward or the spiritual content of the civilization in question. This would presuppose, however, in the majority of cases, a return of the collectivity itself to this living spring; in the present cyclical circumstances this would mean purely and simply returning to the golden age, which unfortunately is an impossibility.

Another point that we still wish to mention is the following: in metaphysical knowledge, reasoning can play no other role than that of occasional cause of intellection; the latter intervenes in a sudden—not continuous or progressive—way as soon as the mental operation, conditioned in turn by an intellectual intuition, possesses the quality or perfection that makes of it an effective symbol. When the heat produced by rubbing together two pieces of wood—or by a lens capturing a ray of sunshine—reaches the precise degree that is its culminating point, a flame suddenly bursts forth; likewise intellection, as soon as the mental operation is capable of supplying an adequate support, will instantly graft itself onto this support. It is thus that human intelligence assimilates its own universal Essence thanks to a sort of reciprocity between thought and Reality. As for rationalism, on the contrary, it seeks on its own plane the culminating point of the cognitive process; it looks for Truth in the realm of mental formulations and rejects *a priori* the possibility of a knowledge accessible beyond these formulations and consequently eluding—at least to a certain extent—the resources of human language; one might as well look for a word that is entirely what it designates! It is from this fundamental contradiction that derives the incapacity, firstly to produce mental forms that can properly serve as vehicles for intellectual intuition and hence for Truth—for badly posed questions are not conducive to light any more than they derive from it—and then to perceive the intellectual dimensions virtually attained by this or that formulation, even if defective. Rationalism proceeds like the man who would seek to draw the geometric point by striving to make it as small as possible, or who would try to reach, on some plane or other within relativity, an absolute perfection, by denying the necessary imperfection of this plane on the one hand and the transcendence of pure Perfection on the other. One cannot state too clearly that a doctrinal formulation is perfect, not because it exhausts the infinite Truth on the plane of logic, which is impossible, but because it realizes a mental form capable of communicating, to whoever is intellectually apt to receive it, a ray of that Truth, and thereby a virtuality of the total Truth. This explains why the traditional doctrines are always apparently naive, at least from the point of view of philosophers—that is to say, of men who do not understand that the goal and sufficient reason of wisdom do not lie on the plane of its formal affirmation; and that, by definition, there is no common measure and no continuity between thought—whose operations have no more than a symbolic value—and pure Truth, which is identical with That which "is" and thereby includes him who thinks.

In conclusion, a few succinct remarks on the qualities indispensable for spirituality in general: firstly, a mental attitude that for want of a better term could be designated by the word "objectivity": this is a perfectly disinterested attitude of the intelligence, and hence one that is free from ambition and bias and thereby accompanied by serenity. Secondly, we would mention a quality concerning the psychic life of the individual: this is nobility, or the capacity of the soul to rise above all things that are petty and mean; basically this is a discernment, in psychic mode, between the essential and the accidental, or between the real and the unreal. Finally, there is the virtue of simplicity: man is freed from all unconscious tenseness stemming from self-love; towards creatures and things he has a perfectly original and spontaneous attitude, in other words, he is without artifice; he is free from all pretension, ostentation, or dissimulation; in a word, he is without pride. This simplicity, however, is never an affected humility, but an absence of innate prejudices, and hence a natural effacement of self—of the "hardened heart" of the Scriptures—a naive effacement whereby man is symbolically linked with childhood. Every spiritual method demands above all an attitude of poverty, humility, and simplicity or effacement, an attitude that is like an anticipation of Extinction in God.

Microcosm and Symbol

Every truth can have incalculable consequences, and on the spiritual plane no truth can be inopportune in an absolute fashion. Spiritual truths are interdependent, and there are circumstances in which he who would tell the truth must either say nothing or tell the whole truth; now these circumstances are precisely those of the world today: the affirmation of the grossest errors calls for the affirmation of the subtlest truths, for cosmic reasons, moreover, and independently of the practical aspect of things.

In order to state our thought clearly while being as brief as possible, we might also express ourselves in the following way: as it is our intention to affirm traditional wisdom as such, we are compelled to speak of things that, for the immense majority of men today, are not an effective possibility, but which nonetheless should be known theoretically, at least to some extent, if only for a fuller comprehension of traditional ideas and facts in general.

To define the difference between the metaphysical and initiatic or mystical perspectives, it could be said that the first distinguishes between Principle and Manifestation, whereas the second considers these two terms in "subjective" mode and hence distinguishes either *a priori* between the human "I" and the divine "He", or *a posteriori* between the human "he" and the divine "I", the " reality experienced" having been displaced as it were from the human to the Divine; the human ego having then become just another ordinary "him", and the divine "He" henceforth being known as unique, absolute, and infinite.[1] In cosmology, there is an analogous—not identical—relationship between the Macrocosm, which serves as divine Model, and the

---

[1] The use of personal pronouns is entirely provisional here, at any rate as regards the divine Reality, which is obviously beyond "objective" and "subjective" points of view; in Sufi language this transcendence is expressed by the word *Huwa*, "He", while the said points of view are respectively designated by the words *anta*, "Thou", and *anā*, "I".

microcosm: however, it is the latter that is active and the former that is passive, in the sense that the microcosm,[2] being so to speak the inner limit of the cosmos—the outer limit being the manifested divine Spirit—also constitutes the way of exit from the cosmic illusion; and this exit is brought about through the Spirit which, for its part, is the direct manifestation of the Word.

The divine Spirit identifies itself thus with the transcendent, universal, cosmic "I" that the relative being bears virtually within himself, so that the inner limit of the cosmos—the microcosm—must identify itself, in its process of deification, with the outer limit—the Empyrean—of this very cosmos. If we say that the microcosm is active and the Macrocosm passive, this is true in only one respect, namely insofar as the relative being determines the flux of forms intellectually, but not insofar as, being a form himself, he is in turn determined by the cosmic Intelligence, in which respect it is clearly the Macrocosm that is active and the microcosm that is passive.[3]

Every schema of spiritual realization starts in principle from the distinction between the body and the soul, then distinguishes in the latter between the sensorial soul (psychic and mental) and the immortal soul (the true ego), and finally, in the latter, between the individual soul and the Spirit (the Intellect), or in other words, between the "brain" and the "heart". Strictly speaking, the heart does not come within the limits of the ego, but constitutes its transcendent center, vehicle of the uncreated Intellect. All these distinctions also pertain to the realm of cosmology, a science that is to metaphysics what psychology—in the spiritual and "alchemical" sense that this word can bear—is to Realization; but while cosmology considers the soul only *ad extra* and in principle goes no further than its threshold, Realization considers it *ad intra*, all the way to the shores of the Ineffable.

---

[2] It is always the human microcosm that we have in view here; but what we say about it applies in the same way to any other total microcosm, that is, any microcosm constituted by the central state of a world. Now it is man who is this central state in relation to the terrestrial world; animals, plants, and minerals mark states that are more and more peripheral, and are consequently partial, not total, microcosms.

[3] Let us recall in this respect that the cosmic Mind or the divine Spirit is an aspect of the Word, of which it is said: "No man cometh unto the Father but by me", or in other words, an aspect of the Prophet, of whom it is said: "No man shall meet *Allāh* who hath not met the Prophet"; but in their highest meaning, these formulas mean that no one may reach the "Essence" who has not realized the "Attributes".

In order to make this sequence of ideas more easily accessible, we will set out the following table:

Principle

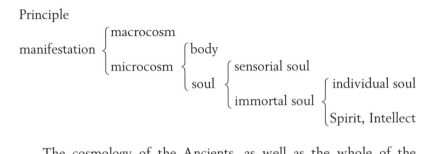

The cosmology of the Ancients, as well as the whole of the Middle Ages of the West and the Near East, conceived of the earthly state as the center from which the planetary spheres rose to the Empyrean, the symbolic seat of the Divinity, who was thus conceived as the Infinite "enveloping" or "containing" the finite. Analogously, Hindu doctrine takes the bodily or gross state (*sthūla-sharīra*) as the starting point of a series of increasingly universal degrees of existence ending up in the metacosmic, absolutely transcendent, infinite Reality that "envelops" not only the world but Being itself.

In the initiatic perspective, the point of departure is also the body—at least in a certain sense—since the body forms part of the microcosm and is as it were its "shell"; but the "direction" of the degrees of universality will be apparently the reverse, at least in the beginning, where the supreme Reality, rather than being conceived of as the most outward, farthest, or most incommensurable Void, appears on the contrary as the most inward, nearest Center, in short, as the unique, indivisible, absolute Subject. In the last analysis, beyond the individuality there is neither subject nor object, neither inward nor outward; the Intellect, which realization conceives of *a priori* as inward, is none other, as we have said, than the universal Spirit that envelops the worlds.

All that we have just said will enable one to understand that, from the initiatic point of view, there is strictly speaking no other field of action than the soul, the microcosm; as for the external world, it will not be taken into consideration except insofar as it influences the internal world, or again, insofar as it is viewed in its turn as being consubstantial with this internal world, hence as the cosmic aspect of the ego. According to this perspective, it will no longer be a question of simply passing from "evil" to "good", on the basis of an individuality that is still maintained, but on the contrary of transcending the individuality itself, so that what was a passage from "evil" to "good" will be replaced by a passage from the I to the Self.[4] It is precisely the analogy between these two passages that allows esoterism to make use of the symbols of exoterism as supports, aside from the fact that the former necessarily and *a fortiori* implies the realizations of the latter. The microcosm, having thus become the whole world, will serve as the ground for the transmutation brought about thanks to the Symbol; in other words, the soul is the fabric that will freely fashion itself in the image of the Symbol and that will be determined, transmuted, regenerated, and absorbed by it.

We must now reply to the question as to what exactly the Symbol is, or more precisely, what the initiatic symbol is; we shall define it as a double manifestation of God, firstly with regard to "form" and then with regard to "Presence". The form, in order to act as a vehicle of the Presence, must, in its own order, directly reflect a divine Reality; now since the Presence is the cause and sufficient reason of the form, and not the other way round, the form can only derive from a revelation sent by That which wills to be "present"; neither the form nor *a fortiori* the Presence can depend on a human willing. This Presence will manifest itself in the immediate materiality of the sacred Symbol, and thereby in the individual who is qualified, that is, in conformity—by nature as well as through initiation and the disciplines it demands—with the nature of the Symbol. This implies three conditions, two of which concern the Symbol and one the individual, namely: firstly the exactness of the Symbol, secondly its consecration, and thirdly the consecration of the individual—of the microcosm—who is to assimilate the Symbol: thus, the host must be made of a special

---

[4] According to a *hadīth*, "thine existence is a sin (*dhanb*) with which no other sin can be compared". This is the most peremptory affirmation possible of an esoteric and supra-moral perspective. We would hasten to add that what we schematically call a "passage from the I to the Self" does not imply the destruction pure and simple of the first of the two terms, for the phenomenon of the "I" is in no way opposed to the realization of the Self, as is proven by the case of the *jīvan-mukta* and of the *Avatāra*.

bread—azyme in the Latin Church—and not of ordinary bread; next, it must be consecrated, which presupposes precisely that it be made in such a way as to fulfill the conditions required for consecration; and finally, whoever desires to take communion must be in a state of sanctifying grace,[5] which implies the complementary rites of baptism and confirmation. Or again, to cite an example of a very different but nonetheless analogous order: the sacred image—such as an icon of the Virgin or a representation of the Buddha—must be made according to the strict rules of the corresponding sacred art; next, it must be blessed or consecrated; finally, whoever contemplates it ritually must have the "right" to do so, that is, he must have received the image from the very hands of the tradition, or in other words, he must be a Christian in the first case and a Buddhist in the second. Or let us take the example of a symbol that is not fixed or static, but "acted" or "actualized", such as an incantatory rite: the divine Name to be invoked must be correctly pronounced, otherwise the condition of formal exactness is not fulfilled; then it must be consecrated by the adequate intention of the individual, an intention that is expressed by concentration, fervor, and perseverance; the consecration here, since it is a question of a dynamic symbol, is necessarily subjective; finally, he who invokes must have a right to this method, that is, he must have received it from a master who likewise received it, which presupposes an initiation regularly transmitted throughout the centuries since the origin of the corresponding Revelation.

Before going further, we must forestall the following objection: is symbolism not inherent in the natural form of the symbolic thing, so that it cannot depend on a superadded value? Now what is in question here is spiritual symbolism and not symbolism pure and simple; every initiatic symbol, by its mere form, is necessarily a "natural" or "existential" symbol, but not every natural symbol is necessarily an initiatic symbol, otherwise, in the final analysis, every appearance would be such a symbol.[6]

---

[5] There are ritual symbols that can be both esoteric and exoteric in application, in accordance with certain modes of spiritual radiation.

[6] "If it be true that it (the Trinity) is present in all things, all things are not present in it" (Saint Dionysius the Areopagite, *Concerning the Divine Names*). Several categories of initiatic symbols may be distinguished: visual, auditory, enacted, and combinations thereof; the invocation of a divine Name, for instance, brings into play a faculty of sensation as well as a faculty of action, namely the primordial faculties of hearing and

The Symbol "is" God and thereby is identified with the "Son" without whom no one may come to the "Father"; and this is so owing to the "vertical identity" in which only the essential nature counts, and not the existential plane on which that nature is manifested. It is not as man that Christ is God; and, on the other hand, the fact that he is man does not prevent his being really God; the levels of existence are therefore comparable to so many horizontal planes of divine reverberation: but the Light, which is vertical in relation to them, is everywhere identical by nature. The fact that this essential or vertical identity can be either indirect or natural as is the case of every thing insofar as it is necessarily—by its mere existence as well as by its positive qualities—a manifestation of "That which is", or either directly and supernaturally as is the case of divine manifestations such as the God-Men and the saving Symbols they have bequeathed to their posterity—this fact, we repeat, does not enter into the essential definition of "vertical identity" and merely indicates its fundamental modes or degrees.

The relationship between the Symbol and the microcosm corresponds analogically to the relationship between the male and female principles; this makes it easier to understand the meaning, in every spiritual path, of the activity and transcendence of the Symbol on the

---

speech; as for the visual symbol (the Hindu and Buddhist *yantra*), it may be either a sculpted or painted image, or a geometric form, or yet again an inscription, depending upon the different schools, and above all too, depending upon the religions, which do not all make the same use of all the modes of symbolism. As regards enacted symbols, we may mention the Hindu and Buddhist *mudrās* and, in a very general way, sacred dances such as those of the dervishes. Apart from this, it is necessary to distinguish between fundamental or central symbols and complementary and secondary ones, not forgetting the different applications, either sensible or purely mental. We may add to what we said above on the invocation of a divine Name, that the ritual chanting of sacred texts also constitutes an incantatory mode: for instance, the long Buddhist *sūtras* with their ceaseless repetitions interlacing in a series of monotonous and varied arabesques, allow of an imperceptible and all the more profound infiltration of the Spirit into the finer modalities of the contemplative, and thus contribute to the liberating transmutation of the ignorant ego; the wisdom that should be transmitted imperceptibly, emerges not only from the meaning of the formulas, but also and perhaps even primarily from their transcendent quality—"magic", one might say in a transposed sense—a quality that is revealed in parallel fashion in the teachings of the literal meaning. These remarks apply *mutatis mutandis* to all symbols; and let us add, "bodily beauty"—hence outward beauty—is one of the ways whereby the Buddhas save souls, which is true of every sacred form.

one hand, and the passivity, virginity, and fecundity of the microcosm on the other, and also to grasp in an altogether general manner, the universal scope of the symbolism of Love.

We said above that for the contemplative the world is reduced to his microcosm, ground of the "theogenesis", and that the external world is either regarded in practice as non-existent, in a certain manner at least, or else considered as internal, according to case and circumstance; on the other hand, the microcosm, since it is practically "the world", is conceived of as external, and only the Symbol is considered as the real ego. This does not in the least contradict the fact that the world, from this point of view, is reduced to the microcosm, for the external world, to the extent that it has to be taken into consideration and hence is spiritually likened to the individual "I", is no more than a secondary and passive aspect of the interior and transcendent "I" represented by the Symbol. It follows that, for the spiritual man, the ego consists on the one hand of the Symbol with which he must identify himself, and on the other, of the Macrocosm that he must not regard as external, and therefore as "other than myself"; the world, whose existence no one can humanly deny, is thus neutralized as to its illusorily external character, and at the same time becomes an expression of the doctrine, since it is the differentiated projection of the Intellect which, for its part, is synthetically actualized by the Symbol.[7]

If the world is become "I" for the contemplative, he will regard its imperfections as "his own" in a certain sense, the cosmic possibilities being the same everywhere; he is thus led to expect everything of himself and nothing of others, which is not unrelated to the symbolism of the "Lamb of God which taketh away the sin of the world". This inversion is but one expression among others of the fundamental inversion brought about by the initiatic process, in accordance with

---

[7] From this it follows that spiritual liberation cannot be an act of "selfishness"; every spiritual path by definition is undertaken "for others", and is incomparably more profitable to them than those apparently most useful activities in which men engage at the price of the "one thing needful". Upon contact with the Symbol, the individual himself becomes symbolic, in the sense that he represents God in the world and the world before God.

the inverse analogy that exists between the Principle and Manifestation and by virtue of which that which seems great in manifestation is small in the Principle, and conversely; this inverse analogy must not be confused with direct analogy, which concerns positive qualities or contents, not limiting containers or modes, and according to which every positive quality is the reflection of a divine Aspect or Attribute.

Analogously, the active becomes passive and the passive active, always insofar as they are limiting modes and not insofar as they reflect the respective principial aspects: the activity reflecting a divine Act cannot legitimately be transmuted into passivity; but specifically human activity necessarily becomes passivity before the divine Will, which thenceforth determines it by giving it meaning and content. Or again: whatever affirms itself *a priori* as positive—namely the apparent reality of the objects of sense and the passions attached thereto— becomes negative in the Truth, and whatever appears as negative from the point of view of sensible experience—namely transcendent, and consequently invisible,[8] Reality, and all the consequences it entails for man—becomes positive to the degree that Knowledge transforms the mental and abstract concept into spiritual and concrete Life. Or again: whatever is dynamic in the ordinary man becomes static in the contemplative and vice versa, in the sense that desires are absorbed into the immutable Beatitude, and doctrinal concepts blossom forth within the Knowledge that transforms them so to speak into tangible, lived realities overflowing with inspiration. Or again, to give another example: what is subjective in the ordinary man—a feeling or an emotion—becomes objective, that is, alien for the sage,[9] and what appears to the ordinary man as objective—some object or other, a natural law, a truth—enters intimately into the life or will of the sage and as a result becomes similar to what was a psychic and therefore subjective disposition for the ordinary mortal; the profane man *a priori* places his love in facts, whereas the spiritual man places his in principles; which leads us to point out that a fact has a deep meaning only insofar as

---

[8] This invisibility does not apply to the "Eye of the Heart", which perceives the Principle in the manifestation, the Cause in the effect, the Absolute in the relative, the Infinite in the finite.

[9] In another respect, this does not prevent an emotional element from being, on the contrary, "universalized" by serving as a support for a participation in the divine Prototype to which it is related.

it manifests a universal law, whereas from the profane point of view principles seem to be just some facts among others.[10]

We said above that whatever appears as small shall become great, and inversely: thus it is that the Symbol, at first little—since *a priori* it appears as a simple fact, a content of the human soul or of human activity—becomes great in the sense that it reveals itself as Principle, as Reality that will envelop and absorb the individual, who in turn becomes little, a mere fact and content. In other words, the microcosm *a priori* is a sphere the Symbol of which will then be like the center or heart; but for the being who has realized the Self, it is the Symbol—or rather its "realized Reality"—that will be comparable to a sphere, limitless in this case, while the microcosm will be reduced to a purely symbolical content, while henceforth possessing, by virtue of this very transmutation, a maximum of quality, an extrinsic attribute of the theogenesis.[11] The entire initiatic process can therefore be defined as a reversal of the poles of attraction: the first pole of attraction, which is external and multiple, but finite, is neutralized by the action of the second pole, which is internal, unique, and infinite.

One question that should not be passed over is the following: what is it in the macrocosmic order that corresponds to the Symbol, in other words, to the means of grace by which and through which a being comes to God? Let us first recall the definition itself of the Symbol: it is the sufficient—and consecrated—vehicle of the real Presence; thus it represents an actualization of the Intellect and, in another aspect, a virtuality of the "divine State". Hence what corresponds to the Symbol in the macrocosmic order is man "made in the image of God"—not exclusively earthly man, of course, but that state of existence which constitutes the center in every integral world, as is

---

[10] This doctrine may be seen admirably formulated in the words of Saint Remy to Clovis: "Bow thy head, proud Sicamber, burn what thou hast worshipped and worship what thou hast burnt"—an inspired formula that sums up in a masterly way the whole spiritual life: firstly, the "abasement" indispensable for the "exit" from the world, and then, the inversion of values which in a certain manner describes all that is essential in the initiatic process.

[11] All the relationships contained in the inversion brought about by the process of spiritual development appear in a very clear manner in the Far-Eastern symbol of the *Yin-Yang*: the white dot is the "real Presence" in the night of ignorance, and the black dot the individual mode as seen in the clear light of Knowledge; for ignorance, the Symbol is contained, whereas in reality, it is container.

precisely the case of the human state in relation to our world; indeed, man manifests, in this world of ours, the universal Intellect, namely the Holy Spirit inasmuch as it manifests itself. It is only through the human state—or through any other central state—that beings in "transmigration" can make their way out of the cosmos, just as in the human state itself, it is only through the Symbol that the soul can leave its state of indefinite tribulation to reintegrate into its immutable and blissful Essence.

Prayer and the Integration of the Psychic Elements

Prayer, in the most usual meaning of the term, appears as a practice that seemingly implies an anthropomorphic and sentimental point of view: anthropomorphic because it seems to attribute to God a temporal nature and human understanding; and sentimental because it readily takes on expressions pertaining to sentiment. Now, it is legitimate and even necessary to conceive Divinity in a more or less personified aspect, since it really comprises such an aspect in relation to ourselves; and in addition, and by virtue of this very point of view, man's attitude can without difficulty be affirmed in ways that are strictly human. Thus conceived, prayer in nowise implies by definition the conception of a God arbitrarily humanized and divested of His infinite transcendence, any more than it implies the presence in man of a specifically emotional disposition. In a general way, it is too often forgotten that sentiment as such is not to be identified with its deviations, and that on the contrary it is a normal psychic fact, hence capable of playing a positive role in spirituality; the mere fact that in praying man makes use of all his inward faculties in his striving towards God, and consequently also of his natural sentimentality, which he cannot abolish or treat as nonexistent, in no way means that sentiment should be taken as an end in itself and thus entail a more or less individualistic alteration of doctrinal truths.[1] Prayer could never be contrary to the purest intellectuality; without contradicting any transcendent truth, prayer has its reason for being in the existence of the human "I" which, since it exists, must be channeled towards its ultimate sufficient reason; in other words, the individual as such never ceases to be "I", and as prayer is the spiritual act of the "I", it must be practiced as long as the individual exists, that is, to the extent that he maintains the idea of the ego.[2] Man's attitude in prayer must in some sense remain egocentric by definition; in metaphysical meditation, on

---

[1] For example, Sri Shankaracharya who implores the mercy of Shiva or who beseeches the divine Mother. We are far from the naive error according to which prayer is incompatible with "pure" *jnāna*; as for Shankara, either he was a *jnānin* or there never has been one. When the God-Man prays, his prayer is cosmic; whence the use in revealed prayers, such as the *Pater* or the *Fātihah*, of the first person plural.

[2] This is closely related to the theory of the two natures of Christ.

the contrary, man places himself symbolically at the "standpoint" of the nature of things.

On the other hand, when it is said that forms are supports, it must never be forgotten that a support, to be such, must be entirely what it is in itself, and that it must not and cannot be a "part" of that which it must transmit, just as a light cannot be the means for reflecting another light; thus prayer must always remain a conversation with God, or an appeal addressed to Him, and it is only on condition that prayer be first entirely what its most immediate possibility makes it— namely the translation and expression of an individual intention—that it can serve as support for intellections transcending the individual plane. By this we mean that prayer cannot be replaced by impersonal and abstract meditation, for the immediate objectives of the two differ; but this does not exclude that meditation can be integrated, in suitable ways, into prayer, or that the formulas of revealed prayers do not contain a universal meaning.

All we have just said makes it easier to understand that there is no need to continuously invoke the opposition between reason and sentiment; if the relatively lower psychic faculties can constitute an obstacle to the activity of reason, seat of theoretical knowledge, reason itself constitutes no less an obstacle once effective knowledge is at issue; for it is then the whole mental faculty as such that can become an obstacle, reason being but the most direct reflection of the Intellect which, itself, is beyond all cerebral contingencies.

The Intellect, being universal in its essence, necessarily penetrates the entire being and embraces all its constituent elements; for to exist is to know, and every aspect of our existence is a state of knowing or, in relation to absolute Knowledge, a state of ignorance. If it is true that reason is the central mirror of the Intellect, whose organ is the subtle heart, the other faculties are nonetheless also planes of manifestation for the Intellect; the individual being cannot be reintegrated into the Absolute without all his faculties participating in due measure in this process. Spiritual knowledge, far from opposing any particular mode of conformity—or participation—on the contrary brings into play all that we are, hence all the constituent elements, psychic, and even physical, of our being, for nothing positive can be excluded from the process of transmutation; nothing can be destroyed, and therefore the psychic faculties or energies that form part of our reality and whose existence must have a meaning for us, have to be determined and channeled by the same governing Idea that determines and transforms thought. Man must transpose onto a higher plane all the positive reactions that the surrounding reality elicit in him, by remembering divine Realities through sensible things;[3] it could also be said that if spiritual things have to be humanized in some way, then conversely human things have to be spiritualized; the first symbolic mode envelops Truth and the second reveals it.

We have seen that the very existence of individual or psychic elements is a sufficient reason for taking them into consideration and that we must necessarily do so in a way that is not purely negative, since these elements are none other than ourselves insofar as we are individuals; if we were able, such as we are, to be absolutely spiritual—an obviously contradictory supposition—we would be identical with the divine Principle, and we would not have to be delivered from anything whatsoever. To be more precise, we may add: the man who, through ignorance or theoretical preconceptions, neglects to integrate the psychic elements of his personality into his spiritual attitude, possesses them nonetheless within himself, whether he allows them to wander about as they please alongside theoretical conceptions and in contradiction to them, or whether he represses them so that they slumber in his subconscious as more or less latent obstacles. In any spiritual realization it is important that man not be fixed, so to speak, within one restricted area of his self; on the contrary, all his possibilities must be awakened, recapitulated, and channeled in accordance with their respective natures, for man is all that constitutes him; his faculties are interrelated. It is not possible to open the intelligence to the Divine without ennobling the psychic and even physical being; there is no spirituality without greatness and without beauty.

We will illustrate the foregoing considerations by the following example: in too many cases the psychological potentiality of childhood never achieves its normal flowering; the necessary manifestation

---

[3] For instance, the passion of love becomes the love of God, anger becomes "holy wrath", or again, warlike passion finds its meaning and sufficient reason in "holy War".

of this possibility is checked—most often by the damaging effects of school education—and subsists as though stifled or crushed, or like a shrunken and hardened kernel, throughout the further development of the individual; whence a psychic imbalance that will show itself on the one hand by the apparent absence of the childlike element, and on the other by childish reactions, such as are not undergone by the balanced man since his virile possibility will have integrated his childlike possibility, the latter being as it were the background of his virility. Virility—*virtus*—is always an aspect and the fact of an equilibrium; the person who is adult only, that is to say adult to the exclusion of any childlike element, is so only imperfectly and as it were through an inability to remain a child; now an incapacity is never a superiority. The state of childhood must be transcended by integration, by "digestion" if one may say so, and this necessity is already indicated by the fact that there is a perfect continuity between the different ages; this means that the individual must at every age benefit from all the positive contents of the preceding ages,[4] and that he will then react to events not in a way strictly dependent on his age, but with complete balance, uniting for example the spontaneity of youth with the reflectiveness of maturity; in other words, he will possess his temporal "self" in its integral state; every positive attitude, be it childlike or other, is necessary and precious.[5]

Reason, the seat of theoretical knowledge, is too abstract a substance to represent, by itself alone, the "I"; therefore feeling and desire, namely that which is most strictly "I", must be transmuted by the Idea. But this transmutation introduces a most important principle that must never be lost sight of: the psychic faculty as such—which is a limitation—must be distinguished from its possible contents; these contents translate the Idea in their own way and are necessary to a man's psychic and physical equilibrium. Sentiment is more remote from pure knowledge than reason; yet the natural impulses of feeling are less harmful—supposing they are such in themselves—to intellectuality than are rational conceptions; these, when taken too literally in

[4] If childhood did not have a positive aspect peculiar to itself, what meaning could there be in the symbolism of the Child Jesus and in the words of Christ regarding holy childlikeness?

[5] These considerations tend to show that the childlike element is not a residue but a necessary and therefore legitimate element in the adult, who never wholly ceases being a child.

the absence of intellectual intuition, can paralyze the possibilities of understanding, whereas feeling is neutral in this respect.

Psychic conformity that is based on the symbolism of feeling or desire is, however, only possible on condition of a rational conformity, namely a sufficient theoretical knowledge on the one hand, and a conformity of action on the other; and this must be so, because the most clearly individual elements can have their sufficient reason and consequently their ideal determination only through the Intellect, and also because these elements are substantially dependent on the physical world where action takes place. Through the Idea the natural emotions are, on the one hand, reduced to proportions that correspond to the individual's psychic equilibrium and, on the other, endowed with a spiritual essence, if one may say; through action—or by the participation of action in the Idea—hence through action that is symbolic and has become so to speak ritual, the emotions receive as it were a new substance.

For man as such, the question of divine Reality can be stated thus: if other individuals—or objects such as food, for example—possess an immediately tangible and empirically incontestable reality, so that it is perfectly natural to speak to somebody else or to partake of food, God—who is the ultimate Prototype of all things—possesses a reality that is incommensurable in relation to the reality that surrounds us and on which we live. Now, if it is logical to talk to people, or to eat food, because both of these are real, it will be even more logical—or less illusory—to speak to God, who is the infinite Cause of all good, and to live on His Word, which is the infinite Essence of all nourishment.

We said earlier that in prayer, God is conceived, as it were automatically, as personal: indeed, it is in the nature of things for God to reveal Himself in a more or less human aspect once He enters into contact with man, for otherwise there would be no possible meeting point between God and the individual; but this human aspect does not pertain to Divinity any more than a color pertains to light. God hears our prayers and replies to them, while He Himself, needless to say, undergoes no change at all. Our prayers cannot penetrate God, since they are nothing before Him. The divine responses are so many effects of absolute Plenitude; it is we, the reflections, who are affected by the universal Cause, and not inversely. "Before" we even formulated our prayers, the divine responses "were" in eternity; God is for us the eternal, omnipresent Response, and prayer can have no other function than to eliminate all that separates us from this inexhaustible Response.

Transgression and Purification

Depending on the traditional doctrine concerned, the idea of transgression or sin appears in different ways—at least as regards its human aspect, but not as to its essential content—and it even differs somewhat in the various Semitic theologies, despite their closeness to one another. In Christianity, the conception of sin is closely bound to the theory of the fall of Adam and the messianic redemption: sin is envisaged primarily under the aspects of seduction and fall, in other words, under the luciferian and satanic aspects of the symbolism of woman—in this case a malefic symbolism[1]—and this explains the prohibitions and restrictions imposed on woman inasmuch as she is the instrument of voluptuousness; woman, or more precisely, the female body viewed in this way, has almost become the very symbol of transgression or evil. The Islamic point of view is different; here sin appears under the aspect of rebellion or negation:[2] rebellion in the sense that infraction destroys the equilibrium of the attitude of abandonment or submission, *al-islām*, and negation insofar as infraction implies a

[1] It is nevertheless important to note that woman, regarded by Christianity as the pre-eminent vehicle of temptation and sin, is nevertheless spiritualized in the person of the Blessed Virgin, mother of the Life-dispensing Word; if Eve, issued from Adam, symbolizes the Fall, the Blessed Virgin, from whom Christ issued, symbolizes victory over the serpent. In Islam, woman is not regarded under her malefic aspect, since she is not involved in the fall of Adam; it is Iblis alone who causes the fall of the first couple and their exile from the earthly Paradise. In the conception of *Jannah*, the "Garden" or Paradise, woman is spiritualized, not by virtue of an exceptional function analogous to that of "Co-Redemptress", but simply as the instrument of love, in the form of the *Hūris*, "the gazelle-eyed"; moreover, traditional Christian iconography nearly always represents angels with feminine features. It would be easy to give other and quite varied examples of the beatific symbolism of woman, for instance: Sita and Radha; the goddess Kali in the *bhakti* of Sri Ramakrishna; the wives of David, Solomon, Muhammad; the knights' ladies, such as Beatrice in the life and work of Dante.

[2] "And they all bowed down except Iblis who refused and was puffed up with pride and was one of the infidels" (Koran, *Sūrah* "The Cow" [2]:34). The refusal is negation, pride, rebellion. The words *khaṭī'ah*, "lack", and *ithm*, "transgression", respectively concern these two attitudes. One may be surprised that Iblis is called "one of the infidels"; this is because he cannot be opposed in a quasi-symmetrical manner to God, who alone is One; he therefore has to be drowned in a multiplicity of analogous manifestations, each universal cycle (or "Life of Brahmā") implying the manifestation of a subversive tendency.

rejection of That to which this attitude relates—in other words, the divine Norm, Cause of every good. The Islamic conception of sin is moreover made concrete in the two alimentary prohibitions, that of intoxicating beverages and that of pork: intoxicating beverages can be taken to mean seduction or passion, and pork impurity or ignorance, in other words, the chief causes of the violation of the Law; moreover pork, insofar as it incarnates the quality or darkness or the downward tendency implicit in cosmic substance, does not lend itself to any ana-logical transposition onto the spiritual plane; but such is not the case of wine which, representing the quality of passion or the expansive tendency, has even pre-eminently a positive meaning, and frequently symbolizes, in Sufi writings, contemplative drunkenness.[3] We may add that the love resulting from the quality of passion, and not from the quality of darkness, is also transposable onto the spiritual plane, which explains why many Sufi writings—and other esoteric texts—take the form of love poems;[4] be that as it may, love as such is not associated, in the Islamic perspective, with the idea of sin, since it is regarded far more in terms of its cosmic function than in terms of its carnal contingency.

In Hindu thought, infraction is regarded as a rupture of equi-librium due to an individual—or rather individualistic—affirmation contrary to *dharma*, the law inherent in the nature of each being and each category of beings; here "sin" is *adharma*, "non-conformity to a necessary law"; the idea of *dharma*, moreover, is closely akin to that of *islām*. As for Chinese thought, the idea of infraction of the cosmic Law is linked with the conception of "nature" (*sing*), which is the "Law of

---

[3] In this connection, see *In Praise of Wine* (*Al-Khamriyyah*) by Omar ibn al-Farid. The wild boar is so totally different from the domestic pig that it lends itself to a positive symbolism. Generally speaking, symbolism is often based on a single aspect of things: for example, one might be surprised that Saint Dominic—the great defender of Chris-tian orthodoxy against heresy—is represented by a hound spitting fire, in accordance with a vision seen by the saint's mother; but it is patently obvious that the hound here represents the vigilant guardian whose voice protects his master's house; it is therefore an eminent virtue that is here symbolized by this animal, which presupposes that the animal possesses this virtue in a natural manner. In this connection, it may be recalled that in the Middle Ages the Friars Preachers were called the "Hounds of the Lord", *Domini canes*.

[4] This fact is far from being peculiar to Sufism; the most famous examples of this type of poem are perhaps the *Song of Solomon* and the *Gītā Govinda*, without forgetting the poems of the troubadours and the *Fedeli d'Amore*.

Heaven"; infraction is regarded as an act that is contrary to "nature" and that shortens life, or as a forgetting of the *Tao*, which is the divine Root and therefore the inner Law and measure of all things.

One often hears it said that the idea of transgression or sin is mere illusion and sentimentality, morality varying according to race or epoch, and its laws differing to the point of mutual contradiction; this error derives, indirectly and contrarily, from the limitations inherent in the moral point of view itself, in the sense that it reacts improperly against the absolute character that this point of view lends to facts. Without first insisting on the profound necessity for moral divergences, we shall say the following: as soon as transgression is considered in itself, in its cosmic nature and with regard to its general conditions—that is to say, in its subjective reality, which defines it essentially, sin having its root in the intention—social factors no longer enter into its definition; for a legislation constitutes no more than one particular support—obviously symbolic and variable according to the "climate"—of the social or individual equilibrium. While the outward law cannot be identified with the norm itself of human behavior, it nevertheless manifests it according to a given perspective; in any case, the diversity of symbols cannot prejudice the realization of the equilibrium in question. In other words, traditional legislation is the application of the cosmic equilibrium to a human collectivity or to an individual insofar as he is integrated into the perspective from which the law in question derives; but the cosmic equilibrium acts primarily as an inward law, which has nothing legislative about it and which can even, in certain exceptional cases, enter into outward contradiction with the general law, in the same way as the prescriptions of the different religions may contradict one another. Nevertheless, this case concerns only "those who are a law unto themselves", to borrow an expression from Muslim esoterism; as for the individual who does not realize this inward—and overriding—identity with the universal Law, he needs, in order to realize his equilibrium, and failing direct knowledge, symbolic supports adapted to his mentality, and such is the case with the immense majority of men. To deny the profound necessity for different legislations or moralities is to deny the necessary and spontaneous homogeneity of all religions; it is to forget then that the moral or ritual law constitutes but part of a totality, whose own unity, dependent upon a distinctly defined spiritual perspective, cannot be broken. This perspective on the one hand, and ethnic and historic contingencies on the other, are the factors that essentially determine the form of the law, just as, for the individual, it is the degree and nature of his spiritual knowledge on the one hand, and his mental structure on the other, that immediately determine the nature of his inner law.

The act itself, whether it be by commission or omission, necessarily participates in the cosmic qualities or tendencies that the Hindu doctrine distinguishes as the three *guna*s, and which we shall here designate by the terms "intelligence", "passion", and "ignorance"; it is the predominance of one of these qualities that determines the act, not as such, but insofar as it is conformity or transgression.[5] On the other hand, if we define transgression as a non-conformity in the domain of action, we can be more exact if we add that it is a non-conformity with regard to the divine Act; this Act is pure affirmation, whereas sin is negative and passive, in the sense that in it man repudiates in a certain manner his intelligence and abandons himself to deceptive appearance.

Before going further, we must pause for a moment at the Christian idea of original sin: this is the fundamental tendency, peculiar to fallen man, towards illusion, a tendency that is compensated for—and virtually abolished—by baptism; now, the fact that the baptismal rite

---

[5] "The action that makes one ashamed when one has just done it, when one is doing it, and when one is preparing to do it, must be regarded by the wise as marked by the quality of darkness (*tamas*). Every act whereby one desires to acquire fame in the world, the non-success of which, however, will not greatly trouble one, must be regarded as pertaining to the quality of passion (*rajas*). When one desires Knowledge with all one's soul, when one is not ashamed of what one is doing, and when the soul derives satisfaction from it, this action bears the mark of the quality of conformity (*sattva*). The love of pleasure characterizes the quality of darkness; that of riches, the quality of passion; that of virtue, the quality of conformity; superiority of attitude in these things follows the order of enumeration" (*Mānava Dharma Shāstra*, XII:35-38). In the Islamic doctrine, those who are endowed with the quality of conformity are "those upon whom is grace" (*al-ladhīna an'amta 'alayhim*); those who possess the quality of passion are "those who err" (*ad-dāllūn*); and those who are subject to the quality of darkness, ignorance, or non-conformity, are "those against whom Thou art angered" (*al-maghdūbu 'alayhim*).

Virgin and Child
Romanesque statue
Wood covered with metal

constitutes an initiation and that it consequently transcends the moral plane, indicates that original sin, since it is the object of this rite, also corresponds to an initiatic and supra-moral conception. Since such a conception cannot prevail outside the realm of esoterism—the case of Christianity is exceptional—it is always legitimate to disregard it from any standpoint that falls outside this realm: one may therefore deny original sin and go no further than the fact that evil is not actualized in the souls of children of tender years, and this is what is done in Islam, which knows neither original sin nor baptism, except of course in its esoterism, where it necessarily has the equivalents under an appropriate form. Moreover, the idea of the Immaculate Conception, closely linked with the doctrine under discussion, gives rise to analogous remarks: one can see why Greek theology, in conformity with its prudence in matters of dogmatic definition and its fidelity to scriptural symbolism, sought to avoid crystallizing, on the plane of outward doctrine, a truth closely relating to the highly delicate question of "human divinity", if we may so call it; be that as it may, if the Catholic dogma of the Immaculate Conception means that the Virgin is "the perfect creature", the absence of this dogma with the Greeks means in the last analysis that "there is none good but God", according to the Gospel words themselves.

— ⸪ —

The ignorance that is the fundamental condition of transgression is of an altogether different order from simple theoretical ignorance: it is effective ignorance whose root is in the heart and not in the reason or the memory; and it is this ignorance that the monotheistic Scriptures call, with great accuracy, "hardness of heart". Ignorance is manifested in three principal ways: stupidity, weakness, and wickedness; these are respectively the privations of divine Wisdom, divine Power, and divine Mercy or Beauty, the corresponding human qualities being intelligence, strength, and goodness. Stupidity is the inability to discern the essential from the accessory: it consists in attaching oneself to mere facts and in considering them simply in themselves, that is, without the least induction; weakness is abandonment to illusions and lack of intellectual penetration with regard to appearances, and hence a lack of inward homogeneity and consequently of resistance; finally, wickedness, which is by far the gravest "non-conformity"—for it is eminently "active" and "conscious"—is an abstraction that is the reverse of that brought about by intelligence: whereas intelligence permits one to see the inner relationships of things, wickedness represents an expressly limitative, negative, and destructive tendency. Before transgressing, man deceives himself; in order temporarily to falsify his judgment, he develops arguments which, depending on the case or the individual, are characterized either by stupidity, weakness, or wickedness: the stupid man dissolves his discernment in a kind of torpor; the weak man abandons it before illusion; the wicked man breaks it with violence. One might further say that transgression by stupidity is action—or omission—deprived of sufficient reason; and, insofar as it is a reaction, it responds merely to a fact. Transgression by weakness is characterized by an illusory sufficient reason; it proceeds essentially from a reaction to appearance. Finally, transgression by wickedness has as sufficient reason none other than the malefic tendency to negation, in other words, hatred of what appears as an affirmation of the divine Norm.

Every transgression must therefore be considered as expressing in the agent the lack of some positive quality, such as wisdom, strength, purity; now, if every positive quality is related to a divine aspect, the absence of such a quality must be related to a cosmic center that is either luciferian or satanic in nature—a center that is the direct source of the negative quality, and which is illusorily opposes itself to the divine aspect that it denies; vice lives by regular, and in some way rhythmic, communication with the center of darkness, which determines its nature and which, like an invisible vampire, attracts, grips, and swallows the being in a state of transgression and disequilibrium. If it were not so, a simple infraction would remain an isolated fact; but every infraction is by definition a precedent, and establishes a contact with a tenebrous center,[6] and this again clearly illustrates the necessity for purificatory rites, whose effect precisely is to break such contacts and re-establish communication with the divine aspect of which the transgression, in keeping with its cosmic center, has been the negation.

---

[6] Hell is sometimes represented in the form of a monster that speaks and moves; Al-Ghazali describes it thus: "It walks on four feet and is led by seventy thousand tethers. On each tether are seventy thousand rings; if all the iron on earth were brought together, it would not equal the weight of one of those rings. Each ring is held by seventy thousand infernal guardians. . . . It groans, howls, crackles, whispers, sparks, and smokes, so that the skies are made invisible by the darkness it exhales."

But there is another point that we must consider here, which takes us back to original sin in its esoteric sense: if sin were exclusively behavior contrary to a religious law, it would not be possible without contradiction to affirm that "the just man sins seven times a day", for there have always been men capable of perfect conformity to sacred precepts; the word "sin" must therefore be understood here in a much broader sense, and there is an inspired text that provides the key: "To him therefore who knoweth to do good and doeth it not, to him it is sin" (James 4:17). Now, it is impossible always to act in the best possible way, for the human mind is incapable of fixing its attention simultaneously on every possible aspect of a reality; by fixing its attention on one good thing, it may lose sight of another; the imperfection of human action is thus conditioned not exclusively by bad will, but also by the vicissitudes of the created order itself, and this is why certain Scriptures attribute "sins" even to Prophets, whereas others, taking sin in its literal and immediate sense, on the contrary affirm the impeccability of those who, being "divine man", are also "human God". In a word, if "the just man sins seven times a day", it is because there cannot be a "pure quality" in manifestation; a purely qualitative manifestation is a contradiction in terms.

This brings us to the question of the perfection—or imperfection—of the God-Man; it is true that we have already answered it implicitly in the foregoing, but this question, although in some ways outside our subject, is nevertheless of such importance that we must dwell on it for a moment. The human individual as such cannot but possess the limitative attributes that constitute his essential definition, failing which he would not be a human individual but something else; there is no doubt that the God-Man is, in a certain respect and by definition, a human individual, otherwise he would not be a man in any sense, and it would even be impossible to speak of him in any way; Christ is "true God and true man", and we will remember his words: "Why callest thou me good? There is none good but God."[7]

---

[7] According to Hanbalite doctrine, the imperfections apparent in the life of a Prophet are willed by Providence with the sole aim of revealing, on the occasion of these

We may compare these Gospel words with the following saying from an *Upanishad*: "The essence of man is made of desire", without however concluding from the application of this saying to the human nature of Christ that beings like him—"divine men"—are subject to desire; for if it be true that such beings possess an individuality which, as such, necessarily comprises all the constituent elements and all the essential attributes of individuality, and if consequently it is true that their psychism implies a particularization analogous to what in ordinary mortals we term "desire", nonetheless this individuality, in the case of a great spiritual figure—whether he has the function of Revealer or not—is of a different essence than in the ordinary man, and this by reason of the intimate penetration of all his modalities by the Universal. Consequently, when in speaking of a God-Man the ordinary psychological terminology is maintained, the words have only an analogical and approximate value, for there is an eminent and essential, if not an absolute, difference between the psychism of the sinner and that of the deified man. Thus, when the divine man apparently expresses a sentiment or a desire, it is he alone who is right in using human terms, and the same statements would become—always in comparison with the God-Man—more or less false in the mouth

---

imperfections, rules of conduct (*sunnah*) that apply to the most diverse situations of human life. Meister Eckhart expresses the fundamental aspect of this truth in the following terms: "Someone might object: Did Christ have immutable indifference when he cried out: 'My soul is exceeding sorrowful even unto death'? And did Mary, when she stood at the foot of the cross? For there is much talk of her sorrowing. How does all this accord with immutable indifference? Well, according to the masters, there are fundamentally two men within every man: firstly, outward or sensorial man; he is served by the five senses, which in fact also derive their strength from the soul; secondly, the inward man, or the inwardness of man. . . . The outward man may perform some action, while the inward man remains perfectly free and immutable in regard to it. In Christ too there was an outward man and an inward man, and similarly in our Blessed Lady, and all that they manifested with regard to external things, they did through the outward man, while the inward man remained in immutable indifference. It was thus that Christ uttered the words: 'My soul is exceeding sorrowful even unto death'; and whatever were the lamentations and bewailings of our Lady, she nevertheless remained the whole time in immutable indifference in her inward soul. Take an example: a door needs a hinge on which to turn; I compare the door to the outward man and the hinge to the inward man. When the door opens and closes, the door is in movement, but the hinge remains immutable in one place and is not affected by the movement" (*Von der Abgeschiedenheit*).

of an ordinary man;[8] the latter cannot know the dimensions that individual facts, thanks to their transcendent quality, have for the "human God"; in short, it is the very substance of the individuality which, in the divine man, is transmuted by the real Presence. To say that a divine man is beyond individuality, that he is perfectly "united", amounts to saying that his "I"—which he possesses by the same right as he does his physical body—is not an obstacle for him. But this does not mean that this individuality, or what manifests itself as such, is inexistent, for this would be contradictory, given that anything that is inexistent cannot be manifested in any way whatsoever; an appearance cannot be "nothing but an appearance", any more than a shadow can proceed from itself; individuality—the presence of which, in some mode or other, is an obvious thing in every man, since the human state is an individual one—cannot but be what it is by definition. These considerations will help us better to understand that the Gospel words quoted above, and which are closely related to a large number of other texts, concern the individuality as such, and not insofar as it is penetrated and determined by the Universal; and it goes without saying that they in nowise concern the God-Man's state of supreme identity. This is why it is possible and legitimate to say that the individuality exists outside the state of supreme identity, and that consequently the divine man, who is such precisely because of this Identity, is unaffected by it; so that it would be much less inexact to say of him that he "has" an individuality than to say that he "is" an individual; be that as it may, it is difficult to define in what manner and in what respect one should attribute individuality to the divine man. One may indeed try, in human language, to specify in what manner the divine man is individual and in what manner he is not, but it will always be impossible to express this adequately and completely, because the infinitely complex and apparently highly paradoxical realities involved transcend the bounds of simple human reason, of which language is

---

[8] When the sage says: "I desire", he speaks truly, but when the ordinary man says of him: "he desires", he is mistaken. One might also say that the sage, when he "desires" something, does so with divine consent (*bi-idhni 'Llāh*) or by divine order (*bi-amri 'Llāh*), and to the extent that his individuality does desire, it has simultaneously sacrificed the object of its desire; this is expressed in the words of Christ: "Not my will, but Thine be done", words that characterize the disposition of the perfect sage in all his wishing, and which compel us to admit that, from the ordinary human point of view, the perfect sage is beyond desire.

the instrument. Perhaps we could summarize all these considerations in the following words: the divine man is "true God and true man"; and, being "God", and despite being "man", he is not "man" in the same way as other men are who are not "God".[9]

Let us now return to the question of transgression, or rather to that of purification, which is inseparable from it: purificatory rites neutralize the effects of sin—insofar as these effects concern the agent, and without modifying the permanent cause of evil, no rite having the power to abolish ignorance—and thus open the way to the elimination of the cause itself; this amounts to saying that they effect a virtual reintegration into the Edenic state. But the extirpation of the root of sin necessitates the intervention of even more positive help, either in the form of a spiritual influence, or in the form of a means proper to the actualization of the divine Presence that we carry within us, and

---

[9] "The esoteric reality, perceived in contemplation, is the following: the servant subsists through the subsistence that *Allāh* grants him, and loves Him out of love He has for him, and looks at Him through the gaze by which He sees him, without there remaining to the servant, in himself, anything that he could consider his own" (Ibn al-Arif). "Examine well what you and your companions admit unanimously: *Allāh*, because of His sublime Transcendence and the sanctity of His Reality, cannot subsist in the body; as for man, he sees through his visual faculty, which subsists in the bodily organ of his eyes, and he hears through hearing, which subsists in his ears, and he speaks through his locutive faculty, which exists in his tongue, his lips, and other vocal organs. But then it happens that this same man accomplishes an act of virtue, not one of those that are strictly obligatory, but one that is supererogatory and devotional that *Allāh* advises and invites him to practice, and that this act of virtue has as a consequence for him the privation of hearing, vision, language, and all the other spiritual or physical faculties that one says necessarily belong to him and in virtue of which one qualifies him—in all propriety—with the terms hearer, seer, speaker. This is to say that now he has begun to hear and to see through *Allāh*, after having heretofore heard and seen with his sense of hearing and of sight; and this without prejudice regarding what we know with certitude, that *Allāh* is too sublime and holy for created things to be subjects wherein He subsists or for Him Himself to be a subject wherein created things reside. Nonetheless, the servant now hears and sees and speaks with That which does not subsist within him, for *Allāh* is now his hearing, his sight, and his hand" (Muhyiddin ibn Arabi in his *Futūhāt al-Makkiyah*).

thus to the establishing of a sort of contact with God.[10] The first case is that of Christian communion, and the second that of the Lord's Prayer, or, in Islam, that of the ritual prayer, to mention only these examples. It should not be forgotten, however, that the aim of these spiritual means is not to abolish the transgression, but to sanctify the soul with a view to its final ends; moreover, like the purificatory rites, they require of the individual two attitudes that belong strictly to himself, namely the right intention and the effort that translates this into act.

Muslim ablution and Christian confession[11] prepare respectively for ritual prayer and holy communion, and even condition them: in the ablution, which is also found to a certain extent in the Christian use of holy water, the water produces a contact with Edenic purity and does so thanks to "parallel analogy" and to the repercussions going from the sensible to the spiritual; the ablution "separates from the world", according to the expression of the Sufi Abu Bakr Ash-Shibli, as a preparation for approaching God, who is Unity and Purity. If water can be a ritual support for purification, the reason is that, being an element, water is simple and therefore indivisible and incorruptible in its substance; and it is for the same reason that the other elements, except ether, which is not immediately sensible and which in any case is omnipresent, may also serve as ritual supports, as is shown by the substitution in the Muslim ablution—permissible under certain circumstances—of water by sand, or again by the breathing practices of *hatha-yoga*, not forgetting the purification by fire that takes place in the Hindu incineration of the dead. In this order of ideas, we must call attention to the main vital act, that of breathing, which purifies the blood and puts man in contact, in a rhythmical way, with air, and by analogical transposition, with the purity of the Spirit. Thus there is a reason why, in Hesychasm as well as in Eastern methods, breathing is closely linked with meditation itself; spiritualized breathing in its turn influences the circulation of the blood and penetrates, with its spiritual perfume, every corner of our body, which thus becomes a tabernacle of the "real Presence".

---

[10] We say "a sort", because such a contact could never be direct, otherwise there would be a common measure between God and man.

[11] We cite the ablution first because of the universality of its symbolism; the case of Christian confession is rather complex by reason of the particular character of Christian eso-exoterism.

Transgression is essentially non-conformity of action; and as Knowledge alone can deliver from the bonds of action, it alone can definitively eliminate the very possibility of transgression. "Though thou shouldst have committed more transgressions than all transgressors, thou shalt traverse, in the vessel of Knowledge, all transgression. As a lighted fire reduces wood to ash, so, Arjuna, the fire of Knowledge consumes all actions. For there is no lustral water like unto Knowledge" (*Bhagavad Gītā*, IV:36-38).[12]

---

[12] In an analogous sense, but in bhaktic mode, Saint Theresa of the Child Jesus said: "Even if I had committed all crimes, I would lose none of my trust in God, for I know what I can expect of His infinite Mercy." One will note the relation between "trust" and "knowing"; mystical certitude is analogous to metaphysical certitude.

On Sacrifice

There is a mode of purification that concerns life itself: this is sacrifice, the purpose of which is to compensate for what one might call, by analogy with the moral order, "existential transgression" or "cosmic sin", that is to say, our very manifestation insofar as, in a sort of titanesque or luciferian way, it seems to usurp or contradict the divine Life. Sacrifice is like a voluntary and symbolic death within the framework of life: everything that exists vibrates between the Principle, which is situated beyond the existence that it determines, and Manifestation which, on the contrary, tends towards total existence, yet without ever being able to realize it, since the Principle alone is entirely itself.[1] That which exists can only sustain and extend its existence by means of reminiscences—or recapitulations—of its initial existence, or rather of its principial non-existence; each thing carries organically within itself the trace of its nothingness; absolute density is something inconceivable, because contradictory. Sound, for example, in order to extend in duration, must affirm itself by means of interruptions or spaces, which in a certain way prolong it, in accordance with the law of compensation—or vibration—that rules all existence; without these spaces in the very substance of manifestation, it would be reduced to a sort of instantaneous explosion that would centralize within itself all the power or all the vitality of the created—a power that, under normal conditions, is affirmed precisely by the different modes of extension of the latter; thus it is that sound manifested in duration may be considered as the broken refraction of instantaneous sound whose existence we provisionally suppose. Nevertheless it cannot be said that such an instantaneous or central manifestation is absolutely impossible, because Universal Possibility alone being absolute, every impossibility has a limit marked by a possibility that seems to belie it, whence the adage: "The exception proves the rule."[2]

---

[1] This "total existence" is symbolically realized in the hardest, densest, and most massive bodies, but it goes without saying that their density can only be relative.

[2] Thus, the impossibility of a round square entails the possibility of a quadrilateral with convex sides; the impossibility that black be white entails the possibility of gray; only the impossibility of All-Possibility is absolutely impossible; nevertheless, cosmic impossibilities may, quite obviously, have the quality of being "relatively absolute".

It is therefore necessary that total or massive manifestation, although impossible in itself, should at least be realized in the order of appearances in a symbolic manner, and then it assumes either a benefic or malefic aspect: in both cases—that of the cataclysm as well as that of the miracle—there is "purification", in other words, reintegration of a partial disequilibrium into total equilibrium.[3]

Man is the sole being, in the terrestrial world, who can consciously purify himself from the stains of his existence, and it is for this reason that it is said that "man is the only animal that offers sacrifice" (*Shatapatha Brāhmana*, VII:5); in other words, since life is a gift from the Creator, conscious and responsible beings—in order to realize spiritually the meaning of this gift by referring to its symbolic quality, and in order thereby to make this gift more prosperous and durable[4]—must sacrifice to the Creator a part of what He has given. This sacrifice can take either bloody or non-bloody forms; thus, to mention only the following examples out of a multitude of others, the Hindus, like many other peoples, do not eat until they have offered a share of their meal to the gods, so that basically their food consists only of sacrificial remnants; similarly, Muslims and Jews drain all the blood from meat destined to be eaten. In an analogous sense, the warriors of some North American tribes, at the moment of their warrior initiation, used to sacrifice a finger to the "Great Spirit"; it should be remembered that to a warrior, a man of action, his fingers are in a certain respect his most precious possession; furthermore, the fact that out of ten fingers

This last expression, which logically is a contradiction in terms, calls for the following precision: the affirmation that $1 + 1 = 3$ cannot be an "absolutely absolute" falsity, since there are statements that are even more false, for example, $1 + 1 = 0$; the falsity that $1 + 1 = 3$ is therefore "relatively" absolute, which at any rate means that it is not relative, but absolute in its own order; thus, our reservation has only a metaphysical and not a mathematical meaning.

[3] This allows us to understand the relationship between the miracle—or the cataclysm—and the diamond: the latter belongs to the same order of cosmic facts and can have either a benefic or malefic emanation. So too lightning.

[4] The pruning of trees and shrubs is based on the same reality and, by its unquestionable efficacy, provides a highly instructive illustration of the theory of sacrifice.

one of them is sacrificed—in other words, a tenth of what represents our activity—is quite significant, first because the number ten is that of the accomplished or wholly realized cycle, and then because of the analogy that exists between the sacrifice we have just mentioned and the tithe. This moreover is the exact equivalent of the Muslim *zakāt*, the alms ordered by Koranic Law: in order to preserve and increase one's possessions, one prevents the cycle of prosperity from closing and one does so by sacrificing the tenth part, that is, the part which, precisely, constitutes the completion and end of the cycle. The word *zakāt* has the twofold meaning of "purification" and "growth", expressions whose close relationship can be seen very clearly in the pruning of plants; the word *zakāt* derives etymologically from the verb *zakā*, which means "to prosper" or "to purify" or, in another acceptation, "to raise" or "to pay" the sacred contribution, or yet again "to increase". In this connection, we may also recall the Arabic expression *dīn*, which means not only religion, but also "judgement", and—with a slightly different voweling that causes the word to be pronounced *dayn*—"debt"; here too, the respective meanings of the word are linked, religion being considered as man's debt towards God; and the "Day of Judgement" (*Yawm ad-Dīn*)—a "Day" of which *Allāh* is called the "King" (*Mālik*)—is none other than the day of the "payment of the debt" of the individual towards Him to whom he owes everything and who is his ultimate reason for being.

To return to bloody sacrifice—which is more particularly related to life—there is obviously nothing arbitrary in the fact that it is blood which is poured out to the creative and donating Principle, for blood is the most immediate vehicle of life; it is also in the blood that the psychic elements enter into connection with the corporal modality, and this is one of the reasons why, in certain religions, its consumption is forbidden. There is in sacrifice itself something analogous to blood-letting: the human collectivity is the body that gives of its blood, either by shedding that of some of its members or by substituting animals for them. The latter case could logically give rise to the objection that for a human collectivity only human beings are capable of serving as payment of the "tenth"; this is true for a society in which the cyclical conditions have not yet necessitated an alleviating readaptation of the bloody sacrifice, in other words, a transference, as far as the victim is concerned, from man to animal; in any case, this transference, where it is appropriate, is perfectly valid from the technical point of view, given that animals, without quite obviously belonging to the human species, nevertheless belong just as we do to the living and terrestrial collectivity and, more particularly, to the collectivity of beings characterized by the same warm blood. To elucidate this question completely, it would be necessary to refer to the theory of the terrestrial collectivity considered as a unique state with multiple, hierarchical modalities, a state whose central modality is humanity; but this would take us too far afield and we must confine ourselves to the indication just given, which is in any case sufficiently intelligible in itself. As regards human sacrifice, one might ask the following question: by what "right" may a sacrificer immolate an individual against his will? To this it must be answered that the sacrificer does not act as an individual, but as an instrument of the collectivity which, being a totality, obviously has certain rights over a part of itself, namely the individual, on condition of course that this totality be unified by a spiritual bond and as a result constitute a real spiritual unity, a "mystical body" so to speak, and that in addition the sacrifice be approved, and therefore required, by God.

In the three monotheistic religions, the passage from human to animal sacrifice is marked by the sacrifice of a sheep substituted for the son of Abraham; in Christianity it is the sacrifice of the God-Man which, in the Eucharist, is substituted for bloody sacrifice as such. It is Christ's sacrifice that allows Christians to slaughter animals without sacrificing them, since Christ, by virtue of his divinity, contains all manifestation; Christians are thus as it were covered—or protected—by Christ's sacrifice, who, as we have said, synthesizes in himself, through his divinity, the totality of beings. Without such a compensation—whatever its form—man has no right to take life since he is incapable of giving it; this is why peoples who live by hunting do not kill like the profane hunters of the modern world: the act of killing game always requires ritual compensations; thus, to give but one example, the American Indian hunter, when he has killed an animal, smokes in front of it the Calumet—the Peace Pipe, a ritual instrument fashioned out of sacred clay—and blows the smoke towards the muzzle of the slain animal, so as to be reconciled with what one may call the "genius of the species"; altogether analogous rites are to be found among the most diverse types of hunting peoples, and sometimes extend even to plants.[5]

---

[5] A mode of sacrifice that should not be forgotten is that of feudal warfare, not insofar

Human sacrifice always runs the risk of deviating—as may happen in principle with any rite—from the "qualitative" to the "quantitative", or from symbol to superstition, so that it may end up being something that is the very opposite of the original sacrifice; this is what occurred in the case of the "heathen" of whom the Bible speaks, as well as with the Aztecs and no doubt with a fairly large number of more or less degenerate peoples. Wherever spirituality has been overtaken by darkness, sacrifice is no longer addressed to the Deity, but to a psychic entity created and maintained by a collective worship which, too, is only psychic. It is true that in a still healthy religion a similar entity also exists, but in this case it is in its normal place, which is secondary, and since this entity is enlightened—and therefore "qualified"—by a spirituality, its very substance cannot be that of a psychic vampire; in fact, it is called upon to act as a support for divine influences, just as, in the individual, the psychic or mental elements must vehicle the irradiations of the Intellect. But when divine influences have withdrawn from a religious cult, and only the psychic entity remains, abandoned to itself and its ignorant servants—who are thereby all the more impassioned—it becomes a true monster and serves as a dwelling place for tenebrous influences; this explains why hideous apparitions have been seen escaping from shattered idols. Decadences of this kind always occur when the forms of worship are no longer adapted to new cyclical conditions; these forms are then no more than vestiges that continue to live from what might be called a purely spasmodic life, just as a decapitated body can still undergo nervous contractions. It is then that there intervenes either a traditional readaptation, in conformity with new cyclical conditions, or a change from without which, in certain conditions, can lead to the destruction pure and simple of the civilization concerned.

as it represents a general manifestation of the unfavorable conditions of our cyclical epoch, but insofar as it has, for the warrior, a positive significance and consequently represents a sort of law, a *modus vivendi* for a given human collectivity. In this order of ideas many more developments could be made concerning other modes of sacrifice of a warrior type, for example, the *seppuku*, generally known in the West as *hara-kiri*, the ritual suicide of the Shintoists; what we have previously said contains implicitly the elements necessary for understanding this very special case of human sacrifice, so we can confine ourselves to one observation: namely that *hara-kiri*, a rite pertaining to a perspective that by definition is a sort of closed and homogeneous system whose elements are not comparable to any other traditional forms—these elements being compossibles only within their own framework—in no way falls under the law of profane and non-ritual suicide, since it is covered by the sacred measures of Shintoism.

The supreme form of sacrifice, of which all the others are but reflections or anticipations, is the one that is situated on the inward plane. It is in order to "lose his life", in the Gospel sense of this term, that man sacrifices himself—or rather it is in order to find it anew in the Immutable which is beyond the cosmic alternations.

The Twin Pitfall

In the fallen nature of man there is a double infirmity and, spiritually speaking, a double obstacle: on the one hand passion, which draws man outside himself while at the same time compressing him, and on the other hand pride, which shuts man within himself, while at the same time dispersing him. Passion reveals itself by attachment, and pride by ambition; even if the latter were spiritual, it still would be worldly, unless one were to give the word ambition—as is sometimes done—a transposed and neutral meaning. In an analogous way, if one understands by the word passion a force in itself neutral and available for use, one can evidently speak of holy passions, or passions sanctified by their object; but it is obviously not this conversion of a natural energy that is in question when we speak here of infirmities or obstacles. In this connection it must be pointed out that pride, for its part, does not admit of such a conversion; it can only be destroyed or dissolved—the first term indicating a privative or penitential ascesis and the second an alchemy of love able to "melt the heart"— depending upon the degrees or modes of hardness. It is true that one can sometimes speak of "legitimate pride", but this is situated on an innocuous plane having nothing to do with vice or sin.

Passion, as it is to be understood here, is to prefer the world to God; pride is to prefer oneself to God or, metaphysically speaking, to prefer sensory consciousness to the immanent Self. Or again, to paraphrase the words of a saint: passion is to flee from God, pride is to rise up against Him. In consequence, one can say that to prefer the world—in the form of some thing or other—to truth or to the good, is passion; to prefer oneself—in the form of some vanity—to truth or to the good, is pride; for truth, or the good, is the trace of God and represents God.

Passion expresses itself not only by attachment, but also, and in a more pernicious way, by insatiability. Pride, for its part, expresses itself not only by ambition, it is yet more vicious when it takes the form of obstinacy. And this shows that the two vices necessarily intermingle: obstinate passion does not go without a measure of pride; insatiable pride does not go without a measure of passion. The man who is without any pride will also be without passion, and he who is wholly without passion will also be without pride.

A prideful person may have all the virtues, even some humility, but he claims them as his own and thus illusorily cuts them off from God, thereby taking away all their intrinsic value and profound efficacy; which means that the virtues of a prideful person are as it were deprived of their content. As for the humble person, he is well aware that the virtues belong to him on loan, just as light belongs in a certain way to the water that reflects it, but he never loses sight of the fact that he is not the author of his virtues—any more than the water is the source of the light—and that the finest virtues are nothing apart from God. Conversely, even if one tries to separate them from God in order to appropriate them to oneself, whatever value they may retain still belongs to God.

A man may have a sincere desire for humility—thus for objectivity towards himself—and may realize thereby a mode of true humility, but at the same time cannot bear any humiliation, even if merited or innocuous. In this case his humility is compromised to a greater or lesser extent by an element of pride, which will also manifest itself by a certain propensity to humiliate others, even if it be only in underestimating them and in interpreting unfavorably something susceptible of a favorable interpretation. That a mixture of humility and pride can exist proves that pride, like passion, comprises degrees: in fact it is necessary to distinguish between a vice that is in the very substance of a person and another that is only an accident; what is accidental can be remedied, the substantial cannot.

We have just said that a criterion of pride—of a pride that is perhaps only accidental and not fundamental—is the propensity to brook no humiliations while readily inflicting them upon others. The right attitude is not to rebel against a humiliation when it manifests the Truth, and to accept in good grace humiliations that do not jeopardize our true dignity, the one God has conferred upon us by His creative act and which is an extension of His own. Nothing harms our dignity as "image of God" so much as pride, because it cuts us off from the divine substance of our dignity. We are well aware that from a certain ascetic and sentimental point of view no humiliation is unmerited, but that is a question of method and not of norm, especially since our perspective is based on the nature of things and not on a voluntarist and emotional automatism.

There are prideful people who appear humble because they avoid disparaging others while being nevertheless steeped in their own importance, as there are on the contrary those who seem humble because they make little of their own worth, while nevertheless underestimating others. Or again there are people who are considered humble because they seem so before God, or before the spiritual master, or before one of the great of this world, whereas they are not at all humble before their peers, which proves precisely that they are sincerely humble neither towards their superiors nor towards God.

Attachment, selfishness, and insatiability belong to passion; ambition, pretension, and obstinacy to pride; both vices, pride and passion, may have stupidity and malice in common, leaving aside the fact that all the vices share in an indirect solidarity.

It is not without reason that popular opinion tends to associate pride with stupidity. One can in fact be pretentious through stupidity just as one can be stupid through pretension; the two things go together. Of course, lack of intelligence does not necessarily lead to pretension, but pretension cannot avoid harming the intelligence. And if, as is commonly admitted, stupidity is the incapacity to discern between the essential and the secondary, or between cause and effect, it includes for that very reason a measure of pride; a stupidity combined with a perfect humility and a perfect detachment would no longer be stupidity, it would be a simplicity of outlook that could trouble no intelligent and virtuous person.

Closely related to pretension is self-satisfaction, with the difference that it is passive, while pretension is active. The self-satisfied person is not one who rightly and with complete humility is conscious of the worth of what he knows or does, but rather one who is full of his own imaginary worth, which he projects onto his scanty knowledge and mediocre activity. Humility, for its part, is in no wise contrary to authority, and could not be so since authority is a positive quality; humility is not modesty, by which we mean that authority excludes modesty, while nonetheless including humility. Setting aside all humilitarianism—automatic and extravagant as it may be, though inevitable and efficacious in the psychological order corresponding to it—humility is the awareness of our real, and not imaginary, littleness in its various aspects, together with the absence of all desire for individual affirmation; modesty, for its part, is the awareness, not of our ontological limitation or of our human insufficiency, but simply of our incompetence or our incapacity, as the case may be. Thus, on the one hand modesty resembles humility, yet on the other hand differs from it, and this may be illustrated by saying that the modest man must of necessity be humble, but the humble man need not necessarily be modest.

There is a certain *de facto* relationship—humanly speaking—between passion and beauty, as likewise between pride and intelligence: in other words, for fallen man, beauty and intelligence have become two-edged swords, which explains the ostracism they often suffer at the hands of moralists, and even at the level of theology. In esoterism, however, intelligence and beauty are thoroughly restored to their real standing and value, for by definition esoterism considers the aseity of things and not their opportuneness on some lower plane; it has always recognized that things that for some can be a seduction and a cause of perdition, can for others be a call to God; herein lies the whole mystery of the metaphysical transparency of phenomena.

Setting aside the weakness of human nature, or the intangible factors of this weakness, as the case may be, the truth of the matter is simple: intelligence and beauty are intrinsically positive; but extrinsically and practically, they are positive or good only on the express condition that, subjectively, they not be separated from God; and that, objectively, they not be envisaged apart from God, and in the end as counter to God, as was precisely the sin with classical Greece and the Renaissance, under the double aspect of thought and art.

To passion, the things of this world appear in some way as absolute; to pride, it is the ego that takes on this aspect. Now, this is obviously incompatible, not only with the concept of God, but even more so with the practices of meditation and realization that pertain thereto. To combine the idolatry and the narcissism of man's fallen nature with practices converging on the Infinite—relating to Immanence as well as to Transcendence—is assuredly the most flagrant of hypocrisies and the most fatal of absurdities.

It follows from most of our preceding considerations that our point of view is not that of individual and sentimental voluntarism: it coincides neither with penitentialism, according to which only the disagreeable leads to God, nor with humilitarianism, according to which every man should think himself the greatest of all sinners. In speaking of passion and attachment, we do not mean a natural attachment to certain goods that every man can experience and that is in no way opposed to the sense of relativity or to serenity of mind, or to detachment generally; we are thinking solely of the passional attachment which, as mentioned, places an absolute value on relative things to the detriment of the love of God. And in speaking of pride, ambition, and pretension, we do not mean natural self-respect, or the awareness that the most objective man may have of his worth, or the sense of dignity or honor, for none of these is in any way opposed to the awareness of our metaphysical nothingness or to true humility in relation to others. We have solely in mind overestimation of oneself, which is inevitably accompanied by underestimation of others and which for that very reason renders sincere effacement before God impossible. Pride is the desire to "keep one's life"; it is to refuse to "die before one dies".

Psychologically or morally speaking, a distinction is made between men who are proud and others who are not, whatever the degree of the vice. In volitive and sentimental mysticism one would say on the contrary that every man is proud, which on the one hand is false—for then the words would practically be devoid of meaning—but which on the other hand is nonetheless true in relation to the virtuality of pride to be found in every man and which can be actualized according to circumstances, even if only to a slight degree. Mystical voluntarism seeks to cut short all ineffective subtlety; spiritual intellectuality, on the other hand, operates by means of truth and not by means of zeal, consequently the remedy it employs will not be a useful and leveling approximation, but a precise knowledge of the malady. The gnostic—in the original and not sectarian sense of the word—does not ask: "What attitude of will and sentiment is the most contrary to pride?" but rather: "What in this particular case is the nature of things, and what consequently is the positive attitude—of mind and soul—of which pride is the negation or the privation?" This is, first, an attitude of the mind: namely, discernment between the Absolute and the relative, and, within the relative, between the essential and the secondary—discernment that entails *ipso facto* the sanctifying and unitive contemplation of the Absolute and of the essential. Then, an attitude of the soul, itself governed by this discernment or by this sense of proportion and equilibrium: namely, self-effacement on the one hand, and generosity on the other; for all the fundamental virtues are included in these two qualities.

Effacement towards God first and then, as a consequence of this vertical quality, effacement towards the world, hence in the horizontal dimension: all virtue and all merit come from God, we are merely reverberating facets; the perspicacious and virtuous man, aware that he cannot in any fashion or in any respect add his personal qualities to the divine Perfection—the only one there is—and that consequently he is nothing before God but a pauper, will not wish to vaunt himself before men either; in other words, he would not think of imposing or putting forward his person as such. He will exercise his function, he will perform his duty; he might perhaps be king, but it will not be his individual person that he will affirm, even if his function obliged him to impose his person as agent and symbol; the king and the pontiff receive in an impersonal manner, and in humbleness before God, the honors due to them. The humble person does not derive any pleasure or any ambition from the fact of being "I", and he has no prejudice with regard to "others".

And the same for generosity: it must be exercised first towards God and then towards men. Everyone knows what generosity is with regard to the neighbor; but what is generosity with regard to God? It is the gift of oneself in contemplation, and extinction—in the measure possible—in the divine Life in the depth of our hearts.

What matters for man and what decides his ultimate fate is his Knowledge, his faith, his character, and his activity. Now the foundation of a noble character is precisely self-effacement and generosity: self-effacement or poverty, which implies detachment, sobriety, patience, and contentment; and generosity or magnanimity, which implies fervor, perseverance, trust, and joy in God.

Passion and pride constitute *a priori* the flaw and the obstacle; mingled with the highest spiritual aspirations, they become an abomination. We will be told that this has always been known, because it is evident; that may be. But the things that have never been unknown seem to be at the same time those that men have the greatest difficulty in learning.

On Meditation

Contrary to what is too often stated, meditation cannot of itself provoke enlightenment; rather, its object is more negative in the sense that it has to remove inner obstacles that stand in the way, not of a new, but of a preexistent and "innate" knowledge of which one has to become aware; thus meditation may be compared not so much to a light kindled in a dark room, as to an opening made in the wall of that room to allow the light to enter—a light that preexists outside and is in no way produced by the action of piercing the wall. Man is by definition a thinking being and consequently he cannot regard thought as useless *a priori*, no matter what his deepest intentions may be; hence his starting point must necessarily be thought, not only for the needs of the outer life, where this is self-evident, but even in his spiritual effort to go beyond the plane of mental limitations. Since he thinks, man must consecrate this faculty to the "one thing needful", as he must consecrate all his other faculties, for everything has to be integrated into the spiritual; whoever takes thought for the world must also take thought for God, and this holds true for every fundamental activity of the human being, since we must go to God with all that we are.

Every spiritual path, independently of its mode or level, comprises three great degrees: purification, which causes "the world to leave man"; unfoldment, which causes "the Divine to enter into man"; and union, which causes "man to enter into God". This might also be expressed somewhat differently: there is something in man that has to die, or has to be destroyed: this is the soul-as-desire, whose existential limit is the sensorial body; there is something in man that has to be converted, or has to be transmuted: this is the soul-as-love—the soul-as-will—whose center of gravity is the ego; finally, there is something in man that has to become conscious of itself; that has to become itself; that has to be purified and freed of what is alien to itself; that has to awaken and expand and become all, because it is all; something that alone must be: this is the soul-as-knowledge,[1] that is to say, the Spirit, whose subject is God and whose object is likewise God.

[1] In the final analysis, this knowledge must not be looked upon as an aspect opposed to love, but rather as the deepest reality of that which on the individual level crystallizes into "will", "love", and "intellection"; thus conceived, knowledge is identified with the divine Light from which all perfections derive.

The role of meditation is thus to open the soul, firstly to the grace that draws it away from the world, secondly to that which brings it nearer to God, and thirdly to that which, so to speak, reintegrates it into God; however, this reintegration may be, according to circumstance, only a fixation in a given "beatific vision", that is to say a still indirect participation in the divine Beauty.

The first thought capable of delivering man from earthly attachments is that of death, and more generally—and correlatively—that of the ephemeral character of all things. This meditation, which also implies the idea of suffering, and which is intimately linked to the attitude of renunciation, sheds light on a fundamental aspect of our existence; it can therefore serve as the basis and the symbol for a spiritual realization, despite its apparently negative character, which is necessarily compensated by a positive aspect: indeed, to withdraw from the world is to open oneself to the divine Ray, it is to be disposed to know the Eternity of God; to flee from the impurity of the created is to take refuge in the Purity of the Uncreated; to leave suffering is to enter into Beatitude.[2]

Now, whatever the intrinsic spiritual virtue of this meditation,[3] it is limited, like every form, and thus cannot constitute the only point of departure possible for the soul seeking the Infinite; it is therefore necessary to consider on the same ascetic plane an active and affirmative attitude, and this attitude will derive not from the idea of death or suffering, but from the idea of meritorious and, in the end, salvific action. Every ascetic attitude, whether active or passive—insofar as

---

[2] If Buddhism makes use of this negative perspective and not some other, it is precisely because, grafting itself onto the most immediately accessible experience, that of pain, it speaks to all beings. Every being can suffer, but not every being necessarily loves God; every being desires to escape suffering which, owing to its quasi-absolute character in the experience of living beings, is like the springboard situated at the diametrical opposite of the Infinite.

[3] We ought rather to speak of a category of meditations; but as we are here considering only fundamental contents and not all their possible modalities and combinations, we may dispense with taking into account the indefinitely diverse variations to which each formulation can give rise.

Sri Swami Bhaskarananda Saraswati
Contemporary sage of Ramakrishna, in Benares

it is possible to see a passivity in asceticism—is equivalent to a stiffening or a freezing that may be likened to the reflex of dread. But the attitude we wish to describe here overcomes fear, not in a negative way by a withdrawn or fixed attitude, as was the case in the meditation on death, but on the contrary by a combative and therefore positive attitude: fear of Judgment—or, what amounts to the same thing, the awareness that God sees us—will have the effect of stimulating a voluntary affirmation capable of opening the soul to Grace, and of eliminating what weakens it. What man has to overcome by this meditation is no longer desire properly so called, as was the case before, but the natural torpor of the soul, its sloth with regard to the "one thing needful", passivity in the face of the seductions of the world. In shaking off this somnolence, man opens himself to the divine Influx, and rouses himself through the spiritual act, which reflects the pure Act of God; he overcomes the world, not by fleeing from it but by opposing it with an affirmation; he does not withdraw from the created, but transforms it by the act, by the intimate and vigorous consent of the soul to God, and by the perseverance that fixes the act in duration. This attitude of vigilance and combat—of "holy anger", if one will—has this in common with the preceding attitude—that of purity—in that it takes its stand in the present as it were, which is pure and strong, and which overcomes the past and the future alike. It is, we repeat, the standpoint of fear, but a fear that has become active and trusting. In other words, in the one case, it is the passive and negative aspect,[4] and in the other, the active and positive aspect of fear; or again, in the one case, it is the perfection of him who avoids evil, and in the other, the perfection of him who accomplishes the good.

After the perspective of fear, we shall consider that of love: its most direct expression is the contemplation of the divine Perfections, which may be designated synthetically by the term "Beauty". This perspective of love is situated beyond fear and negation: instead of having painfully to reject the world on account of the ephemeral

---

[4] According to a Sufi teaching, when one fears a creature one flees from it, but when one fears God one flees towards Him.

and deceptive nature of its always limited perfections, love, on the contrary, attaches itself to the divine Prototypes of these perfections, so that the world, henceforth emptied of its content—since this is to be found again infinitely in God—will be only a play of symbols and an accumulation of husks, and thus will have no further hold over man.[5] He who knows that all he loves here below is lovable only in virtue of the Essences[6]—and therefore preexists infinitely in the Divinity—becomes detached from the earthly shadows almost effortlessly; he knows that nothing is ever lost, the perfections of this world being no more than fleeting reflections of the eternal Perfections. In other words, the beloved thing, or the beloved being, is to be found infinitely more in God than in this world; God is, in infinite measure, every beloved thing and every beloved being. This meditation helps to overcome the world, not by renouncing it *a priori*, but by finding it again beyond the created, in the Principle that is the Cause of all good; the soul thus consoled rests in God, and there finds peace; the soul rests, recollected and satisfied, and freed from all dissipation, in awareness of the infinite Beauty.

In creatures, beauty is above all an outward attribute, and it is really only by extension that one can speak, for example, of beauty of soul; but in this case again, beauty is an appearance that envelops a deeper reality, a kind of inward truth; in a word, for us beauty is what is most easily graspable, and it is quite significant that it appears in the purest, most exclusive, and most perfect—albeit also the simplest and poorest—manner in the most peripheral kingdom, that of minerals, in which beauty is quasi-abstract and absolute. Now this outwardness of beauty is the inverse reflection of the principial relationship; if beauty appears outward in creatures, it is because it is inward in God; or again, if it is immediately graspable in the created, it is, in turn, the most difficult aspect to grasp in the Uncreated. If God's Beauty were as easily accessible as that of creatures, the apparent contradictions of creation—the sufferings that we consider to be unjust or horrible— would be resolved of themselves, or rather, they would vanish away in

---

[5] As an Arab dervish once said to us: "It is not I who have left the world, it is the world that has left me."

[6] "Verily, it is not for love of the husband that the husband is dear, but for love of the *Ātman* in him. Verily, it is not for love of the wife that the wife is dear, but for love of the *Ātman* that is in her. Verily, it is not for love of the sons that the sons are dear, but for love of the *Ātman* that is in them" (*Brihadāranyaka Upanishad*).

total Beauty; it is thus that a woman's beauty can engulf and bring to naught all reasoning, or that the beauty of a piece of music can drown out mental distractions.[7] When we consider the sufferings of this world, we must never forget that God compensates them infinitely by His Beauty; but this is beyond rational demonstration.

Contemplative concentration on divine Beauty or Beatitude implies, in the attitude of the individual and in relation to the divine Prototype, a parallel analogy and an inverse analogy: the first is provided by the quietude, repose, and peace of the soul, for Beauty is balance and harmony; the second analogy is the individual's contentment with that which he possesses in an immediate and ineluctable fashion, and consequently it is resignation towards all that he is according to the will of destiny;[8] this attitude is inversely analogous to the divine Beauty in the sense that the divine Beauty represents an aspect of infinity, hence of extension, if one may express it thus, whereas contentment on the contrary, and by a kind of compensation, realizes a non-expansion or a contraction in the individual.

Another attitude, complementary to the one we have just spoken of, is that of fervor; this likewise derives from the attitude of love, but whereas the preceding attitude rested in the Beauty or Beatitude of God, this new attitude soars towards His Goodness and Mercy: the soul clings with all its life and all its being to faith in the divine Mercy; it strives to "do violence" to that Mercy, to "force the gates of Heaven"[9]. This is the way of ardent trust, of intense hope, which dissolves all hardnesses of soul and is affirmed outwardly by the love of one's neighbor, since it abolishes the individual divisions born of initial hardness of heart; it is the "faith which removes mountains".

Here again, in the attitude of the individual in relation to the divine aspect in view, there is a parallel analogy and an inverse one: Goodness or Mercy is warmth and center and is translated in the individual in parallel mode as fervor, and in inverse mode as generosity, hence as a radiance or an expansion; now the divine Goodness can be said to be

---

[7] According to an Arab proverb, the beauty of man is in his intelligence, and the intelligence of woman in her beauty.

[8] The Sufis call this virtue *ridhā*, "resignation" or "contentment"; it is what the Hesychasts call the "maintaining of the spirit within the body". Diogenes' reply to Alexander expresses very well the attitude in question.

[9] It will be recalled that "the Kingdom of Heaven suffereth violence".

"attractive" since it attracts from the periphery to the Center, or from the current of forms to the blissful and liberating Essence.

On the plane of pure intellectuality, there is a negative attitude that corresponds to renunciation of the passional plane, and which is as it were its core; but what was renunciation for the will, becomes discernment for the intelligence: it is the distinction between the Real and the unreal, and hence the negation of the world, including the "I". According to this perspective, God alone "is"; the world—the microcosm as well as the macrocosm—is merely illusion or "nothingness"; there is no need for renunciation, since nothing is; it suffices to know, through the Intellect, that nothing is real.

The point of view that we have just set forth is discernment, hence separation between the Real and the unreal, and even annihilation of the unreal, and not directly union with the Real. Union derives from a different point of view that may be formulated thus: "outside God" nothing is, except nothingness, and nothingness in no way is; now since I am not nothing, I am all; I am all That is, or in other words, I am not other than He,[10] in my supra-individual Essence, of which the ego is merely a refraction and hence a symbol. Thanks to this knowledge, God penetrates and sanctifies me,[11] while on the other hand absorbing my existence; He makes me become That which I am in reality and from all eternity, namely Himself. The mental act that corresponds to this reality is concentration on the Real, the Absolute, the Infinite; concentration in fact corresponds to a quasi-existential realization of God, which in any case presupposes the intellectual discernment we have considered previously. According to this supreme point of view—which constitutes the esoteric complement of the

---

[10] Let us recall the following formulas: *Aham Brahmāsmi* ("I am *Brahman*"), *Shivo'ham* ("I am *Shiva*"), and in Sufism, the Hallajian expression *Anā'l-Haqq* ("I am God-Truth"), or again the expression *Subhānī* ("Glory be to me") of Bayazid.

[11] On condition that the knowledge be metaphysically exact! Otherwise, man will enter into a darkness much deeper than that of simple ignorance. Aside from the fact that spiritual dilettantism possesses neither greatness nor beauty, whosoever appropriates to himself spiritual attitudes to which he has no right, becomes the sport of powers of illusion and runs the risk of foundering in a darkness from which there is no return.

affirmative attitude we discussed above—it is only in God that I am really "I"; in the illusion of individuality I am as though separated from myself, and the created "I" is only a veil that hides me from "Myself" who am uncreated. It is no longer a question here of distinguishing That which is from that which is not, but of "being" That which is. We may also express this idea in the form of the following reasoning: it is certain that I am not nothing; not being nothing, I am all; being all, I am not other than He. This meditation is plenitude and not emptiness like the preceding one; it is totality and not unicity; it is like the sun filling space, flooding it with light; it is inaccessible and even fatal for the profane mind, whence the theological denials and prohibitions that always have in view the common interest, never that of a minority. And yet, there is no restriction here that is inherent to Christianity as such, for according to Saint Macarius of Egypt, "the crowns and diadems that the Christians receive are uncreated"; according to Saint Gregory Palamas, "the saints who participate in the divine Grace become, in conformity with Grace, infinite and without origin"; and according to Meister Eckhart, "we are totally transformed in God and changed into Him; in the same way as in the sacrament the bread is changed into the body of Christ, I am changed into Him, so that He makes me one with his own Being and not simply like unto Him; by the living God, it is true that there is now no longer any distinction".

This gradation of spiritual attitudes, far from being merely the fact of a more or less arbitrary systematization, on the contrary corresponds rigorously to the nature of things, and every possible spiritual attitude can be reduced in the final analysis to one of the points of view we have just considered. We may designate these six fundamental attitudes respectively by the following terms: "negation", "affirmation"; "passivity", "activity"; "emptiness," "plenitude";[12] this amounts to saying that in "fear" there is an attitude that is negative and another that is positive; that in "love" there is an attitude that is passive and

---

[12] These six positions could also be designated respectively by the following terms: "cold", "dryness"; "humidity", "heat"; "emptiness", "plenitude"; or again by these symbols: "crystal", "lightning" (or "sword"); "water", "fire"; "night", "sun".

another that is active; that in "knowledge" there is an abstractive, distinctive, or objective attitude and another that is integrative, unitive, or subjective. The negative attitude of "fear" is renunciation, detachment; the affirmative attitude is effort, perseverance. The passive attitude of "love" is contentment, peace; the active attitude is faith, fervor.[13] The distinctive attitude of "knowledge" is discernment between the Real and the unreal, the extinction of the unreal within the Real; the unitive attitude is concentration on That which I am in reality, identity with That which I am.

[13] According to Hesychast doctrine, the two great graces that Christ bequeathed with his Name, and which as it were flow from it, are peace and love: they correspond respectively to the two attitudes that we have just mentioned and which we have dealt with previously, peace being the "static" aspect and love the "dynamic" aspect of one same mode of spirituality, namely *bhakti.*

APPENDIX

Selections from Letters and
Other Previously Unpublished Writings

1

The method must encompass all the elements of individual existence, at the risk of remaining incomplete. In the life of an initiate everything is therefore ritualized, through the consecration of every act, which is thus offered to the Divinity and integrated into the spiritual path. Every act is susceptible to sacralization by virtue of its symbolic character on the one hand, and its relative necessity on the other; an activity that is sought only for its own sake, that is, apart from or even contrary to its symbolism, and which cannot include a sufficient necessity, is no more than a transgression, and it cannot be integrated, together with rites properly speaking, to the traditional method. Every rite, just like all ritualized or sacralized acts, which presuppose the consciousness of their symbolism, is subject to two "technical" conditions: not to be anything other than what it must be, and to be entirely what it is; only in this way can the rite and the ritualized act serve as a support to the spiritual influence conferred by initiation, because only in this way does the rite participate, from the point of view of its "technique", in the divine Principle, which is nothing but what it is, and which is absolutely what it is.

2

Concerning the problem of transmigration, it seems to me that one does not take sufficiently into account the fact that there are between incarnations intermediary states—either celestial or infernal—whose length is described in sacred Texts as being very long. The Bible and the Koran speak of the resurrection of the flesh, which is indeed a "re-incarnation"; but at that moment, the present earth will have ceased to exist. In any case, the facile reincarnationism of most Easterners does not conform to their own Scriptures. Obviously, there are widely diverse theories and symbolisms to be considered here, which indicates just how complex the problem is; perhaps it cannot be expressed in human language, since this language is terrestrial, at least in a certain way. In this sense, it is easier to speak of metaphysics than of cosmology; from a certain point of view, the Absolute is closer to us than are the other worlds.

3

There are for man as it were four fields of experience or four realities with which he must come to terms: God, the world, the "I", the neighbor. God speaks within each of these realities in a particular way: in the world as destiny; in the I as pure Spirit; in the neighbor as need. How does one encounter God in the world? In destiny, which one accepts precisely because one submits to God. How does one encounter God in one's own soul? In pure knowledge, which indeed is pure and suprahuman Truth. How does one encounter God in one's neighbor? In the love of one's neighbor, in good deeds, on whatever plane our gift may be. One cannot serve God if one does not also see Him in destiny, in knowledge, and in one's neighbor. When destiny comes, God says: "Here too am I." When man acts on the basis of truth, God says: "Here too am I." When the neighbor comes in need, God says: "Here too am I." To serve God in the world means to thank Him for every aspect of destiny; to serve Him in one's own soul means to know and will the True, to fulfill the law, and to invoke the supreme Name; to serve God in the neighbor means to provide him with what we have and what he needs, whether with food or the Spirit. All these things are inseparable.

Expressed differently: we must always give something to our neighbor, for "Inasmuch as ye have done it unto one of the least of these my brethren, ye have done it unto me." But in order to give our neighbor the best that we have, it is not enough to draw from out of the doctrine, as one would write a book; rather we owe our neighbor in a certain way what we owe to God: what we fulfill for God in secret we can also then give our neighbor. What we do spiritually also benefits our neighbor. He who out of carelessness neglects spiritual duties should say to himself that he also owes their fulfillment to his neighbor; what we do not wish to do for ourselves, we should at least do for others. We therefore owe our fellow men in a twofold way: first the intention to give something, and secondly the gift. The first is not enough if one does not have the second, and the second is not enough if one does not have the first.

Or stated differently yet: our fellow brother also stands before us in a twofold way, first as the one who receives in God, and secondly as the one who teaches us on God's behalf; in the first case the thanks come from God, and in the second case the teaching is from God. For every man, even the most ignorant, can teach us in some way; this is what the Hindus call an *upaguru*. Animals and plants are our neighbors also, and as such have a claim to our confraternity and can teach us something.

Thus is God in our neighbor. God is also in our own soul in a twofold way: first in the center of our being, in the pure Spirit which is one with Truth, and secondly in worship, in the fulfillment of duty, in good deeds, and above all in the invocation of the supreme Name. Man must repose in the Spirit, and he must perform good deeds.

God is also in the environment in a twofold way: on the one hand in the destiny we experience every day, and on the other hand in the symbols, the "signs", that we see and hear every day. In both of these we must think of God: in experience and in what we see; in destiny and symbols. The environment reminds us of God, and this is its spiritual function, its mystical significance.

God, the world, I, thou; fundamentally, however, there are only two things, God and the soul, everything else being for us in some way either God or the soul. And fundamentally there is only God.

4

The certitudes that we may have *a priori* need to be nourished by faith; faith is an attitude of calmness, trust, resignation, of "poverty" and of existential simplicity. Man is so made that intellectual certitude does not suffice; man is not just a thinking being, he also lives. Life is situated outside of our certitudes, thus it must come to meet them through faith. Faith is the feminine element which is added to the masculine element that is certitude. Within a traditional civilization, faith is something easy, it is so to speak in the air one breathes, but in the modern world it is doubt that is in the air, this doubt that exacerbates our need for logical explanations and our critical sense. Faith is a kind of beauty, whereas doubt has something of miserliness and envy, it is a kind of vindictive bitterness. Faith is nourished by metaphysical certitude on the one hand and by life in God on the other; the pivot of life in God is prayer and virtue. Virtue consists in giving up the tension and heaviness that the fall has superimposed on our primordial nature; prayer is the fixation of the powers of our soul in God; the quintessence of prayer is the invocation, "ejaculatory orison"; it could also be called "pure prayer" or the "synthesis of prayers".

5

The reasonings characteristic of a humble man—and hence the criteria of humility—are the following:

God has willed that I exist; I accept, then, this intention of God, for in no case can my will be better than His. The fact that I exist proves that I must exist.

God has given me enough natural gifts to save my soul; and this is all He asks of me. He does not ask me to be great in any way, nor to have particular gifts, but He does ask me to abstain from evil and to practice prayer, and this is something every man can do; man by very definition is capable of his salvation, thanks to the means that God has put at his disposal.

A humble man tends to rely on the insights of others; he does not readily take important initiatives and he never needlessly presents others with a *fait accompli*; he does not get angry merely because someone blames him, for what matters is not whether or not others scold us, but whether they are right or wrong.

There is a false, egocentric, introverted, and psychologizing humility that is simply indirect pride. A humble person never closes himself to his peers, and still less to his superiors, on the pretext that he is of no importance; he never thinks he has problems that others would be incapable of understanding, for such problems do not exist; to believe so is pride and insolence. Similarly, a humble disciple never decides for himself what is important and what is not, he submits to the judgment of a peer or of a superior; otherwise every disciple could decide, on the pretext of humility, that serious matters—if sometimes small in appearance—are unimportant.

Humility is not a specialty of modestly endowed men; it is incumbent on every man. For even the most intelligent and most spiritual of men will ask for advice when he considers taking action of any kind; he will do so not because he believes that someone else is necessarily superior to himself, but because it is natural for a person to communicate with others, as it is always possible that others have insights that escape us. To rely on oneself without any verification from the outside is inhuman and monstrous, and it is what is called pride.

Moreover, it is not enough to want to be humble, one must furthermore know what humility is, and to this end one has to inform oneself; for knowledge is transmitted.

To suffer from the feeling of our littleness to the point of not being able to overcome it by simply accomplishing what God asks of us, and to the point of putting into question our very existence, is a form of pride. A humble man—hence every man of good will—accepts his own human scope, even if it be quite modest, and confines himself to doing what, being human and not an animal, he must certainly do. Life has no other meaning.

And besides, it is not for us to judge whether we are great or small; it is God who will judge this. We are obliged solely to follow the Path that every man must follow; and "My yoke is easy, and My burden is light".

6

Temptations against faith are possible because faith is situated in the will and not in the intellect. Faith is a matter of grace, will, and reason, and only indirectly of knowledge; it has an aspect of "obscurity", which implies the possibility of "temptations", rather as the fallibility of reason implies the possibility of errors, or as the freedom to do evil implies the possibility of sin.

Hindu *bhakta*s do not have this temptation—they have others—because Hindus are more intuitive than Westerners. Westerners are rationalists, which the Hindus are not.

The Christian saints do not fall into this temptation, precisely because their sanctity preserves them from it. Sanctity replaces, at the level of faith, the intellectual certitude of the *jnānin*. Once the crisis is overcome, mystics have certitude through grace; it is then much deeper than that of certain metaphysical theoreticians.

From the human point of view, sanctity is perfect conformity of the will to the divine Truth. One can be a saint before having attained the primordial state, but one will certainly attain this state—be it only at the moment of death—owing to the perfection of the will directed towards God.

In the case of the *jnānin*, intellectuality is an aspect of sanctity, but it is never its sole constituent; also necessary are abstention from transgressions, and the perfection of concentration on the Absolute.

7

All is love, and there is nothing outside of it; in this profound meaning of the term, love should not be understood in a human manner, obviously, but in its most elementary sense; indeed, love is finally nothing other than the tendency of a subject towards an object in view of their union, and knowledge is nothing other than the purest and most perfect mode of this union. Therefore, one must understand that there is no divergence between knowledge and love in their synthetic and profound reality, for both terms designate this selfsame reality in relation to different modes or degrees; and if the Judeo-Christian Scriptures have stressed love more often than knowledge, this is because love is the most immediately tangible expression of this reality. Humanity, whose terrestrial state is the starting point of our spiritual journey, procreates itself through love and therefore exists through love, so that the vilest man is raised above himself and is sanctified by natural love; through love he partakes in that which transcends and dissolves his individual imperfection, and for such a man, it is even the only possible manner to become as it were symbolically divine, albeit in a way that is clearly transitory and more or less accidental. Maternal love too has something sacred as does all natural love, from which it derives; the mother loves her child more than herself, which indicates that in this love she transcends her singular "ego".

8

The relationship *Ātmā-Māyā* is reflected at every ontological Degree and in everything that is contained in Relativity or "Illusion": thus the creating Principle has its creative potentialities as well as its divine essence, and "Heaven" comprises angelic and paradisal possibilities as well as the universal Intellect (*Buddhi, Trimūrti*); this is the same as the Islamic distinction between the angels and the blessed—taken together—and the "Spirit" of God (*Rūh*). The same distinction exists—*mutatis mutandis*—between the mental faculties and the Intellect, or between the differentiated elements and the underlying ether. The relationship *Ātmā-Māyā* reverberates even in the opposition between good and evil, which pertains only to the "terrestrial" domain, in the universal sense that we give to this term.

If between *Ātmā* and *Māyā* there is a relationship of analogy, there is also a relationship of inversion owing to the fact that the cosmogonic process cannot but lead away from the divine Source; whence arise the three qualities or tendencies characteristic of Relativity-Illusion, namely *Sattva, Rajas,* and *Tamas:* "Luminosity", "Heat", and "Darkness". *Māyā* is "luminous" because it conveys the reflection of *Ātmā*—of necessity, since it is a projection of it; further, it is "hot" or "igneous" because it produces manifestation and because it "desires" it and "expands" it; and lastly, *Māyā* is "dark" insofar as it leads away from *Ātmā*, and this is its aspect of inversion, which contradicts the tendency of the Supreme Principle "towards itself".

Thus *Māyā* contains on the one hand the divine aspects of "Power", "Consciousness", and "Beatitude", which it reflects, and on the other hand the tendencies of "Luminosity", "Heat", and "Darkness", which are its own characteristics; it is thus that *Māyā* comprises two trinities, one "horizontal" and homogeneous since its reason for being is to reflect *Ātmā*, and another that is "vertical" and contradictory since its reason for being is also to differentiate from *Ātmā*. These two trinities are consequently to be met with wherever there is Relativity and Existence; Existence emerging from Relativity, for the Creator is not "existing", but He is "relative" in relation to His transpersonal Essence, the pure Absolute.

9

Men are forever swaying to and fro between the consciousness of being a divine manifestation and the command—or the necessity—to submit to God. Thus there are many confusions, misunderstandings, and false presumptions; man often thinks he is absolutely good because in his genius he manifests something divine; he forgets that man as such is always man. So is it also with civilizations: they are at the same time good and not good; they are struck down on account of the bad they contain, but survive the blow because they are good and divine. Caesar was divine, and yet a man.

10

When it is said: "Judge not that ye be not judged", this does not mean that we should not use our God-given powers of discrimination to judge things aright, but merely that we should not let ourselves be led by passion into unjustly condemning them; the meaning is: judge as you yourself would wish to be judged, that is, from the standpoint of truth and with as much indulgence as possible; I do not say: with all indulgence, for love of one's neighbor must never be allowed to falsify the truth. We may and must see the extenuating circumstances that are there, and thus in the nature of things, but we have no right to invent such circumstances; that is an essential distinction. There are also extenuating circumstances that are too general to have any weight; to take them into account would be to confuse different planes; but justice is, above all, to put each thing in its proper place.

11

When one closes one's eyes and pronounces the supreme Name—as such or as part of a sacred formula—one stands then before God; this standing before God is everything; it is the highest, best, and most real thing that this life can offer us; it is the hereafter and eternity. Standing before God is our primary function on earth, it belongs to being human. Symbolically, closing the eyes corresponds to the Holy Virgin—the image of Buddha expresses the same thing—in the sense of the well-known saying from the Song of Songs; at first this closing of the eyes is darkness, then it becomes inner music and golden depth. It is no accident that when one listens to a beautiful piece of music one is apt to close one's eyes; for music is the inner experience of what, in the visible world, we encounter as beauty of forms. "Verily God is beautiful and He loves beauty."

12

When experiencing mental difficulties, it is important not to forget that there are three principal ways of confronting them, according to the ternaries *Makhāfah, Mahabbah, Ma'rifah*, and *Karma, Bhakti, Jnāna*: that is to say, one always needs 1. a measure of constraint, discipline, know-how, and of action as well, then 2. a measure of joy—for joy lies within us, so that it suffices to extract it from our substance and to project it into the *mantra*—and finally 3. a measure of consciousness of the nature of things, hence discernment, analysis, a searching for the causes; and depending on our state, preeminence must be granted to one or another of these three means. Thus: when the mind is agitated, we must ask ourselves why it is so, and to be aware of the illusory character of that which agitates it, or of the disproportion between the object agitating us and the infinite Essence of our nature, or between the relative and the Absolute; for agitation cannot but cease when its cause is perfectly understood, and once it is reduced to its correct proportions; in any case, whatever the causes may be, we have no choice, since we are made for Eternity. Next— or first, depending on what sequence is more effective, it does not matter—we must throw ourselves with perfect carefreeness into the *mantra*; let the *samsāra* be what it will, we will not change it, and the essential is that the Infinite welcome us. This is the point of view of faith and trust, of joy and also beauty; this is connected to the beauty of the sacred Image, the language of which is direct and somehow musical; we are husks, Reality is music. In any case, one must act, and thus at all costs practice the *japa*; the whole question, I repeat, is that of knowing which of the two other supports—one intellectual and the other affective—we shall give our preference to, depending on circumstances or depending on our character.

13

Exoterically, the word *Īmān* means: the acceptance of the dogmas of Islam; esoterically, it means: metaphysical knowledge; doctrinal discernment; total Truth; for the latter contains all dogma possible.

Exoterically, the word *Islām* means: the practice of the prescriptions of Islam; esoterically, it means: the conformation of the soul to

Truth, Virtue; for Virtue is the perfect abandonment (*islām*) to the Will of God.

Exoterically, the word *Ihsān* means: "believing" (*Īmān*) and "doing" (*Islām*) as perfectly as possible, hence practicing the religion with sincerity; esoterically, it means: concentration upon the Real, hence the invocation; for the latter summarizes all religion.

Īmān, Islām, Ihsān: Comprehension of the Real; Conformation to the Real; Concentration upon the Real or the Invocation. Metaphysical Doctrine; moral Comportment or Beauty of character; invocatory Method. Intelligence; Soul; Will.

14

Wisdom cannot bear fruit in a soul without virtues, for the object of Wisdom is God, and God is virtuous. God is virtuous, not because virtues limit Him, which is impossible, but because there is no virtue that does not derive from Him, and that does not exist in Him in an infinite manner. The fundamental divine virtue is Beauty; it explains everything. It is from it that are derived Goodness and Strength, Mercy and Justice, Love and Will. As for Wisdom, it is not a virtue, it is Being itself: God being wise in Himself, He is wise in each virtue; there is no virtue that excludes His wisdom. Justice excludes Mercy—not in an absolute fashion, but in a certain respect—while neither Justice nor Mercy exclude Wisdom, any more than they exclude Sanctity or Infinity.

Metaphysical wisdom is certainly independent of human virtues, but the man who wishes to realize this wisdom is not independent of the virtues, since it is through them that he participates humanly in the Truth.

EDITOR'S NOTES

Numbers in bold indicate pages in the text for which the following citations and explanations are provided.

Author's Preface

xv: For an extended discussion of what the term *rationalism* properly entails, see the author's "Rationalism Real and Apparent", in *Logic and Transcendence: A New Translation with Selected Letters*, ed. James S. Cutsinger (Bloomington, Indiana: World Wisdom, 2009), pp. 28-45.

xvii: For a more detailed exposition on *existentialism*, see the author's "Letter on Existentialism", in *The Essential Frithjof Schuon*, ed. Seyyed Hossein Nasr (Bloomington, Indiana: World Wisdom, 2005), pp. 492-95.

The Eye of the Heart

5: Note 8: *Augustine* (354-430) was Bishop of the North African city of Hippo and one of the greatest of the Western Church *Fathers*.

The *"Eye of the Heart"* is referred to in *Plotinian doctrine* as ὁ μόνος ὀφθαλμός (*ho mónos ophthalmós*). Plotinus (c. 205-270), founder of the Neoplatonic school, endeavored to synthesize the teachings of Plato and Aristotle in his monumental *Enneads*, a collection of discourses compiled by his disciple Porphyry.

In his *Letter to the Ephesians*, the Apostle *Paul* writes, "That the God of our Lord Jesus Christ, the Father of glory, may give unto you the spirit of wisdom and revelation in the knowledge of him: The *eyes of your heart* being enlightened" (1:17-18).

In the *eighth beatitude* of the *Sermon on the Mount*, Christ says: "Blessed are the *pure* in *heart*: for *they shall see God*" (Matt. 5:8).

Note 10: The *divine essence* is referred to as ὕπαρξις (*húparxis*) *in* Orthodox *Greek theology* (see the author's chapter below, "*Nirvāna*", p. 36).

6: Note 12: *Meister Eckhart* (c. 1260-1327), a German Dominican writer whom the author regarded as the greatest of Christian metaphysicians and

175

esoterists, proclaimed that "There is something in the soul which is uncreated and uncreatable; if the whole soul were such, it would be uncreated and uncreatable, and this is the Intellect" (*Aliquid est in anima quod est increatum et increabile; si tota anima esset talis, esset increata et increabilis, et hoc est Intellectus*).

7: Note 14: The passage beginning "*I am blind and I do not see the things of this world . . .*" comes from an unpublished statement by the *wise man of the Oglala Sioux*, Nicholas Black Elk (c. 1863-1950), recorded by Joseph Epes Brown in a letter which was in the possession of the author. Brown, an associate of the author, was responsible for compiling *The Sacred Pipe: Black Elk's Account of the Seven Rites of the Oglala Sioux*, first published in 1953.

8: Note 14: *John Climacus* (c. 570-649), a monk and later abbot of Sinai, is best known for his *Ladder of Paradise*, a treatise on the spiritual life in which the thirty steps (chapters) of the "ladder" (*klimax* in Greek) correspond to the age of Christ at his Baptism.

9: In Hindu iconography the *Eye of Shiva*, sometimes called the *third eye*, is the organ of mystical insight and is usually depicted on the forehead.

Shiva is the third god of the Hindu trinity (*trimūrti*)—Brahmā being the first and Vishnu the second—and is associated with the powers of generation and destruction.

"*Iron age*": in its most representative form, the Hindu doctrine of cosmic cycles divides time qualitatively into *mahāyuga*s or "great ages", each comprising four lesser ages (*yuga*s) or periods of time, namely, the *Krita-Yuga* (the "golden" age of Western tradition), *Tretā-Yuga* ("silver"), *Dvāpara-Yuga* ("bronze"), and *Kali-Yuga* ("iron"), the latter "*dark age*" being characterized by *fallen humanity*'s loss of the *consciousness of eternity*.

10: *Mansur Al-Hallaj* (858-922), the first Sufi martyr, was dismembered and crucified for his mystical pronouncement, "I am the Truth" (*Anā'l-Haqq*).

On Knowledge

13: For further reflections on *All-Possibility, Infinity, evil,* and *nothingness,* see the author's "The Question of Theodices", in *Form and Substance in the Religions* (Bloomington, Indiana: World Wisdom, 2002), pp. 151-63 and "The Two Problems", in *In the Face of the Absolute: A New Translation with Selected Letters*, ed. Harry Oldmeadow (Bloomington, Indiana: World Wisdom, 2014), pp. 27-31.

An-Nūr

15: Note 1: For a fuller discussion of *Mary* as *Virgin* and as *Mother*, see the author's "Christic and Virginal Mysteries", in *Gnosis: Divine Wisdom: A New Translation with Selected Letters*, ed. James S. Cutsinger (Bloomington, Indiana: World Wisdom, 2006), pp. 119-24.

16: Abd Allah *Ibn Abbas* (c. 618-c. 688), a cousin of the Prophet, was revered by Muslims for his knowledge and expertise in Koranic exegesis.

Note 1 (cont.): The Arabic term *Al-Hayūlā* is derived from the Greek ὕλη (*hylé*), meaning "*first Matter*".

Muhyi al-Din *Ibn Arabi* (1165-1240) was a prolific and profoundly influential Sufi mystic, known in tradition as the Shaykh al-Akbar ("great master"). He is the author of numerous works, including *Meccan Revelations* and *Bezels of Wisdom*.

17: Sunan *Said ibn Mansur* (d.c. 842) was the compiler of an early collection of nearly three thousand *ahādīth*, or sayings of the Prophet.

Note 5: For *Shiva*, see editor's note for "The Eye of the Heart", p. 9.

Ali Ibn Abi Talib (597-661) was the cousin and son-in-law of the Prophet Muhammad and the fourth caliph of Islam.

18: Note 5 (cont.): For the Angel Gabriel's *annunciation* that *the Virgin Mary* would miraculously conceive and give birth to a son named Jesus, see Luke 1:26-38 and Matt. 1:18-23.

Note 8: "*In truth, before Abraham was, I am*" (John 8:58).

19: Note 8 (cont.): The *Immaculate Conception* is the Roman Catholic dogma that, from the first moment of her conception, the Blessed Virgin Mary was free from all stain of original sin.

20: Note 9: For *Plotinus*, see editor's note for "The Eye of the Heart", p. 5, Note 8.

The "*Universal Soul*" of the Plotinian system is referred to as ψυχή (*psukhè*).

Note 10: *Apophatic theology* or the "way of negation" (*via negativa*), is a means of approaching God by stating what He is not.

21: Abu Muhammad Abd ar-Rahman *Ibn Abi Hatim* ar-Razi (854-938) was the author of an extensive *commentary* (*tafsīr*) on the Koran.

22: Note 12: The *Études traditionnelles* articles *"Ar-Rūh"* and *"Note sur l'angélologie de l'alphabet arabe"* ("Notes on Angelic Number Symbolism in the Arabic Alphabet") first appeared in English in *Insights into Islamic Esoterism and Taoism*, ed. Samuel D. Fohr (Hillsdale, New York: Sophia Perennis, 2001), pp. 24-32.

René Guénon (1886-1951), a French metaphysician and prolific scholar of religions, was one of the formative authorities of the perennialist school and a frequent contributor to the traditionalist journal *Études traditionnelles* ("Traditional Studies").

Abu Hamid Muhammad *Al-Ghazali* (c. 1058-1111), often regarded as the greatest religious authority in Islam after the Prophet Muhammad, was a jurist and theologian before entering upon the Sufi path.

23: The *"Lesser Mysteries"* of Western Antiquity, secondary to the *"Greater Mysteries"*, were secret cultic rites associated with the Greek city of Eleusis.

Brahmā is the first god of the Hindu trinity (*trimūrti*)—Vishnu being the second and Shiva the third—and is associated with the power of creation.

The Latin *fiat lux*, "let there be light" (Gen. 1:3), appears in the Vulgate translation of the Old Testament.

24: *"The day when the Spirit and the angels will raise themselves in ranks"* (Koran, *Sūrah* "The Tiding" [78]:38).

"Allāh, *Lord of the degrees* (ma'ārij) *by which the angels and the Spirit will mount towards Him"* (Koran, *Sūrah* "The Ascending Ways" [70]:3-4).

"*The angels and the Spirit have descended in it* (*in the night of the Revelation*)" (Koran, *Sūrah* "Power" [97]:4).

Note 16: *Dionysius the Areopagite*, a disciple of Saint Paul (Acts 17:34, though dated c. 500 by many scholars) and perhaps the greatest of all Christian masters of apophatic theology, was the author of several important mystical works including *The Divine Names*, *The Mystical Theology*, and *The Celestial Hierarchy*.

25: *"The Spirit of God moved upon the face of the waters"* (Gen. 1:2).

Vishnu is the second deity in the Hindu trinity (*trimūrti*)—Brahmā being the first and Shiva the third—and is associated with the preservation and maintenance of the cosmos.

26: Note 17: Mount *Kailasa*, a Himalayan peak in Tibet, is sacred to Hindus, Buddhists, and Jains.

28: Note 19 (cont.): The saying, *"There is no divinity but God, and Muhammad is the Prophet of God"* is referred to as the Islamic testification of faith (*Shahādah*).

Note 20: *Kali* is the destructive and transformative manifestation of the Hindu goddess Parvati, consort of Shiva.

Yama is the Vedic god of death, Lord of the Underworld, and one of the eight guardians of the universe.

29: Note 23: For *the bull of the* Dharma *in the Hindu tradition*, see editor's note for "The Eye of the Heart", p. 9.

Note 24: Jalal ad-Din *As-Suyuti* (1445-1505) was a Persian-Egyptian medieval theologian and teacher in the Islamic tradition.

Nirvāna

33: Note 1: *Macarius of Egypt* (c. 300-c. 390), or *Macarius* the Great, a Desert Father renowned for his sanctity and miracles, founded an ascetic community which became one of the chief centers of early Egyptian monasticism.

Palamite theology is the doctrine of Gregory Palamas (c. 1296-1359), an Athonite monk and later Archbishop of Thessalonica, best known for his defense of the contemplative techniques used by the Hesychast Fathers and for his distinction *in divinis* between the Divine Essence and the "Energies".

Areopagitic theology stems from Dionysius the Areopagite (see editor's note for "*An-Nūr*", p. 24).

Patristic theology refers to the religious writings of the early Church Fathers.

34: Note 4: *"Why callest thou me good? God alone is good"* (Mark 10:18, Luke 18:19).

36: *"For in Heaven there is no marrying or giving in marriage"* (Matt. 22:30).

The theology of the Christian East makes *the distinction between the Processions or proódoi* (προόδοι), *and the impenetrable Substratum or húparxis* (ὕπαρξις), *that is, between the Energies and the Essence, or between Being and Beyond-Being.*

38: Abu Zakariya Yahya *Muadh Ar-Razi* (830-871) was a *Sufi* teacher and writer in central Asia.

Christ could say that He is the "Life": "Jesus saith unto him, I am the way, the truth, and *the life*: no man cometh unto the Father, but by me" (John 14:6).

39: "*Brahman is not in the world*": Elsewhere the author writes: "It is useless to seek to realize that 'I am *Brahma*' before understanding that 'I am not *Brahma*'; it is useless to seek to realize that '*Brahma* is my true Self' before understanding that '*Brahma* is outside me'; it is useless to seek to realize that '*Brahma* is pure Consciousness' before understanding that '*Brahma* is the almighty Creator'. It is not possible to understand that the statement 'I am not *Brahma*' is false before having understood that it is true. Likewise it is not possible to understand that the statement '*Brahma* is outside me' is not precise before having understood that it is; and likewise again it is not possible to understand that the statement '*Brahma* is the almighty Creator' contains an error before having understood that it expresses a truth" (*Spiritual Perspectives and Human Facts: A New Translation with Selected Letters*, ed. James S. Cutsinger [Bloomington, Indiana: World Wisdom, 2007], p. 116).

40: Paramahamsa *Ramakrishna* (1834-86), a *bhakta* of the Hindu Goddess Kali, was one of the great Hindu saints of modern times. See the author's "*Vedānta*", in *Spiritual Perspectives and Human Facts: A New Translation with Selected Letters*, ed. James S. Cutsinger (Bloomington, Indiana: World Wisdom, 2007), pp. 124-26.

For further reflections on *the Holy Virgin*, see the author's "Christic and Virginal Mysteries", in *Gnosis: Divine Wisdom: A New Translation with Selected Letters*, ed. James S. Cutsinger (Bloomington, Indiana: World Wisdom, 2006), pp. 119-24.

41: The *Kabbalah* is a mystical stream of esoteric teachings within the Judaic tradition.

Lakshmi, regarded in most Hindu traditions as the wife of Vishnu, is the Goddess of good fortune and the embodiment of beauty.

Although never defined as dogma, popular recognition of the Blessed *Virgin as "Co-Redemptress"* dates from ancient times and can be found in both the Eastern and the Western Churches.

The third of the Ecumenical Councils, meeting in Ephesus (431), declared that the *Virgin* Mary is rightly called *Mater Dei* or "*Mother of God*".

Christian tradition refers to the *Virgin* Mary as *"Spouse of the Holy Spirit"* since it was the Holy Spirit, and not her husband Joseph, who brought about the conception of Jesus in her womb (see Matt. 1:18, 20, Luke 1:34).

Note 13: In Judaism, the *Shekhinah* is the dwelling-place or presence of God in the world; traditionally it was thought to dwell in the Holy of Holies in the Temple of Jerusalem.

Durga, "the unfathomable one", is one of the most widely used names in Hinduism for the Divine *Mother*. The consort of Shiva, she destroys the demon of ignorance and confers blessings of knowledge and love on spiritual devotees.

Kwan-Yin (*Chinese*), *Kwannon* (Japanese), or *Avalokiteshvara* (*Sanskrit*) is the Buddhist goddess or *Bodhisattva* of Mercy.

In Tibetan Buddhism, *Tara*, the "Mother of all the Buddhas" or "Mother of Compassion", is the female counterpart of the *Bodhisattva Avalokiteshvara*.

Pté-San-Win is the heavenly White Buffalo Cow Woman who brought the *Sacred Pipe* to the Plains Indians of North America. For an explication of this ritual instrument's symbolism and religious significance, see the author's "The Sacred Pipe", in *The Feathered Sun* (Bloomington, Indiana: World Wisdom, 1990), pp. 44-70. Two of the author's paintings of *Pté-San-Win* can be found in the same volume on pp. 131, 137.

Krishna is the eighth *avatāra* of the Hindu God Vishnu.

The Posthumous States

44: Note 4 (cont.): The *Law of Manu* (*Mānava Dharma Shāstra* or *Manu-smriti*) is an ancient collection of moral, social, and legal prescriptions under-stood to be binding on all orthodox Hindus.

45: Note 5: *Thomas Aquinas* (c. 1225-74) was an immensely influential Italian Dominican priest and scholastic theologian, known in Catholic tradition as the "Angelic Doctor". His best-known works are the *Summa theologiae* and the *Summa Contra Gentiles.*

Wisdom after the flesh: "In simplicity and godly sincerity, not with fleshly wisdom, but by the grace of God, we have had our conversation in the world" (2 Cor. 1:12).

48: Note 11: The author provides a masterly account of the principles informing the widely-misunderstood Hindu *caste* system in his essay "The Meaning of Caste", in *Language of the Self* (Bloomington, Indiana: World Wisdom, 1999), pp. 113-46.

49: *To be perfectly man is "to become God"*: This essential teaching is common to many Church Fathers, including Irenaeus (c. 130-c. 200), according to whom "the Son of God became the Son of man so that man, by entering into communion with the Word and thus receiving divine sonship, might become a son of God" (*Against Heresies*, 3:19); and Athanasius (c. 296-373), who wrote, "The Son of God became man in order that we might become God" (*On the Incarnation*, 54:3).

Note 12: *Basil* the Great (c. 330-79), one of the Cappadocian Fathers, and *Cyril of Alexandria* (d. 444), Patriarch of that city, were key figures in promoting the classical Patristic teaching that the purpose of the Incarnation is the deification of man.

Christianity and Buddhism

53: *The "kingdom" of the Buddha, like that of Christ, "is not of this world"*: "My *kingdom is not of this world*; if my kingdom were of this world, then would my servants fight, that I should not be delivered to the Jews: but now is my kingdom not from thence" (John 18:36).

Note 1: *Rama* is the seventh *avatāra* or incarnation of the Hindu God Vishnu and the hero of the *Rāmāyana*, the oldest of the Hindu epics.

For *Krishna*, see editor's note for "*Nirvāna*", p. 41, Note 13.

The prophet *Abraham* is a Biblical patriarch in the monotheistic traditions of Judaism, Christianity, and Islam, and is considered the father of both the Jews and the Arabs through his sons Isaac and Ishmael.

Moses is a prophet, religious leader, and law-giver within the Abrahamic monotheisms, renowned for leading the Israelites out of Egypt and receiving the Ten Commandments on Mt. Sinai.

Muhammad (570-632), the prophet and founder of Islam, received a series of divine revelations from 610 to 632 which comprise the Koran.

54: "*Dead letter*": "The *letter* killeth, but the spirit giveth life" (2 Cor. 3:6).

The *Mosaic Law* refers to the *Torah* or first five books of the Hebrew Bible, traditionally attributed to Moses.

Note 2: *Shankara* (788-820) is the pre-eminent exponent of *Advaita Vedānta* and regarded by the author as the greatest of Hindu metaphysicians.

Note 3: For *the apophatic sense*, see editor's note for "*An-Nūr*", p. 20, Note 10.

55: "Give not that which is holy unto the *dogs*, neither cast ye your pearls before *swine*, lest they trample under their feet, and turn again and rend you" (Matt. 7:6).

"*Wisdom according to the flesh*": "For our rejoicing is this, the testimony of our conscience, that in simplicity and godly sincerity, not with *fleshly wisdom*, but by the grace of God, we have had our conversation in the world" (2 Cor. 1:12).

Wisdom "*according to the Spirit*": "For those who live according to the flesh set their minds on the things of the flesh, but those who live *according to the spirit* set their minds on the things of the spirit" (Rom. 8:5).

Note 5: *Judas* Iscariot, one of the twelve disciples, betrayed Christ to the Sanhedrin in the Garden of Gethsemane. At the Last Supper Christ handed Judas *bread*, saying, "I speak not of you all: I know whom I have chosen: but that the scripture may be fulfilled, He that eateth bread with me hath lifted up his heel against me" (John 13:18).

56: For the *caste system*, see editor's note for "The Posthumous States", p. 48, Note 11.

Note 6: *What Saint Paul says of circumcision*: "For he is not a Jew, which is one outwardly; neither is that *circumcision* which is outward *in the flesh*: But he is a Jew which is one inwardly; and *circumcision* is that of the heart, *in the spirit*, and not in the letter; whose praise is not of men, but of God" (Rom. 2:28-29).

57: *Psychologism* may be defined as the assumption that man's nature and behavior can be explained by psychological factors which can only be laid bare by a scientific and empirical psychology. Elsewhere the author speaks of psychologism as "the prejudice of wishing to bring everything back to psychological causes, which can only be individual and profane. Everything then becomes the fruit of a contingent elaboration: Revelation becomes poetry, religions are inventions, sages are 'thinkers' and 'researchers', that is, mere logicians, if indeed they are still such; infallibility and inspiration no longer exist; error becomes an 'interesting' and quantitative 'contribution' to 'culture', and so on; if every mental phenomenon is not reduced to material causes, there is at least the denial of any supernatural or even simply supra-sensory cause and, by the same token, the negation of any principial truth. According to this way of seeing things, man is doubtless more than just his body, but he is nonetheless reduced to being a human animal, which means that he is no longer anything; for man limited to himself is no longer truly human" ("The Five Divine Presences", in *Form and Substance in the Religions* [Bloomington, Indiana: World Wisdom, 2002], p. 64).

Know how to tell a wolf from a lamb: "Beware of false prophets, which come to you in sheep's clothing, but inwardly they are ravening wolves" (Matt. 7:15).

The law of *karma*, or the *mechanism of concordant actions and reactions*, most immediately concerning the equilibrium of natural forces and energies, is found everywhere in the East but particularly in the Taoist tradition. As the French metaphysician René Guénon (1886-1951) remarked, it is "a principle that does not concern the corporeal world alone, but indeed the totality of manifestation in all its modes and states" ("On Mathematical Notation", in *Miscellanea* [Hillsdale, New York: Sophia Perennis, 2003], p. 7

Christ's Law—requiring that one love one's enemy and turn the other cheek: "But I say unto you, That ye resist not evil: but whosoever shall smite thee on thy right cheek, turn to him the other also. . . . Love your enemies, bless them that curse you, do good to them that hate you . . ." (Matt. 5:39, 44).

"For the love of God": "Thou shalt *love* the Lord thy *God* with all thy heart, and with all thy soul, and with all thy strength, and with all thy mind" (Luke 10:27; cf. Matt. 22:37, Mark 12:30, Deut. 6:5).

58: The *"letter killeth, but the spirit giveth life"* (2 Cor. 3:6).

59: A *categorical imperative* refers to an absolute or unconditional require-ment. The phrase is most commonly associated with the German philoso-pher, Immanuel Kant (1724-1804) and his *Groundwork for the Metaphysics of Morals* (1785).

60: Note 14: The apostle *Luke* was one of the four evangelists, or ascribed authors of the canonical Gospels, as well as the author of "The Acts of the Apostles" in the *New Testament*.

King Prasenajit of Shravasti (sixth century B.C.), sometimes known as Pas-enadi, belonged to the Aiksvaka dynasty and ruled Kosala (modern-day Oudh).

King Udayana of Kaushambi was the ruler of Vatsa and a contemporary of Gautama Buddha.

Note 15: "And he took bread, and when he had given thanks, he brake it, and gave to them, saying, This is my body which is given for you: *this* do *in remembrance of me*" (Luke 22:19).

61: The "*gift of tongues*", mentioned in the Epistles of Paul and Peter (1 Cor. 14:27, 1 Pet. 4:10), is the miraculous ability to speak in a foreign and unknown language.

"And the *Word* was *made flesh*, and dwelt among us" (John 1:14).

Note 16: *Tao-Cho* (562-645) was the second patriarch of Pure Land Buddhism.

Daisetz Teitaro Suzuki (1870-1966) was a leading Japanese scholar who promoted Western interest in Chinese and Japanese forms of Buddhism. He published three volumes of *Essays in Zen Buddhism* between 1927 and 1933.

62: The *Paraclete* refers, in Christian tradition, to the Holy Spirit (see John 14:16, 26).

Hesychasm is the spiritual practice of certain monks of the Christian East whose aim is to attain a state of *hesychia*, or inner stillness, through the practice of the Jesus Prayer or other "prayer of the heart".

Note 18: "*God within us*": "Behold, the kingdom of *God* is *within you*" (Luke 17:21).

The Mystery of the *Bodhisattva*

63: *Shakyamuni*, meaning "the sage of the Shakyas", is one of the epithets by which the Buddha is known, as well as by his name "Siddhartha Gautama".

Buddhism distinguishes three ages after the passing of Shakyamuni Buddha: a first age when the "Law of the Buddha" is fulfilled; a second age when it is merely "imitated"; and a third age—the "*Latter Times*"—when it is "forgotten" (see author's note 11 below).

64: Note 2: *Brahmanism* is the doctrine of Hindu brahmins or priests.

65: *Amitabha* (Sanskrit), or *Amida* (Japanese), is the Buddha of "infinite light" who, as a *Bodhisattva* named Dharmakara, vowed not to enter *nirvāna* until he had brought all who invoked his Name into the *Paradise* of his Pure Land.

66: Note 3: *Nagarjuna* (c. 150-250), founder of the *Mādhyamika* or "middle way" school of Buddhism and widely regarded in the *Mahāyāna* tradition as a "second Buddha", is best known for his doctrine of *shūnyatā*, "voidness" or "emptiness", and for the correlative teaching that *Nirvāna* and *samsāra* are essentially identical.

67: Note 6: The *Mahā Prajnā Pāramitā Hridaya Sūtra*, "the Heart of Perfect Wisdom", is a celebrated *Mahāyāna* Buddhist *sūtra* or manual of aphorisms.

The *Vajracchedikā Prajnāpāramitā Sūtra* or "Diamond *Sūtra*" is a key text in *Mahāyāna* Buddhism, and especially Zen; it contains the discourse of the Buddha to a senior monk, Subhuti.

Note 7: *Christ strikes the Temple merchants*: "And Jesus went into the temple of God, and cast out all them that sold and bought in the temple, and overthrew the tables of the moneychangers, and the seats of them that sold doves, And said unto them, It is written, My house shall be called the house of prayer; but ye have made it a den of thieves" (Matt. 21:12-13; cf. Mark 11:15-17, Luke 19:45-46, John 2:13-16).

The *Scholastic distinction* of two kinds of truth identifies a truth *secundum fidem* ("according to faith") and a truth *secundum rationem* ("according to reason"), each thought to be valid within its respective domain.

68: Note 10: The *Family* (*āl*) of the Prophet Muhammad refers to the line of his descendants through his eldest daughter Fatimah and son-in-law Ali ibn Abi Talib.

The *Companions* (*sahb*) were the Prophet Muhammad's followers, that is, the early Muslims who lived in close proximity to him in Mecca and Medina in seventh century Arabia.

Note 11: For *Ali* ibn Abi Talib, see editor's note for "*An-Nūr*", p. 17.

Note 13: The *Tao Te Ching*, traditionally ascribed to the ancient Chinese sage Lao-Tzu, is the foundational text of the Taoist tradition.

69: *Shinran* (1173-1262), a disciple of Honen and founder of the *Jōdo-Shinshū* or "true pure land school" of Japanese Buddhism, rejected all "ways of effort" and advocated complete reliance on the "power of the other" as manifest in the Name of the Buddha Amida, a single pronunciation of which is sufficient for rebirth in the Buddha's paradise, *Sukhāvatī*.

70: *Honen* Shonin (1133-1212), founder of the *Jōdo* or "Pure Land school" in Japan, taught that everyone without exception, whether *celibate* or *married*, can be reborn into Amida's paradise simply by faithful repetition of his Name. For further commentary on Honen by the author, see "David, Honen, Shankara", in *To Have a Center: A New Translation with Selected Letters*, ed. Harry Oldmeadow (Bloomington, Indiana: World Wisdom, 2015), pp. 105-112.

71: The doctrine of *Apocatastasis*, universal salvation, was expounded by Origen (185-252), the most prolific and influential of the early Church Fathers. Esoterically the doctrine is linked with the recovery, through sleepless attention, of man's primordial unity in God.

Note 17: *Gregory of Nyssa* (c. 330-c. 395), a bishop of the early church and an influential mystical and ascetical writer, taught that the *nous* or intellect is the fundamental reason for man's intrinsic dignity as the "image of God".

Note 18: *Jacques Bacot* (1877-1965) was a French explorer and Tibetologist.

72: Note 20: *Milarepa* (c. 1052-c. 1135) was a renowned poet, ascetic, and *yogin* who became a great sage and one of the most revered figures in the Tibetan tradition.

73: Note 23: *Chaitanya* (1486-1533), a Vaishnavite Hindu spiritual teacher and ecstatic devotee of Krishna, was regarded by his followers as an *avatāra* of both Krishna and his consort Radha.

74: For *Avalokiteshvara*, see editor's note for "*Nirvāna*", p. 41, Note 13.

Manjushri is the *Bodhisattva* of discriminating wisdom, usually portrayed brandishing a sword that cuts through the knots of ignorance.

Note 24: *Theresa of Lisieux* (1873-1897), also known as "Theresa of the Child Jesus" and "The Little Flower", was a Carmelite nun who was drawn to the life of prayer as a very young child.

76: Note 26: For *Shankara*, see editor's note for "Christianity and Buddhism", p. 54, Note 2.

Catholic tradition associates *Mary Magdalene* with three distinct figures mentioned in the Scriptures: "a woman in the city, which was a sinner", who washed Jesus' feet "with tears, and did wipe them with the hairs of her head, and kissed his feet, and anointed them with ointment" (Luke 7:37-38); "Mary called Magdalene, out of whom went seven devils" (Luke 8:2); and the sister of Lazarus and Martha, who "sat at Jesus' feet, and heard his word", whom Christ commended, saying, "One thing is needful: and Mary hath chosen that good part, which shall not be taken from her" (Luke 10:39, 42; cf. John 11:1-2).

78: For *Ramakrishna*, see editor's note for "*Nirvāna*", p. 40.

Ramana Maharshi (1879-1950), widely regarded as the greatest Hindu sage of the twentieth century, experienced the identity of *Ātmā* and *Brahma* while still in his teens, and the fruit of this experience remained with him as a permanent spiritual station throughout his life.

For *Rama*, see editor's note for "Christianity and Buddhism", p. 53, Note 1.

For *Krishna*, see editor's note for "*Nirvāna*", p. 41, Note 13.

For the *Mother of Jesus* as "*Co-Redemptress*", see editor's note for "*Nirvāna*", p. 41.

79: *Truth "become flesh"*: "And the Word was made *flesh*" (John 1:14).

"*Each thing is* Ātmā": "*Ātmā* was indeed *Brahma* in the beginning. It knew only that 'I am *Brahma*'. Therefore It became all. And whoever among the gods knew It also became That; and the same with sages and men. . . . And to this day whoever in like manner knows 'I am *Brahma*' becomes all this universe. Even the gods cannot prevail against him, for he becomes their *Ātmā*" (*Brihadāranyaka Upanishad*, 1.4.10).

"*The world is false*; Brahma *is true*; the soul is not other than *Brahma*" is a summation of *Advaita Vedānta* traditionally ascribed to Shankara.

The Islamic testimony of faith (*Shahādah*) proclaims that "*There is no divinity save the one Divinity*" or "There is no god but God" (*Lā ilāha illā 'Llāh*).

The "celestial weight" of Revelation: "If We had caused this Koran to descend upon a mountain, thou (O Muhammad) verily hadst seen it humbled, rent asunder by the fear of God" (*Sūrah* "The Gathering" [59]:21).

81: The *breaking of the first Tables of the Law* refers to the two pieces of stone inscribed with the Ten Commandments revealed to *Moses on Mount Sinai*. The first tablet, inscribed by God, was smashed by Moses when he became enraged by the sight of the Israelites worshipping the Golden Calf (see Exod. 32:15-19).

"*Those who have ears to hear*": "He that hath *ears to hear*, let him hear" (Matt. 11:15, *passim*).

82: *Kshitigarbha* is a *Bodhisattva* who made a vow to postpone Buddhahood until all the hells are emptied of human souls; he is the guardian of children, deceased children, and hell-beings.

Akashagarbha is a *Bodhisattva* associated with infinite wisdom and compassion, and the twin brother of Kshitigarbha.

83: The *Gordian knot* stems from the legend of the Phrygian Gordias, whose son Midas tied his father's ox-cart to a post with an intricate knot which no one could untie. After Alexander the Great failed to unravel the knot, he cut through it with his sword.

"Though I speak with the tongues of men and of angels, and have not charity, I am become as *sounding brass, or a tinkling cymbal*" (1 Cor. 13:1).

Elementary Remarks on the Enigma of the *Kōan*

87: *Shinto*, the "way of the gods", is the indigenous religion of Japan, about which the author has written extensively in Part II of *Treasures of Buddhism: A New Translation with Selected Letters*, ed. Harry Oldmeadow (Bloomington, Indiana: World Wisdom, 2018).

"The Buddha's gesture, his smile, and by the flower he held in his hand" refers to the "Flower Sermon", a silent discourse in which the Buddha held up a white flower to signify the ineffable nature of *tathātā*, or "suchness". The origin of Zen Buddhism is attributed to this wordless teaching.

88: *Aristotle* (384-322 B.C.) was an ancient Greek philosopher whose works had a profound influence on the intellectual tradition of the three Semitic monotheisms.

Note 4: *Ta-Hui* (1089-1163) was a twelfth century Zen master.

Mahaprajnaparamita, "great transcendent wisdom", is the *shakti* or consort of the supreme *Ādi-Buddha*.

In the *Vajrayāna* tradition, *Vajradhara* ("diamond holder") is identified with the primordial or *Ādi-Buddha* and also with the *Dharmakāya* or "nirvanic" body of the Buddha.

Note 5: Carl G. *Jung* (1875-1961) was a one-time colleague of Sigmund Freud, the founder of psychoanalysis.

Jiddu *Krishnamurti* (1895-1986) was proclaimed by the Theosophical Society as the "New World Teacher" of the "Order of the Star of the East", a role which he disavowed. He later became an iconoclastic teacher and speaker on "spiritual" themes, and was popular in the West in the two decades before his death.

For *psychologism*, see editor's note for "Christianity and Buddhism", p. 57.

Īmān, Islām, Ihsān

90: Note 4: "*Blessed are they that have not seen, and yet have believed*" (John 20:29).

93: "He that loveth not knoweth not God; for *God is love*" (1 John 4:8).

Intellectuality and Civilization

96: *God alone is good*: "Why callest thou me good? There is none good but one, that is, God" (Matt. 19:17; Mark 10:18).

97: "*One thing needful*": "One thing is needful: and Mary hath chosen that good part, which shall not be taken from her" (Luke 10:42).

Modes of Spiritual Realization

101: *There are as many paths to God as there are human souls* (*At-turuqu ila 'Llāhi ka-nufūsi bani Adam*) is an Islamic formula often cited in Sufi circles.

102: "*Whatsoever ye have done to the least of these, ye have done it unto Me*" (Matt. 25:40).

Note 2: For *Shintoism*, see editor's note for "Elementary Remarks on the Enigma of the *Kōan*", p. 87.

The author has written extensively on *the almost extinct religion of the American Indians* in *The Feathered Sun: Plains Indians in Art and Philosophy* (Bloomington, Indiana: World Wisdom, 1990).

104: *Shankarian advaitism* is the Hindu perspective of "non-dualism" as expounded by Shankara (see editor's note for "Christianity and Buddhism", p. 54, Note 2).

Ramanuja (1017-c. 1157) is the classic exponent of *Vishishta Advaita*, the Hindu *darshana* or perspective of "qualified non-dualism", in which emphasis is placed on the personal nature of God.

Note 4: For *Ramakrishna*, see editor's note for "*Nirvāna*", p. 40.

Note 5: In Hindu tradition, *Radha* was one of the *gopīs*, or cowherd girls, who loved *Krishna*, the eighth of the incarnations of Vishnu, and she was the one whom he especially loved in return; although not an *avatāra*, she is understood to be the *shakti*, or radiant power, of Krishna and an embodiment of *Ānanda*.

105: Note 6: Swami *Vivekananda* (1863-1902), a disciple of Ramakrishna, was greatly influenced by the ideas of such modern Western social theorists as John Stuart Mill, which led to his joining the *Brahmo Samāj*, a nineteenth century Hindu reform movement. Concerning the relationship between Ramakrishna and Vivekananda, the author writes elsewhere, "The insufficiently doctrinal character of Ramakrishnian *jnāna*, and his lack of discernment with regard to conceptual forms—which did not seem to exist for him—then his ill-defined and somewhat imprudent universalism, and finally the dynamic and sentimental tendencies of Vivekananda: all this would have been free from danger within the framework of a Hinduism that was complete, closed, free from fissures; the environment would have rectified, neutralized, and counterbalanced whatever there might have been that was 'subjective', 'fragile', and 'hazardous' in certain attitudes of the *Paramahamsa*. Furthermore an integral or total Hinduism would not have allowed Vivekananda to open his mind to Western influences, which were unknown and incomprehensible to Ramakrishna but which stimulated in the disciple exactly those tendencies whose development had at times been feared by the master. . . . The *Paramahamsa* thus found himself at the crossroads of two worlds between which there was no common measure. His altogether primordial simplicity and candor, even his modesty, were not 'up to'—we ought to say 'down to'—dealing with these conditions; he grasped in them neither the principle nor the complexity" (*Spiritual Perspectives and Human Facts: A New Translation with Selected Letters*, ed. James S. Cutsinger [Bloomington, Indiana: World Wisdom, 2007], pp. 125-26).

Menander (*Milinda*) is thought to have been a second-century or first-century B.C. king of the Eastern Punjab, known to tradition because of his debate with *the Buddhist monk* Nagasena, who successfully countered each of the eight-two problems the king had posed, thus converting him to Buddhism.

106: *Christ—the Wisdom of God—was born by beauty—the Virgin*: the author explicates the "relationships" in question in "Christic and Virginal Mysteries", in *Gnosis: Divine Wisdom: A New Translation with Selected Letter,* ed. James S. Cutsinger (Bloomington, Indiana: World Wisdom, 2006), pp. 119-24.

107: *Meister Eckhart* (see editor's note for "The Eye of the Heart", p. 6, Note 12) adds elsewhere, "God speaks the truth and swears by himself, who is the Truth. If God were to fall short of His Word, His Truth, He would fall short of His divinity and would not be God, for He is His Word, His Truth" (*The Book of Divine Consolation*, Sect. 2).

108: "My kingdom is *not of this world*" (John 18:36).

Note 7: The Latin phrase *nihil est in intellectu quod non prius fuerit in sensu,* "nothing is in the intellect that was not before in the senses", expresses the fundamental conviction of empiricists such as John Locke (1632-1704).

Note 8: "*Love they neighbor as thyself*" (Matt. 19:19, Matt. 22:39, Mark 12:31; cf. Luke 10:27).

109: For *the Hindu caste system,* see editor's note for "The Posthumous States", p. 48, Note 11.

110: *The "hardened heart" of the Scriptures:* "He hath blinded their eyes, and hardened their heart; that they should not see with their eyes, nor understand with their heart, and be converted, and I should heal them" (John 12:40; cf. Exod. 7:13, Deut. 2:30, 2 Chron. 36:13, Isa. 63:17 passim); "For the hardness of your heart [Moses] wrote you this precept" (Mark 10:5).

Microcosm and Symbol

112: Note 3: "Jesus saith unto him, I am the way, and the truth, and the life: *no man cometh unto the Father, but by me*" (John 14:6).

"*No man shall meet Allāh who hath not met the Prophet*" (*hadīth*).

114: Note 4: The saying, "*thine existence is a sin* (dhanb) *with which no other sin can be compared*", is attributed by the author and some Sufis such as al-Kashani to the Prophet, while others ascribe it to the early Muslim mystic Rabiah al-Adawiyyah.

115: Note 6: For *Dionysius the Areopagite,* see editor's note for "*An-Nūr*", p. 24, Note 16.

117: "The next day John [the Baptist] seeth Jesus coming unto him, and saith,

Behold the *Lamb of God, which taketh away the sin of the world*" (John 1:29).

Note 7: "*One thing needful*": "One thing is needful: and Mary hath chosen that good part, which shall not be taken from her" (Luke 10:42).

119: "*Made in the image of God*": "And God said, Let us make man in our image, after our likeness" (Gen. 1:26).

Note 10: *Remy*, or Remigius (c. 438-c. 533), known as the "Apostle of the Franks", was Metropolitan of Reims when he baptized King *Clovis* I (c. 466-511), founder of the Frankish monarchy, together with three thousand of his subjects.

Prayer and the Integration of the Psychic Elements

121: Note 1: For *Shankara* or *Sri Shankaracharya*, see editor's note for "Christianity and Buddhism", p. 54, Note 2.

For *Shiva*, see editor's note for "The Eye of the Heart", p. 9.

The *Pater*, or *Pater Noster*—"Our Father" in Latin—is the Lord's Prayer, the most common of Christian canonical prayers (cf. Matt. 6:9-13; Luke 11:2-4); the *Fātihah*—"The Opening" in Arabic—is the first *sūrah*, or chapter, of the Koran, consisting of seven short verses used in all Muslim prayers.

Note 2: According to traditional Christian teaching, *two natures*, one Divine and one human, are united in the single Person of *Christ*, who is the *Logos* or Son of God. For more on this subject, see the author's "The Mystery of the Two Natures", in *Form and Substance in the Religions* (Bloomington, Indiana: World Wisdom, 2002), pp. 141-50.

124: Note 4: *The words of Christ concerning holy childlikeness*: "Whosoever shall not receive the kingdom of God as a little child, he shall not enter therein" (Mark 10:15; cf. Luke 18:17).

Transgression and Purification

127: Note 1: For some commentary on the mystery of *Eve*, see the author's "The Primordial Tree", in *Esoterism as Principle and as Way: A New Translation with Selected Letters*, ed. Harry Oldmeadow (Bloomington, Indiana: World Wisdom), pp. 71-82.

The fall refers to the eating of the forbidden fruit by Adam and Eve in the

Garden of Eden (cf. Gen. 2-3, *Sūrah* "The Heights" [7]:19-26) and their subsequent banishment from the earthly Paradise.

In Islam, *Iblis* is a personal name of Satan (*shaytān*) or the devil, who was cast out of Heaven for refusing to bow down to Adam (Koran, *Sūrah* "The Cow" [2]:34; cf. Is. 14:12-15).

For the *Blessed Virgin* as "*Co-Redemptress*", see editor's note for "*Nirvāna*", p. 41.

In the Hindu tradition *Sita*, an incarnation of the goddess Lakshmi, is the *shakti* or consort of the god Rama.

For *Radha*, see editor's note for "Modes of Spiritual Realization", p. 104, Note 5.

For *Kali*, see editor's note for "*An-Nūr*", p. 28, Note 20.

For *Ramakrishna*, see editor's notes for "*Nirvāna*", p. 40.

David (c. 1040-970 B.C.) was the second king of Israel and Judah, the composer of the *Psalms*, and, according to Christian tradition, an ancestor of Jesus Christ. He had several wives and concubines (see 2 Samuel 5:13).

Solomon (c. 970-931 B.C.), who succeeded his father David as the King of Israel, "had seven hundred wives, princesses, and three hundred concubines" (1 Kings 11:3).

Muhammad, the Prophet of Islam, was married to Khadija bint Khuwaylid (d. 619) for twenty-five years, but took several wives following her death.

Dante Alighieri (1265-1321) celebrated his love for the young woman *Beatrice* in his *La Vita Nuova* ("The New Life"), promising her a poem (*The Divine Comedy*) "such as has been written for no lady before" and making her his spiritual guide in *Paradise*, thus transposing the courtly ideal of love for the earthly beloved into a means of deepening one's love for God.

128: Note 3: *Omar ibn al-Farid* (c. 1182-1235) was a mystical poet and author of *Al-Khamriyyah*, an ode "*In Praise of Wine*".

Dominic (1170-1221) was founder of the Dominican Order of *Friars Preachers*, a mendicant order noted for its intellectual defense of *Christian orthodoxy against heresy*.

Note 4: The Song of Songs, or *Song of Solomon*, a book of the Hebrew Bible, is an allegorical love poem, traditionally interpreted by Jews and Christians to signify the mystical relationship between God and the soul.

The *Gītā Govinda* ("Song of Govinda"), written by the Sanskrit poet Jayadeva (b.c. 1200), is a twelfth century work concerning the love of Krishna, an *avatāra* or incarnation of Vishnu, for his consort Radha.

The *Fedeli d'Amore* (Italian for "the faithful of love") were a group of Medieval poets, including Dante, who transposed the courtly ideal of love for the earthly beloved—in Dante's case, Beatrice—into a means of deepening one's love for God.

130: Note 5: "The path of *those upon whom is* (Thy) *grace; not* (the path) of *those who err* nor of *those against whom Thou art angered*" (*Sūrah* "The Opening" [1]:7).

132: For *Immaculate Conception*, see editor's note for "*An-Nūr*", p. 19, Note 8.

"Why callest thou me good? *There is none good but God*" (Mark 10:18, Luke 18:19).

"*Hardness of heart*": "He hath blinded their eyes, and hardened their heart; that they should not see with their eyes, nor understand with their heart, and be converted, and I should heal them" (John 12:40; cf. Exod. 7:13, Deut. 2:30, 2 Chron. 36:13, Isa. 63:17 passim); "For the hardness of your heart [Moses] wrote you this precept" (Mark 10:5).

133: Note 6: For *Al-Ghazali*, see editor's note for "*An-Nūr*", p. 22, Note 12.

134: "*The just man sins seven times a day*": "For a just man falleth seven times, and riseth up again: but the wicked shall fall into mischief" (Prov. 24:16).

According to the Definition of Chalcedon, promulgated by the fourth of the Ecumenical Councils (451 A.D.), *Christ* the *Logos* is at once "*true God and true man*".

"*Why callest thou me good? There is none good but God*" (Mark 10:18, Luke 18:19).

Note 7: *Hanbalite doctrine* refers to the perspective of Ahmad Ibn Hanbal (d. 855), whose school of Islamic law accentuated a literal interpretation of the Koran.

135: Note 7 (cont.): In his German treatise, *"Von der Abgeschiedenheit"* ("On Detachment"), *Meister Eckhart* (see editor's note for "The Eye of the Heart", p. 6, Note 12) expounds on the spiritual quality of *indifference*.

"My soul is exceeding sorrowful even unto death" (Matt. 26:38).

136: Note 8: "Father, if thou be willing, remove this cup from me: nevertheless *not my will, but Thine be done"* (Luke 22:42; cf. Matt. 26:39, Mark 14:36).

137: Note 9: *Ibn al-Arif* (1088-1141) was an Andalusian Sufi master, best known for his writings on the science of the virtues.

For *Muhyiddin ibn Arabi*, see editor's note for *"An-Nūr"*, p. 16, Note 1.

138: *Abu Bakr Ash-Shibli* (c. 861-945), an important Sufi of Baghdad and the author of a number of paradoxical aphorisms, was a high government official before entering the spiritual path.

For *Hesychasm*, see editor's note for "Christianity and Buddhism", p. 62.

The *"real Presence"* refers to the Christian doctrine that in the Eucharist the Son of God "becomes bread" in the sacrament even as he "became flesh" (cf. John 1:14) in Jesus.

139: The *Bhagavad Gītā*, the best known and arguably the most important of all Hindu sacred texts and part of the much longer epic *Mahābhārata*, consists of a dialogue between the prince *Arjuna* and his charioteer, the *avatāra* Krishna, concerning the different paths to God.

Note 12: For *Theresa of the Child Jesus*, see editor's note for "The Mystery of the Bodhisattva", p. 74, Note 24.

On Sacrifice

143: The *"Day of Judgement"* (Yawm ad-Dīn)—*a "Day" of which* Allāh *is called the "King"* (Mālik): "Praise be to God (*Allāh*), Lord of the worlds . . . King of the Day of Judgment" (Koran, *Sūrah* "The Opening" [1]:2, 4).

144: *The sacrifice of a sheep substituted for the son of Abraham* is related in the Book of Genesis (22:1-18) and also in the Koran (*Sūrah* "Those Ranged in Ranks" [37]:102-11).

For *the Calumet—the Peace Pipe*, see the editor's note for "The Eye of the Heart", p. 41, Note 13.

146: *"Lose his life"*: "For whoever will save his life shall lose it: and whoever will lose his life for my sake shall find it" (Matt.16:25; see also Matt. 10:39, Mark 8:35, Luke 17:33, John 12:25).

The Twin Pitfall

148: *"Image of God"*: "And God said, Let us make man in our image, after our likeness" (Gen. 1:26).

150: For more detailed commentary on *the sin with classical Greece and the Renaissance* of separating *intelligence and beauty from God*, see the author's "Concerning Forms in Art", in *The Transcendent Unity of Religions* (Wheaton, Illinois: Theosophical Publishing House, 1993), pp. 61-78, and "Aesthetics and Symbolism in Art and Nature", in *Spiritual Perspectives and Human Facts: A New Translation with Selected Letters*, ed. James S. Cutsinger (Bloomington, Indiana: World Wisdom, 2007), pp. 21-48.

151: *"Keep one's life"*: "For whosoever will save his life shall lose it: and whosoever will lose his life for my sake shall find it" (Matt. 16:25; cf. Mark 8:35, Luke 9:24, and John 12:25).

"Die before ye die" (*hadīth*).

On Meditation

153: "But *one thing* is *needful*: and Mary hath chosen that good part, which shall not be taken away from her" (Luke 10:42).

158: *"Faith which removes mountains"*: "If ye have faith as a grain of mustard seed, ye shall say unto this mountain, Remove hence to yonder place; and it shall remove: and nothing shall be impossible unto you" (Matt. 17:20).

Note 8: For *Hesychasts*, see editor's note for "Christianity and Buddhism", p. 62.

Diogenes' reply to Alexander. According to Plutarch, the Greek cynic philosopher *Diogenes* of Sinope (c. 412-323 B.C.), having refused to join other notable statesmen and philosophers in an audience with *Alexander* the Great (356-323 B.C.), was visited by the emperor, who found him lounging in the sun and asked him whether there was any boon he wished granted; Diogenes replied, "Yes, I would have you stand so that you do not block the sun."

Note 9: "And from the days of John the Baptist until now *the kingdom of heaven suffereth violence, and the violent take it by force*" (Matt. 11:12).

159: Note 10: The Sanskrit phrase *Aham Brahmāsmi* ("I am *Brahman*"), is found in the *Brihadāranyaka Upanishad* (1.4.10).

Shivo'ham ("I am Shiva"), is the refrain of "*Nirvāna Satakam*", a devotional hymn by Shankara (see editor's note for "Christianity and Buddhism", p. 54, Note 2).

For the *Hallajian expression* "Anā'l-Haqq" ("*I am God-Truth*"), see editor's note for "The Eye of the Heart", p. 10.

Bayazid (Abu Yazid) al-Bastami (d. 874), known as the "sultan of the gnostics", is said to have been the first of the great Sufi masters to teach the doctrine of *fanā'* or spiritual extinction in God.

160: For *Macarius of Egypt*, see editor's note for "*Nirvāna*", p. 33, Note 1.

For *Gregory Palamas*, see editor's note for "*Nirvāna*", p. 33, Note 1.

For *Meister Eckhart*, see editor's note for "The Eye of the Heart", p. 6, Note 12.

161: Note 13: For *Hesychast doctrine*, see editor's note for "Christianity and Buddhism", p. 62.

Selections from Letters and Other Previously Unpublished Writings

165: Selection 1: "Ed-Dīn", *Études traditionnelles*, March, 1936.

Selection 2: Letter of November 8, 1959.

"*The Bible and the Koran speak of the resurrection of the flesh*": "I believe in the Holy Spirit, the holy Catholic Church, the communion of saints, the forgiveness of sins, *the resurrection of the body*, and the life everlasting" (Apostles' Creed, Art. 3; cf. 1 Cor. 15:35-50). "And We send down from the sky blessed water whereby We give growth unto gardens and the grain of crops, and lofty date palms with ranged clusters, provision (made) for men; and therewith We quicken a dead land. Even so will be the resurrection of the dead" (*Sūrah* "*Qaf*" [50]:9-11, *passim*).

166: Selection 3: Letter of July 23, 1951.

"Inasmuch as ye have done it unto one of the least of these my brethren, ye have done it unto me" (Matt. 25:40; cf. Matt. 25:45).

167: Selection 4: Letter, c. 1956.

168: Selection 5: *The Book of Keys*, No. 1061, "Succinct Remarks on Humility".

169: *"My yoke is easy, and My is burden light"* (Matt.11:30).

Selection 6: Undated, untitled note.

170: Selection 7: Unpublished article "On Love", c. 1945.

Selection 8: *The Book of Keys*, No. 1045, "Hypostatic Modes, Ontological Degrees".

The relationship Ātmā-Māyā is more fully expounded in the author's "Tracing *Māyā*", in *Light on the Ancient Worlds: A New Translation with Selected Letters*, ed. Deborah Casey (Bloomington, Indiana: World Wisdom, 2006), pp. 75-82 and "*Ātmā-Māyā*", in *Form and Substance in the Religions* (Bloomington, Indiana: World Wisdom, 2002), pp. 31-41.

171: Selection 9: "Travel Meditations", *Studies in Comparative Religion*, Vol. 12, Nos. 1 & 2, Winter-Spring, 1978.

172: Gaius Julius *Caesar* (100-44 B.C.) was Roman Emperor from 49 B.C.

Selection 10: "Travel Meditations", *Studies in Comparative Religion*, Vol. 12, Nos. 1 & 2, Winter-Spring, 1978.

"Judge not, that ye be not judged" (Matt. 7:1).

Selection 11: Letter of January 17, 1981.

For *Song of Songs*, see editor's note for "Transgression and Purification", p. 128, Note 4.

"Verily God is beautiful and He loves beauty" (*hadīth*).

173: Selection 12: Letter of January 31, 1965.

The Book of Keys, No. 810, "Esoteric Meanings".

174: Selection 13: Letter of November 3, 1950.

GLOSSARY OF FOREIGN TERMS AND PHRASES

'Abd (Arabic): "servant" or "slave"; as used in Islam, the servant or worshiper of God in His aspect of *Rabb* or "Lord".

Ad extra (Latin): "at the extremity"; from the point of view of a boundary or limit; considered from without.

Ad intra: (Latin): "at the interior"; considered from within.

Adharma (Sanskrit): non-conformity to a necessary law.

Ādi-Buddha (Sanskrit): in Buddhist cosmology, the universal or primordial Buddha, in whom is personified supreme suchness or emptiness, and from whom come forth both the *Dhyāni-Buddha*s and the historical Buddhas, including Siddhartha Gautama.

Advaita (Sanskrit): "non-dualist" interpretation of the *Vedānta*; Hindu doctrine according to which the seeming multiplicity of things is regarded as the product of ignorance, the only true reality being *Brahma*, the One, the Absolute, the Infinite, which is the unchanging ground of appearance.

A fortiori (Latin): literally, "from greater reason"; used when drawing a conclusion inferred to be even stronger than the one already put forward.

Ahadiyyah (Arabic): the supreme divine Unity of the pure Absolute; see *Wāhidiyyah*.

Aham Brahmāsmi (Sanskrit): "I am *Brahma*"; in *Advaita Vedānta*, one of the four principal "great sayings" (*mahāvākya*s) of the Upanishads.

Ahankāra or *Ahamkāra* (Sanskrit): literally, "I maker"; in Indian philosophy, the ego or ego principle; the ontological root of the individual being.

'Ālam al-'izzah (Arabic): the "world of glory"; in Islam, the realm of Being or the personal God.

'Ālam al-ghayb (Arabic): the "world of the invisible".

'Ālam al-jabbarūt (Arabic): the "world of power"; in Islam, supraformal or celestial manifestation.

'Ālam al-malakūt (Arabic): the "world of royalty"; in Islam, subtle manifestation.

'Ālam al-mulk (Arabic): the "world of the manifested"; in Islam, corporeal manifestation.

Anā'l-Haqq (Arabic): "I am the Truth."

Ānanda (Sanskrit): "bliss, beatitude, joy"; one of the three essential aspects of *Apara-Brahma*, together with *sat*, "being", and *chit*, "consciousness".

Ānandamaya-kosha (Sanskrit): the "sheath" (*kosha*) of "bliss" (*ānanda*); in *Vedānta*, one of the five sheaths, or levels of reality, successively surrounding or enveloping *Ātmā*; in "descending" order these are: *ānandamaya-kosha* ("sheath of bliss"), *vijnānamaya-kosha* ("sheath of intelligence"), *manomaya-kosha* ("sheath of mind"), *prānamaya-kosha* ("sheath of vital breath"), and *annamaya-kosha* ("sheath of food") or the body.

A posteriori (Latin): literally, "from after"; subsequently; proceeding from effect to cause or from experience to principle.

A priori (Latin): literally, "from before"; in the first instance; proceeding from cause to effect or from principle to experience.

Apara-Brahma (Sanskrit): the "non-supreme" or penultimate *Brahma*, also called *Brahma saguna*; in the author's teaching, the "relative Absolute".

Apsarā (Sanskrit): in Hinduism, a celestial maiden in Indra's heaven skilled in the performance of music and dance.

'Aql (Arabic): intellect; in Sufism, either the uncreated Intellect (*al-'Aql al-awwal* or "first Intellect"), corresponding to the Pen (*Qalam*), or the supra-rational intelligence within man.

Arahant (Pali) or *Arhat* (Sanskrit): in Buddhism, a perfected saint who has realized enlightenment.

'Arsh (Arabic): in Islam, the divine "Throne" of the Lord.

Asmā' (Arabic, singular *ism*): literally, "names"; in Islam, the divine Names of God, traditionally numbered at ninety-nine, and including the supreme Names of the Essence (*Asmā' dhātiyyah*) and the non-supreme Names of the Qualities (*Asmā' sīfātiyyah*).

Ātmā or *Ātman* (Sanskrit): the real or true "Self", underlying the ego and its manifestations; in the perspective of *Advaita Vedānta*, identical with *Brahma*.

Avatāra (Sanskrit): the earthly "descent", incarnation, or manifestation of God, especially of Vishnu in the Hindu tradition.

Avidyā (Sanskrit): "ignorance" of the truth; spiritual delusion, unawareness of *Brahma*.

A'yān thābitah (Arabic): the "immutable essences" or "permanent entities"; the archetypal realities contained in the divine Essence.

'Ayn al-Qalb (Arabic): "eye of the heart"; the intellect; the highest faculty in man, by which truth can be directly known.

Baqā' (Arabic): "permanence", "subsistence"; in Sufism, the spiritual station or degree of realization following upon "extinction" (*fanā'*), in which the being is reintegrated or united with God.

Barzakh (Arabic): as used in the Koran, a "barrier" or "separation" between paradise and hell, or this life and the next, or the two seas (fresh and salt); in the interpretation of Sufism, an "isthmus" connecting different planes of reality.

Basmalah (Arabic): traditional Muslim formula of blessing, found at the beginning of all but one of the *sūrah*s of the Koran, the full form being *Bismi 'Llāhi 'r-Rahmāni 'r-Rahīm*, "In the Name of God, the Beneficent, the Merciful".

Bātin (Arabic): literally "hidden, inward"; in Islam, the divine Name "the Inward"; the Principle insofar as it is veiled by its manifestation; see *Zāhir*.

Bhakta (Sanskrit): a follower of the spiritual path of *bhakti*; a person whose relationship with God is based primarily on adoration and love.

Bhakti or *bhakti-mārga* (Sanskrit): the spiritual "path" (*mārga*) of "love" (*bhakti*) and devotion; see *jnāna* and *karma*.

Bi-amri 'Llāh (Arabic): "by the command of God", the divine Command (*al-Amr*) itself being the active pole of the Principle, or the divine Word (cf. Koran *Sūrah "Yā Sīn"* [36]:82).

Bodhi (Sanskrit, Pali): "awakened, enlightened"; in Buddhism, the attainment of perfect clarity of mind, in which things are seen as they truly are.

Bodhisattva (Sanskrit, Pali): literally, "enlightenment-being"; in *Mahāyāna* Buddhism, one who postpones his own final enlightenment and entry into *Nirvāna* in order to aid all other sentient beings in their quest for Buddhahood.

Brahmā (Sanskrit): God in the aspect of Creator, the first divine "person" of the *Trimūrti*; to be distinguished from *Brahma*, the Supreme Reality.

Brahma or *Brahman* (Sanskrit): the Supreme Reality, the Absolute.

Brahma-Loka (Sanskrit): "domain of *Brahmā*"; Hindu heaven in the company of God as creator.

Buddhānusmriti (Sanskrit): "remembrance or mindfulness of the Buddha", based upon the repeated invocation of his Name; central to the Pure Land school of Buddhism; known in Chinese as *nien-fo* and in Japanese as *nembutsu*.

Buddhi (Sanskrit): "Intellect"; the highest faculty of knowledge, to be contrasted with *manas*, that is, mind or reason.

Chit (Sanskrit): "consciousness"; one of the three essential aspects of *Apara-Brahma*, together with *sat*, "being", and *ānanda*, "bliss, beatitude, joy".

Dākinī (Sanskrit): in Tibetan Buddhism, a female spirit who attends and inspires the *yogin*, transmitting to him secret teachings in dreams.

Darshan or *darshana* (Sanskrit): a spiritual "perspective", point of view, or school of thought; also the "viewing" of a holy person, object, or place, together with the resulting blessing or merit.

De facto (Latin): literally, "from the fact"; denoting something that is such "in fact", if not necessarily "by right".

De jure (Latin): literally, "by right"; an expression often used in contradistinction with *de facto*.

Deva (Sanskrit): literally, "shining one"; in Hinduism, a celestial being; any of the gods of the *Veda*s, traditionally reckoned as thirty-three.

Dharma (Sanskrit): in Hinduism, the underlying "law" or "order" of the cosmos as expressed in sacred rites and in actions appropriate to various social relationships and human vocations; moral duty; in Buddhism, the practice and realization of Truth.

Dharmakāya (Sanskrit): literally, "*dharma* body"; in *Mahāyāna* Buddhism, the supreme and non-manifest form of the Buddhas, personified as the *Ādi Buddha*; see *Sambhogakāya* and *Nirmānakāya*.

*Dharma*s (Sanskrit): in Buddhism, the elementary qualities or factors of existence.

Dhāt (Arabic): the supra-personal divine Essence; see *Ahadīyah*.

Dhikr (Arabic): "remembrance" of God, based upon the repeated invocation of His Name; central to Sufi practice, where the remembrance is often supported by the single word *Allāh.*

Dhyāna (Sanskrit): literally, "meditation", "contemplation"; one of the six *pāramitā*s or spiritual virtues of the *Bodhisattva*; also the term from which *Ch'an* (Chinese) and *Zen* (Japanese) Buddhism derive their name.

Dhyāni-Buddha (Sanskrit): Buddha "of meditation"; a Buddha, such as Amitabha (Amida in Japanese), who appears to the eye of contemplative vision, but is not accessible in a historical form.

Dīn (Arabic): "religion"; the exoteric tradition of Islam.

Dvija (Sanskrit): "twice-born"; in Hinduism, an initiated member of one of the three higher castes.

Fanā' (Arabic): "extinction, annihilation, evanescence"; in Sufism, the spiritual station or degree of realization in which all individual attributes and limitations are extinguished in union with God; see *Nirvāna.*

Fard (Arabic): "alone"; in Sufism, one who realizes the truth on his own and without membership in a *tarīqah*, or even without belonging to a revealed religion, receiving illumination directly from God.

Fiat lux (Latin): "Let there be light" (cf. Gen. 1:3).

Gandharva (Sanskrit): celestial musician; in Hinduism, the male counterpart of the female *apsarā* in Indra's heaven, also skilled in the performance of music and dance.

Gnosis (Greek): "knowledge"; spiritual insight, principial comprehension, divine wisdom.

Grosso modo (Italian): "roughly speaking".

Guna (Sanskrit): literally, "strand"; quality, characteristic, attribute; in Hinduism, the *guna*s are the three constituents of *Prakriti: sattva* (the ascending, luminous quality), *rajas* (the expansive, passional quality), and *tamas* (the descending, dark quality).

Guru (Sanskrit): literally, "weighty", grave, venerable; in Hinduism, a spiritual master; one who gives initiation and instruction in the spiritual path and in whom is embodied the supreme goal of realization or perfection.

Hadīth (Arabic, plural *ahādīth*): "saying, narrative"; an account of the words or deeds of the Prophet Muhammad, transmitted through a traditional chain of known intermediaries.

Haqīqah (Arabic): "truth, reality"; in Sufism, the inward essence of a thing, corresponding to an archetypal Truth in God.

Haqq (Arabic): "the True, the Real"; in Islam, one of the Names of God, who alone is truly real.

Hara-kiri (Japanese): "abdomen cutting"; a traditional form of Japanese ritual suicide by disembowelment; also referred to as *seppuku*, "cutting the belly".

Hatha-yoga (Sanskrit): in Hinduism, various postures (*āsana*s) and breathing exercises (*prānāyāma*) aimed at preparing the psycho-physical being for the more advanced spiritual practices of *rāja-yoga* such as meditation, concentration, and contemplation; see *yoga*.

Hayūlā (Arabic): Arabized form of Greek *hylé*, "first matter"; see *materia prima*.

Hīnayāna (Sanskrit): "lesser or small vehicle"; in Buddhism, the early monastic way comprised of branches including the *Theravāda*, *Mahāsānghika*, and *Sarvāstivāda*; the *Theravāda* is today prevalent in regions such as Sri Lanka, Burma, Thailand, Cambodia, and Laos; see *Mahāyāna*.

Hiranyagarbha (Sanskrit): in Hindu cosmogony, the "golden embryo" from which the world proceeds.

Ho mónos ophthalmós (Greek): "the eye of the heart"; the intellect.

Húparxis or *hyparxis* (Greek): in Eastern Orthodox Christian theology, the supreme divine Essence, as distinguished *in divinis* from the non-supreme divine "Energies" (*dynameis*) or "Processions" (*proódoi*).

*Hūri*s (Arabic): in Islam, the "gazelle-eyed" celestial maidens in Paradise.

Huwa (Arabic): literally, "He"; the divine Self; the exclusive divine Essence inasmuch as it transcends the servant-Lord dichotomy.

Hylé (Greek): literally, "first matter"; in Platonic cosmology, the undifferentiated and primordial substance serving as a "receptacle" for the shaping force of divine forms or ideas; universal potentiality.

Ihsān (Arabic): "excellence, perfection"; in Islam, virtuous or beautiful action; spiritual excellence.

Īmān (Arabic): "faith"; in Islam, faith and trust in God and in the Prophet Muhammad, hence in the content of his message.

In divinis (Latin): literally, "in or among divine things"; within the divine Principle; the plural form is used insofar as the Principle comprises both *Para-Brahma*, Beyond-Being or the Absolute, and *Apara-Brahma*, Being or the relative Absolute.

In saecula saeculorum (Latin): literally, "into ages of ages"; for ever and ever.

Ipso facto (Latin): by that very fact.

Islām (Arabic): "submission, peace"; the peace that comes from submission or surrender to God.

Jannah (Arabic): "garden"; in Islam, the heavenly Paradise of the blessed.

Jannat adh-Dhāt (Arabic): "garden of the Essence"; in Islam, the supreme Paradise of the supra-personal divine Essence.

Japa (Sanskrit): "repetition" of a *mantra* or sacred formula, often containing one of the Names of God; see *buddhānusmriti, dhikr.*

Jawhar al-habā' (Arabic): literally, "Substance comparable to a cloud of dust"; the undifferentiated Substance of universal manifestation; see *Lawh al-Mahfūz.*

Jawhar al-hayūlāni (Arabic): literally, "material Substance"; Substance insofar as it is differentiated or actualized in its productions; see *materia secunda.*

Jinn (Arabic, singular *jinnī*): in Islam, subtle creatures of fire, capable of changing size and shape, who can help or harm human beings.

Jīvan-mukta (Sanskrit): one who is "liberated" while still in this "life"; a person who has attained a state of spiritual perfection or self-realization before death; in contrast to *videha-mukta*, one who is liberated at the moment of death; see *krama-mukta.*

Jnāna or *jnāna-mārga* (Sanskrit): the spiritual "path" (*mārga*) of "knowledge" (*jnāna*) and intellection; see *bhakti* and *karma.*

Jnānī or *Jnānin* (Sanskrit): a follower of the path of *jnāna*; a person whose relationship with God is based primarily on sapiential knowledge or gnosis.

Jōdo (Japanese): "pure land"; the untainted, transcendent realm created by the Buddha Amida (Amitabha in Sanskrit), into which His devotees aspire to be born in their next life; see *Sukhāvatī*.

Kāfir (Arabic): literally, one who "covers" or "conceals"; in Islam, the person who deliberately covers the truth and is thus in fundamental opposition to God and in danger of damnation.

Karma (Sanskrit): "action, work"; one of the principal *mārga*s or spiritual "paths", characterized by its stress on righteous deeds (see *bhakti* and *jnāna*); in Hinduism and Buddhism, the law of consequence, in which the present is explained by reference to the nature and quality of one's past actions.

Karma-mārga, karma-yoga (Sanskrit): the spiritual "path" (*mārga*) or method of "union" (*yoga*) based upon right "action, work" (*karma*); see *bhakti* and *jnāna*.

Kōan (Japanese): literally, "precedent for public use", case study; in Zen Buddhism, a question or anecdote often based on the experience or sayings of a notable master and involving a paradox or puzzle which cannot be solved in conventional terms or with ordinary thinking.

Krama-mukta (Sanskrit): one who obtains "deferred" or "gradual liberation"; one who is liberated by intermediate stages through various posthumous states; see *jīvan-mukta*.

Kursī (Arabic): in Islam, the divine "Footstool" of the Lord (cf. Koran *Sūrah* "The Cow" [2]:255).

Lawh al-Mahfūz (Arabic): "the Guarded Tablet"; in Islam, the universal Substance serving as receptacle for the complementary divine forms or ideas, symbolized by the Pen (*Qalam*); universal potentiality.

Lingam (Sanskrit): "sign, symbol"; in Hinduism, the symbol of masculine generative energy, associated with Shiva.

Logos (Greek): "word, reason"; in Christian theology, the divine, uncreated Word of God (cf. John 1:1); the transcendent Principle of creation and revelation; in its created aspect, the various prophets insofar as they transmit the Word of God to humanity.

Ma'rifah (Arabic): "knowledge"; in Sufism, the spiritual way based upon knowledge or *gnosis*, analogous to the Hindu *jnāna-mārga*; see *mahabbah* and *makhāfah*.

Mahabbah (Arabic): "love"; in Sufism, the spiritual way based upon love and devotion, analogous to the Hindu *bhakti-mārga*; see *makhāfah* and *ma'rifah*.

Glossary of Foreign Terms and Phrases

Mahāpralaya (Sanskrit): in Hinduism, the "great" or final "dissolving" of the universe at the end of a *kalpa*, or "day in the life of *Brahmā*", understood as lasting one thousand *yugas*.

Mahat (Sanskrit): the universal Intellect; see *Buddhi*.

Mahāyāna (Sanskrit): "great vehicle"; the form of Buddhism, including such traditions as Zen and *Jōdo-shinshū*, which regards itself as the fullest or most adequate expression of the Buddha's teaching; distinguished by the idea that *nirvāna* is not other than *samsāra* truly seen as it is.

Maitrī (Sanskrit): kindness, benevolence, love of one's neighbor.

Makhāfah (Arabic): "fear"; in Sufism, the spiritual way based upon the fear of God, analogous to the Hindu *karma-mārga*; see *mahabbah* and *ma'rifah*.

Manas (Sanskrit): the individual mind or inner sense.

Mantra or *mantram* (Sanskrit): "instrument of thought"; a word or phrase of divine origin, often including a Name of God, repeated by those initiated into its proper use as a means of salvation or liberation.

Materia prima (Latin): "first or prime matter"; in Platonic cosmology, the undifferentiated and primordial substance serving as a "receptacle" for the shaping force of divine forms or ideas; universal potentiality.

Materia secunda (Latin): "secondary matter", existence; in Platonic cosmology, the secondary material forms of the physical world, as distinguished from *materia prima*, primordial and formless substance.

Māyā (Sanskrit): universal illusion, relativity, appearance; in *Advaita Vedānta*, the veiling or concealment of *Brahma* in the form or under the appearance of a lower, relative reality; also, as "productive power", the unveiling or manifestation of *Ātmā* as "divine art" or theophany. *Māyā* is neither real nor unreal, and ranges from the Supreme Lord to the "last blade of grass".

Metatron (Hebrew): in Jewish Kabbalah, the Universal Spirit; also characterized as Universal Man and Prince of the Angels.

Miftah ar-Rahmah (Arabic): "Key of Mercy"; one of the names of the Prophet Muhammad.

Modus vivendi (Latin): literally, "mode of living"; a practical compromise; a working arrangement between competing interests.

Moksha (Sanskrit): "release" or "liberation" from *samsāra*; according to Hindu teaching, the most important of the aims of life, attained by following one of the principal *mārga*s or spiritual paths (see *bhakti, jnāna,* and *karma*).

Mu'min (Arabic): in Islam, one who has belief or "faith" (*īmān*), understood as a more inward form of adherence to God than outward "submission" (*islām*).

Mudrā (Sanskrit): in the Hindu and Buddhist traditions, a ritual gesture usually made with the hands, but sometimes involving other parts of the body or the breathing; also a "seal" or "mark" of iconographical authenticity.

Muhsin (Arabic): in Islam, one who practices virtuous or beautiful action (*ihsān*), understood as a deeper form of adherence to God than *islām* and *īmān*; often associated with Sufism.

Muslim (Arabic): a practitioner of the religion of Islam; also, any person or thing who has submitted (*islām*) to God.

Mutatis mutandis (Latin): literally, "those things having been changed which need to be changed".

Nabī (Arabic, plural *anbiyā'*): prophet.

Nafs al-kulliyah (Arabic): "the Universal Soul"; see *psukhè*.

Natura naturans (Latin): literally, "nature naturing"; nature as an active principle of causality that constitutes and governs the phenomena of the physical world; a term associated with the Dutch philosopher Spinoza; see *natura naturata*.

Natura naturata (Latin): literally, "nature natured"; the phenomena of the physical world considered as the passive effect or production of an inward and invisible causal power; a term associated with the Dutch philosopher Spinoza; see *natura naturans*.

Nembutsu (Japanese): "remembrance or mindfulness of the Buddha", based upon the repeated invocation of his Name; same as *buddhānusmriti* in Sanskrit and *nien-fo* in ChNirmānakāya (Sanskrit): the "earthly body" or "body of supernatural metamorphosis" of the Buddha; see *Dharmakāya* and *Sambhogakāya*.

Nirvāna (Sanskrit): literally, "blowing out" or "extinction"; in Indian traditions, especially Buddhism, the extinction of suffering and the resulting, blissful state of liberation from egoism and attachment; extinction in relation to universal manifestation; see *parinirvāna*.

Nishkāma-karma (Sanskrit): action without desire; action accomplished without attachment to its fruits or rewards.

Nothelfer (German): "helpers in need"; in Roman Catholicism, apotropaic saints or "holy helpers" whose intercession is thought to be particularly effective.

Nubuwwah (Arabic): prophecy.

Nūr (Arabic): light, in particular the uncreated divine Light considered as the principle of Existence (cf. Koran *Sūrah "An-Nūr"* [24]:35).

O beata solitudo, o sola beatitudo (Latin): "O blessed solitude, O sole blessedness".

Oculus Cordis (Latin): "eye of the heart"; the intellect.

Para-Brahma (Sanskrit): the "supreme" or ultimate *Brahma*, also called *Brahma nirguna*; in Schuon's teaching, the "pure Absolute".

Paramahamsa (Sanskrit): literally, "highest flyer" or "supreme swan"; in Hinduism, a title given to certain great saints and renunciates, who have attained the supreme state of *moksha*.

Paramātmā (Sanskrit): the "supreme" or ultimate Self; see *Ātmā*.

Pāramitās (Sanskrit): literally, "that which has reached the other shore"; the six virtues or disciplines characteristic of the *Bodhisattva*, namely *dāna* ("charity"), *shīla* ("renunciation"), *kshānti* ("patience"), *vīrya* ("virility"), *dhyāna* ("contemplation"), and *prajnā* ("wisdom").

Parinirvāna (Sanskrit): "supreme extinction", "extinction without residue"; complete extinction in relation to universal manifestation and to Being, especially at the moment of death; see *nirvāna*.

Philosophia perennis (Latin): "perennial philosophy".

Prajnā (Sanskrit): "wisdom, intelligence, understanding"; in Hinduism, the self-awareness of *Ātmā*; knowledge of things as they truly are; in Buddhism, one of the six *pāramitās* or virtues of the *Bodhisattva*.

Prakriti (Sanskrit): literally, "making first" (see *materia prima*); the fundamental, "feminine" substance or material cause of all things; see *Purusha*.

Pratīka (Sanskrit): sacred image.

Pratyeka-Buddha (Sanskrit): "independent Buddha"; in Buddhism, one who attains enlightenment without a teacher and who makes no attempt to instruct disciples.

Proódoi (Greek): in Eastern Orthodox Christian theology, the non-supreme divine "Processions" or "Energies" (*dynameis*), as distinguished *in divinis* from the supreme divine Essence (*húparxis* or *hyparxis*).

Psukhè or *psyche* (Greek): literally, "soul"; in Plotinian cosmology, the "Universal Soul" as principle or differentiating Substance of manifestation.

Purusha (Sanskrit): literally, "man"; the informing or shaping principle of creation; the "masculine" demiurge or fashioner of the universe; see *Prakriti.*

Qalam (Arabic): literally, "pen"; in Islam, the divine Intellect as principle of universal manifestation and containing the divine forms or ideas of creation; see *Lawh al-Mahfūz.*

Rahmah (Arabic): "compassion, mercy"; in Islam, one of the Names of God, who is supreme Compassion, Mercy, and Clemency; see *basmalah.*

Rahmān, Rahīm (Arabic): "clement", "merciful"; found in Islam in the invocatory formula *bismi 'Llāhi 'r-Rahmāni 'r-Rahīm*: "In the Name of God, the Clement, the Merciful", *Rahmān* being the compassion of God insofar as it envelops all things, and *Rahīm* being the beneficence of God insofar as it is directed toward men of good will.

Rajas (Sanskrit): in Hinduism, one of the three *guna*s, or qualities, of *Prakriti*, of which all things are woven; the quality of expansiveness, manifest in the material world as force or movement and in the soul as ambition, initiative, and restlessness.

Rasūl (Arabic, plural *rusul*): "messenger, apostle"; in Islam, one whom God sends with a message for a particular people and who is thus a founder of a religion.

Ridhā (Arabic): the spiritual virtue of resignation or contentment.

Rūh (Arabic): "Spirit"; in Sufism, either the uncreated Spirit of God or the spirit of man.

Salāt 'alā 'n-Nabī (Arabic): a formula of blessing upon the Prophet Muhammad; in Sufism, often recited as part of a rosary during devotional worship.

Sambhogakāya (Sanskrit): the "beatific body" or paradisal "body of bliss" of the Buddha; see *Dharmakāya* and *Nirmānakāya.*

Samsāra (Sanskrit): literally, "wandering"; in Hinduism and Buddhism, transmigration or the cycle of birth, death, and rebirth; also the world of apparent flux and change.

Samyaksambodhi (Sanskrit): literally, "plenary enlightenment"; see *bodhi*.

Samyaksam-Buddha (Sanskrit): literally, "fully awakened one"; a fully enlightened Buddha with the function of enlightening others through preaching the *Dharma*; equivalent to a major *avatāra* in Hinduism and a *rasūl*, or messenger of God who founds a religion, in Islam.

Sangha (Sanskrit, Pali): literally, "gathering"; in Buddhism, the spiritual community of all those who follow the teaching of the Buddha.

Sat (Sanskrit): "being"; one of the three essential aspects of *Apara-Brahma*, together with *Chit*, "consciousness", and *Ānanda*, "bliss, beatitude, joy".

Sat-Chit-Ānanda or *saccidānanda* (Sanskrit): "being-consciousness-bliss"; the three essential aspects of *Apara-Brahma*, that is, *Brahma* insofar as it can be grasped in human experience.

Satori (Japanese): in Zen Buddhism, the sudden experience of enlightenment; a flash of intuitive insight often gained through the employment of a *kōan* during *zazen* or "sitting meditation"; see *bodhi*.

Sattva (Sanskrit): in Hinduism, one of the three *guna*s, or qualities, of *Prakriti*, of which all things are woven; the quality of luminosity, manifest in the material world as buoyancy or lightness and in the soul as intelligence and virtue.

Sayyidnā (Arabic): "our liege lord"; in Islam, a title of respect used for prophets, angels, and for the descendants of the Prophet Muhammad through his daughter Fatima and son-in-law Ali ibn Abi Talib.

Seppuku (Japanese): "cutting the belly"; a traditional form of Japanese ritual suicide by disembowelment; also referred to popularly as *hara-kiri* ("abdomen cutting").

Shahādah (Arabic): the fundamental "profession" or "testimony" of faith in Islam, consisting of the words *lā ilāha illā 'Llāh, Muhammadan rasūlu 'Llāh*: "There is no god but God; Muhammad is the messenger of God."

Shakti (Sanskrit): creative "power", expressed in Hinduism in the form of divine femininity.

Sharī'ah (Arabic): "path"; in Islam, the proper mode and norm of life, the path or way willed and marked out by God for man's return to Him; Muslim law or exoterism.

Shirk (Arabic): literally, "association"; the association of something relative with God; in Islam, considered as the worst of sins.

Shramana (Sanskrit): in Buddhism, a monk or ascetic.

Shrāvaka (Sanskrit): "hearer" or "disciple"; in early Buddhism, a disciple of the Buddha, or a disciple of a disciple of the Buddha, who attained to enlightenment and became an *arahant* or perfected saint; in later Buddhism, a disciple who accepts the essential precepts of the Buddhist *Dharma*.

Shūdra (Sanskrit): a member of the lowest of the four Hindu castes; an unskilled laborer or serf.

Sifāt (Arabic, singular *Sifah*): the divine Qualities of Being, or the personal God; see *Asmā'* and *Dhāt*.

Sine qua non (Latin): an indispensable or essential condition.

Sophia perennis (Latin): "perennial wisdom".

Sthūla-sharīra (Sanskrit): in Hinduism, the corporeal or "gross body" surrounding or enveloping *Ātmā*.

Sub specie aeternitatis (Latin): literally, "under the gaze of eternity", that is, from an eternal perspective.

Sukhāvatī (Sanskrit): "place of bliss"; the Western Paradise, or Pure Land, of Amitabha Buddha.

Sukshma sharīra (Sanskrit): in Hinduism, the "subtle body" surrounding or enveloping *Ātmā* and comprised of thinking, feeling, and desiring; intermediate between the *kārana sharīra* ("blissful body") and the *sthūla sharīra* ("gross body").

Sūtra (Sanskrit): literally, "thread"; a Hindu or Buddhist sacred text; in Hinduism, any short, aphoristic verse or collection of verses, often elliptical in style; in Buddhism, a collection of the discourses of the Buddha.

Tabī'at al-kull (Arabic): literally, "total" or "universal Nature"; the differentiating Substance of universal Manifestation; the efficient cause of manifested things.

Tamas (Sanskrit): in Hinduism, one of the three *guna*s, or qualities, of *Prakriti*, of which all things are woven; the quality of darkness or heaviness, manifest in the material world as inertia or rigidity and in the soul as sloth, stupidity, and vice.

Tao (Chinese): literally, "way"; in Taoism, the ultimate Source of all things, from which they come and to which they return; the Way of the universe and the sage.

Tarīqah (Arabic): "path"; in exoteric Islam, a virtual synonym for *Sharī'ah*, equivalent to the "straight path" mentioned in the *Fātihah*; in Sufism, the mystical path leading from observance of the *Sharī'ah* to self-realization in God; also a Sufi brotherhood.

Tasawwuf (Arabic): a term of disputed etymology, though perhaps from *sūf* for "wool", after the garment worn by many early Sufis; traditional Muslim word for Sufism.

Tathāgata (Sanskrit): literally, "thus gone" or "thus come"; according to Buddhist tradition, the title the Buddha chose for himself, interpreted to mean: he who has won through to the supreme liberation; he who has come with the supreme teaching; he who has gone before and found the true path.

Tawhīd (Arabic): "unification, union"; in Islam, the affirmation of divine unity as expressed in the first phrase of the *Shahādah*, "There is no god but God" (*lā ilāha illā 'Llāh*); in Sufism, the doctrine of mystical union; see *fanā'*.

Theravāda (Pali): "teaching of the elders"; the oldest surviving school of Buddhism.

Trimūrti (Sanskrit): literally, "having three forms"; in Hindu tradition, a triadic expression of the Divine, especially in the form of Brahmā, the creator, Vishnu, the preserver, and Shiva, the transformer.

Umm al-Kitāb (Arabic): "mother of the Book"; in Islam, the divine archetype or principle of the Koran; also, the fundamental, "feminine" substance or material cause of all things; see *materia prima*.

Ummī (Arabic): "unlettered, illiterate"; a term used in the Koran (*Sūrah* "The Heights" [7]:157-58) to describe the Prophet Muhammad, who is traditionally thought to have been unable to read or write.

'Unsur al-a'zam (Arabic): "the supreme Element"; the undifferentiated Substance of universal manifestation; see *Lawh al-Mahfūz*.

Upaguru (Sanskrit): in Hinduism, any person or thing who incidentally performs the role of spiritual guide or instructor for a seeker; see *guru*.

Upanishad (Sanskrit): literally, "to sit close by"; hence, any esoteric doctrine requiring direct transmission from master to disciple; in Hinduism, the genre of sacred texts that end or complete the *Vedas*; see *Vedānta*.

Upāya (Sanskrit): "means, expedient, method"; in Buddhist tradition, the adaptation of spiritual teaching to a form suited to the level of one's audience.

Upekshā (Sanskrit): impassivity.

Veda (Sanskrit): "knowledge"; in Hinduism, the body of sacred knowledge held to be the basis of orthodoxy and right practice.

Vedānta (Sanskrit): "end or culmination of the *Vedas*"; one of the major schools of traditional Hindu philosophy, based in part on the Upanishads; see *advaita*.

Videha-Mukta (Sanskrit): one who is "liberated" at the moment of death; see *jīvan-mukta*.

Vijñānamaya-kosha (Sanskrit): the "sheath" (*kosha*) of "intelligence" (*vijñāna*) or discriminative knowledge; in *Vedānta*, one of the five sheaths, or levels of reality, successively surrounding or enveloping *Ātmā*; in "descending" order these are: *ānandamaya-kosha* ("sheath of bliss"), *vijñānamaya-kosha* ("sheath of intelligence"), *manomaya-kosha* ("sheath of mind"), *prānamaya-kosha* ("sheath of vital breath"), and *annamaya-kosha* ("sheath of food") or the body.

Vikriti (Sanskrit): in Hinduism, Substance insofar as it is differentiated or actualized in its productions; in contrast to *Prakriti*, the undifferentiated universal Substance; see *natura naturata* and *natura naturans*.

Virtus (Latin): "manly excellence, strength, valor".

Wahdat al-wujūd (Arabic): "oneness of existence, unity of being"; in Sufism, the doctrine that all existence is the manifestation or outward radiation of the one and only true Being; associated above all with Ibn Arabi.

Wāhidiyyah (Arabic): the non-supreme Divine Unicity of the "relative Absolute"; see *Ahadiyyah*.

Walī (Arabic): literally, "friend"; in Islam, a saint.

Wilāyah (Arabic): sainthood.

Yantra (Sanskrit): literally, "instrument of support"; a geometrical design, often representing the cosmos, used in Tantric Hinduism and Tibetan Buddhism as a visual support or focus for meditation.

Yawm al-Qiyāmah (Arabic): the "Day of Resurrection".

Yin-Yang (Chinese): in Chinese tradition, two opposite but complementary forces or qualities, from whose interpenetration the universe and all its diverse forms emerge; *Yin* corresponds to the feminine, the yielding, the moon, liquidity; *Yang* corresponds to the masculine, the resisting, the sun, solidity.

Yoga (Sanskrit): literally, "yoking, union"; in Indian traditions, any meditative and ascetic technique designed to bring the soul and body into a state of concentration; one of the six orthodox *darshana*s, or perspectives, of classical Hinduism.

Yogī or *yogin* (Sanskrit): one who is "yoked" or "joined"; a practitioner of *yoga*, especially a form of *yoga* involving meditative and ascetic techniques designed to bring the soul and body into a state of concentration.

Yuga (Sanskrit): an "age" in Hinduism, one of the four periods into which a cycle of time is divided.

Zāhir (Arabic): literally, "manifest, outward"; in Islam, the divine Name "the Outward"; the Principle insofar as it is "externalized" by its manifestation; see *Bātin*.

Zakāt (Arabic): in Islam, the tithe or alms tax; one of the five pillars of the religion, along with the testimony of faith (*shahādah*), prayer (*salāh*), fasting (*sawm*), and pilgrimage (*hajj*).

Zazen (Japanese): literally, "sitting meditation"; in Zen Buddhism, a contemplative practice, often used in conjunction with the *kōan*, and seen as the most direct path to enlightenment.

For a glossary of all key foreign words used in books published by World Wisdom, including metaphysical terms in English, consult: www.DictionaryofSpiritualTerms.org. This on-line Dictionary of Spiritual Terms provides extensive definitions, examples, and related terms in other languages.

INDEX

Abraham, 18, 53, 144, 177, 182, 196
Absolute, the, vii, viii, xi, 39, 40, 54, 59, 63, 69, 70, 71, 72, 75, 80, 84, 86, 87, 118, 122, 152, 159, 166, 170, 173, 176, 201, 204, 207
Adam, 18, 21, 24, 27, 29, 32, 44, 127, 190, 193, 194
Ādi-Buddha, 69, 76, 82, 84, 88, 201
Advaita, 36, 183, 188, 190, 201, 202, 209. See also *Vedānta*
Ahadiyyah, al-, 36, 201, 216. See also *Wāhidiyyah, al-*
Akashagarbha, 82, 189
'ālam al-'izzah, 21, 201
'ālam al-jabbarūt, 21, 201
'ālam al-malakūt, 21, 201
'ālam al-mulk, 21, 202
Ali ibn Abi Talib, 17, 68, 177, 186, 213
Allāh, 15, 16, 17, 18, 19, 21, 22, 23, 24, 26, 27, 28, 29, 30, 31, 32, 39, 70, 89, 112, 137, 143, 178, 192, 196, 205
All-Possibility, viii, 8, 13, 16, 17, 46, 141, 176
ambition, 110, 147, 149, 151, 152, 212
American Indians, the, xvi, 29, 102, 190
Amitabha, 6, 35, 65, 69, 70, 185, 205, 207, 214
Ānanda, 18, 191, 202, 213
ānandamaya-kosha, 21, 202, 216
angels, the, 21, 22, 24, 26, 28, 29, 30, 32, 37, 44, 49, 60, 81, 171, 178

Apocatastasis, the, 71, 82, 187
apsarā(s), 36, 202, 205
'Aql, 16, 202
Arahant, 64, 67, 72, 73, 76, 80, 202
archangels, the, 23, 24, 25, 32, 74, 75
Aristotle, 88, 175, 189
'Arsh, al-, 16, 20, 21, 23, 26, 31, 32, 202. See also Throne
asceticism, 156
Asmā', 17, 36, 202, 214. See also Names, the divine
Ātmā, xi, 79, 108, 170, 171, 188, 199, 202, 209, 211, 214, 216
attachment, 102, 147, 151, 210, 211
Augustine, St., ix, 5, 175
Avalokiteshvara, 41, 74, 76, 82, 181, 187
Avatāra(s), 9, 39, 53, 54, 64, 74, 75, 82, 104, 114, 202
avidyā, 75, 203
'Ayn al-Qalb, 5, 203. See also Eye of the Heart
A'yān thābitah, al-, 20, 203
Aztecs, the, 145

Bacot, Jacques, 71, 187
baptism, 48, 56, 115, 130, 132
baqā', 38, 203
barzakh, 22, 203
Basil the Great, St., 49, 182
Being, 5, 6, 8, 14, 15, 17, 21, 31, 34, 36, 54, 58, 73, 74, 75, 107, 113, 160, 174, 179, 201, 207, 211, 214, 216
Beyond-Being, 17, 34, 36, 74, 179, 207
Bhagavad Gītā, the, 139, 196

208
God-Man, the, 60, 121, 134, 135,
136
Gordian knot, the, 83, 189
Gospel, the, 90, 96, 132, 135, 136,
146
Gregory of Nyssa, St., 71, 187
Gregory Palamas, St., 160, 179, 198
Guarded Tablet, the, 15, 16, 17, 18,
19, 20, 24, 208. See also *Lawh
al-Mahfūz*
Guénon, René, x, 2, 22, 178, 184
guna(s), 15, 21, 130, 205, 212, 213,
214

hadīth, xi, 15, 18, 22, 31, 32, 45,
62, 89, 114, 192, 197, 199, 206
haqīqah, 93, 206
hara-kiri, 145, 206
hatha-yoga, 138, 206
Heaven, 36, 38, 41, 43, 45, 46, 59,
73, 74, 75, 129, 158, 170, 179,
194
Hell, 26, 27, 43, 44, 45, 133
Hesychasm, 62, 138, 185, 196
Hīnayāna, 65, 84, 206
Hinduism, 41, 54, 56, 70, 106, 181,
191, 202, 204, 205, 206, 208,
209, 211, 212, 213, 214, 215,
216, 217
Hiranyagarbha, 23, 30, 206
Holy Spirit, the, 6, 25, 39, 41, 44,
120, 181, 185, 198
Holy Virgin, the: *See* Mary, the
Virgin
Honen, 66, 70, 186, 187
human state, the, 9, 43, 44, 46, 47,
48, 120, 136
humilitarianism, 149, 151
humility, 88, 110, 148, 149, 150,
151, 168, 169
hūris, the, 36, 127, 206

Huwa, 111, 206

Iblis, 127, 194
Ibn Abbas, 16, 17, 18, 22, 26, 177
Ibn Abi Hatim, 21, 177
Ibn al-Arif, 137, 196
ibn al-Farid, Omar, 128, 194
Ibn Arabi, Muhyiddin, 16, 20, 137,
177, 196, 216
ignorance, 4, 7, 11, 21, 63, 65, 75,
95, 119, 122, 123, 128, 130,
132, 137, 159, 181, 187, 201,
203
ihsān, al-, 5, 89, 93, 94, 174, 190,
206, 210
īmān, al-, 5, 89, 90, 92, 93, 173,
174, 190, 207, 210
Immaculate Conception, the, 19,
132, 177, 195
Immanence, 32, 87, 150
Infinite, the, 13, 14, 75, 79, 80, 113,
118, 150, 154, 159, 173, 201
Intellect, the, 3, 6, 9, 16, 20, 23,
54, 75, 94, 106, 112, 113, 117,
119, 120, 122, 125, 145, 159,
171, 176, 202, 204, 209, 212
intellection, xvii, 3, 67, 106, 109,
153, 207
intellectual intuition, xvi, 9, 107,
109, 125
intelligence, viii, xvi, xvii, 3, 5, 36,
58, 60, 81, 105, 106, 109, 110,
123, 130, 132, 133, 149, 150,
158, 159, 197, 202, 211, 213,
216
islām, 5, 89, 92, 93, 127, 128, 173,
174, 207, 210
Islam, xi, 16, 17, 20, 30, 36, 41, 43,
48, 54, 56, 57, 70, 106, 127,
132, 138, 173, 177, 178, 182,
194, 201, 202, 203, 205, 206,
207, 208, 210, 212, 213, 214,

Index

Index

BIOGRAPHICAL NOTES

Frithjof Schuon

Born in Basle, Switzerland in 1907, Frithjof Schuon was the twentieth century's pre-eminent spokesman for the perennialist school of comparative religious thought.

The leitmotif of Schuon's work was foreshadowed in an encounter during his youth with a marabout who had accompanied some members of his Senegalese village to Basle for the purpose of demonstrating their African culture. When Schuon talked with him, the venerable old man drew a circle with radii on the ground and explained: "God is the center; all paths lead to Him." Until his later years Schuon traveled widely, from India and the Middle East to America, experiencing traditional cultures and establishing lifelong friendships with Hindu, Buddhist, Christian, Muslim, and American Indian spiritual leaders.

A philosopher in the tradition of Plato, Shankara, and Eckhart, Schuon was a gifted artist and poet as well as the author of over twenty books on religion, metaphysics, sacred art, and the spiritual path. Describing his first book, *The Transcendent Unity of Religions*, T. S. Eliot wrote, "I have met with no more impressive work in the comparative study of Oriental and Occidental religion", and world-renowned religion scholar Huston Smith said of Schuon, "The man is a living wonder; intellectually apropos religion, equally in depth and breadth, the paragon of our time". Schuon's books have been translated into over a dozen languages and are respected by academic and religious authorities alike.

More than a scholar and writer, Schuon was a spiritual guide for seekers from a wide variety of religions and backgrounds throughout the world. He died in 1998.

Harry Oldmeadow was, until his recent retirement, the Coordinator of Philosophy and Religious Studies at La Trobe University Bendigo, in southeast Australia. A widely respected author on the *sophia perennis* and the perennialist school, his publications include *Traditionalism: Religion in the Light of the Perennial Philosophy* (2000) and *Frithjof Schuon and the Perennial Philosophy* (2010). He has edited several anthologies for World Wisdom, the most recent being *Crossing Religious Frontiers* (2010), and has contributed to such journals as *Sophia* and *Sacred Web*. In addition to his studies of perennialism, he has written extensively on the modern encounter of Eastern and Western traditions in works such as *Journeys East: 20th Century Western Encounters with Eastern Religious Traditions* (2004) and *A Christian Pilgrim in India: The Spiritual Journey of Swami Abhishiktananda* (2008).

The Eye of the Heart

Huston Smith (1919-2016) was Thomas J. Watson Professor of Religion and Distinguished Adjunct Professor of Philosophy, Emeritus, at Syracuse University. One of the world's leading scholars on comparative religion, he was author of the bestselling *The World's Religions*, as well as *Forgotten Truth: The Common Vision of the World's Religions, Beyond the Post-Modern Mind*, and *Why Religion Matters: The Fate of the Human Spirit in an Age of Disbelief.* His discovery of Tibetan multiphonic chanting was lauded as "an important landmark in the study of music", and his film documentaries of Hinduism, Tibetan Buddhism, and Sufism have all won international awards.